THE FULL GOSPEL IN ZION

THE FULL GOSPEL IN ZION

A History of Pentecostalism in Utah

Alan J. Clark

The University of Utah Press | Salt Lake City

The Defiance House Man colophon is a registered trademark of the University of Utah Press. It is based on a four-foot-tall Ancient Puebloan pictograph (late PIII) near Glen Canyon, Utah.

Names: Clark, Alan J., author
Title: The Full Gospel in Zion : A History of Pentecostalism in Utah / Alan J. Clark.
Description: Salt Lake City : University of Utah Press, [2023] | Includes bibliographical references and index.
Identifiers: LCCN 2022949724 | ISBN 9781647690922 (hardcover : alk. paper) | ISBN 9781647690946 (ebk) | ISBN 9781647690939 (paperback : alk. paper)
LC record available at https://lccn.loc.gov/2022949724

Errata and further information on this and other titles available online at UofUpress.com

Printed and bound in the United States of America.

CONTENTS

ACKNOWLEDGMENTS

As I canvassed the Utah Pentecostal community in search of resources, many individuals responded to my requests for information about their lives. Robert Smith offered a wealth of resources and contacts to get me started. Henry McAllister joined forces and provided his collection of history. I am indebted to their early support and interest in the project. Leon and Barbara Burrows, Alex Lucero, Roy and Becky Cazares, Pat Christensen, Tommy Vigil, Harley Boyles, William Fitzgerel, David Velasquez, and many others offered their stories as part of the full gospel story in Utah. Glenn Gohr provided answers and resources from the Flower Pentecostal Heritage Center in Springfield, Missouri, and Crystal Napier provided welcome assistance at the Center for the Study of Oneness Pentecostalism in Florissant, Missouri.

I deeply appreciate the fellowships and grants from the Mormon Studies Council at Claremont Graduate University, the Tanner Center for the Humanities at the University of Utah, the college of Religious Education at Brigham Young University, and the Charles Redd Center for Western Studies at Brigham Young University. In its early stages as a dissertation, Patrick Q. Mason read and reread and reread my writing. I have vastly improved my grasp of American religious history thanks to his tutelage. Gastón Espinosa, Phil Zuckerman, and Daniel Ramírez all offered their mentorship and their time reading and reviewing the project as well. Jedediah Rogers at the Utah Historical Society and Tom Krause at the University of Utah Press provided guidance and assistance through the publishing and editing process. Most of all, I am indebted to my wife, Meagan, who taught me to finish what I start.

INTRODUCTION

In the mid-1990s, shortly after the opening of the Latter-day Saint Temple in Bountiful, Utah, the city put up a sign near the corner of 450 East and 400 North. In all capital letters, the sign read "LDS TEMPLE," accompanied by an arrow pointing north along the street. The city intended to help visitors to the newly constructed temple find their way through the Bountiful neighborhood, which led up to the religious structure. A few days after the sign was posted, someone in the community decided to add a few more signs to the post. Above and below the sign for the LDS Temple, they placed signs to help people find their way to the local Community, Baptist, Lutheran, and Catholic churches.

After a few days, the local newspaper noticed and put a small article in the paper commenting on the new signs. With the headline "Diversity in Bountiful?," the brief paragraph reported, "Someone erected signs near 400 North and 400 East in Bountiful last week in response to an arrow sign erected by the city that points in the direction of the Bountiful LDS Temple. The unauthorized signs point to the city's Lutheran, Baptist, and Catholic churches." The night following the newspaper article, someone smashed off all of the unauthorized, non-Latter-day Saint signs. And the day following that, the sign for the LDS Temple also disappeared. The city chose not to replace the "LDS TEMPLE" sign, and the pole returned to an unadorned state.[1]

The nearest Pentecostal church to this location is the Abundant Life Assembly of God church in North Salt Lake, which has been there since the mid-1980s. Only in the last few decades have Pentecostal churches in Utah become a recognizable part of the community. From the Christian Life Center's large campus and school in Layton, to the Salt Lake Christian Center, which maintains facilities for congregations worshiping in twelve different languages, Pentecostal churches now rival in size all but the Church of Jesus Christ of Latter-day Saints and the Catholic Church in the state of Utah.

In some ways, the minor public controversy over religious street signs represents the story of Pentecostal Christians in the state of Utah. Long dominated by the Church of Jesus Christ of Latter-day Saints, religious diversity often feels like a myth to non-Latter-day Saints living along the Wasatch Front and rural corners of the state. Pentecostals first arrived in Utah as early as 1914, but the small congregations that gradually planted themselves in the state went unnoticed for much of the twentieth century. Even today, Latter-day Saints (who are also sometimes known as Mormons) are usually more familiar with the churches like those posted above and below the sign for the temple.[2] Yet whenever politics, culture, and religion intermingled in Utah, the results did more to bury the concept of religious diversity in Utah than to highlight it. Take away the signs and the LDS Temple is still conspicuously located on the hill above. The location of the other churches, however, becomes more obscure without any arrows to point visitors in the right direction.

This book argues that most Pentecostals first came to Utah for the express purpose of converting the Latter-day Saints. American Pentecostal Christians considered the residents of both Utah and many non-Christian nations to be heathens living in heathen lands. The Great Basin region of the American West, predominantly settled by Latter-day Saints, became regarded by many Christian missionaries during the early twentieth century as "the most difficult mission field on the entire globe."[3] For much of the twentieth century, Pentecostal missionaries viewed the residents of Utah as little different spiritually from the non-Christian masses of Asia and Africa. Yet the lives and experiences of the Pentecostal missionaries and converts who evangelized and remained in Utah were quite different from the experiences of foreign missionaries because of the unique religious environment in the state.

Ultimately the goal of complete conversion was too lofty. Pentecostals did not manage to convert the Latter-day Saints en masse. Over the course of the twentieth century, very few Latter-day Saints joined any of the Pentecostal congregations in Utah. Certainly, some did convert, but Pentecostals attracted little interest in their preaching because it was too theoretically similar to the message already being preached by the Latter-day Saints. Both of their communities became defined as religious outsiders within American culture. Latter-day Saints in the nineteenth century viewed themselves not as Catholics or Protestants but as something new and old at the same time. Within the revelations received by Joseph Smith, the Lord declared he would "raise up unto [himself] a pure people" that would embrace the moniker of "a peculiar people" as well.[4] Claiming revelation that restored ancient truths, they recast Christianity in their own image. Pentecostals left behind what they viewed as the spiritually hollow Protestant denominations in pursuit of the genuine experience of Christian Spirit. Proclaiming their message as the whole or the full gospel, they pointed out just how different they were from other Protestants. Their engagement with the Spirit made them "true Christians," distinct from the Protestants they left behind.[5] Both Latter-day Saints and Pentecostals viewed their movements as different.

Both movements also embraced the designation of religious outsider. R. Laurence Moore argued that the labeling of "mainline" and "outsider" religions in American history has developed a misleading understanding of the narrative of American religion. It suggested that within American religiosity there are "mainline" or "normal" types of religions, as well as "outsider" or "aberrational" types of religions. Many religious historians and members of the mainline denominations argued that the narrative of American religion focused on the histories of the mainline denominations because the outsider denominations represented ephemeral curiosities that would fade away over the course of time. Moore, however, argued that the "American religious experience began as dissent, and invented oppositions remained the major source of liveliness in American religion both in the nineteenth and twentieth centuries."[6] American religion maintained its vibrancy and creative energy through the pluralistic controversies that developed between groups that identified themselves as "mainline" and the groups that identified themselves as "outsiders."[7]

Within the factionalism of American religion in the West, both Pentecostals and Latter-day Saints willingly appropriated the role of religious outsiders. "Mormons were different because they said they were different," argued Moore, "and because their claims, frequently advanced in the most obnoxious way possible, prompted others to agree and to treat them as such."[8] Pentecostals in the twentieth century behaved identically. "Holy Spirit–filled believers had come to know, either through inerrant Scripture or through direct revelation, exactly what God wanted them to think and to do," argued Grant Wacker.[9] Their "noble conviction that the Holy Spirit lived within" created an identity apart from other Protestant Christians in America.[10]

Because both groups shared this theoretical perspective, Pentecostals offered no novelties to, and Latter-day Saints desired no substitutes for, the Latter-day

Saint spiritual worldview. Pentecostals were the outsiders of the Protestant community because they believed they were experiencing the resurgence of true, or full, Christian spirituality. They claimed to be embracing spiritual practices ancient in relation to early Christianity, rejected by institutions more concerned with themselves than with God. This was the very same messaging developed by Latter-day Saints eighty years earlier. They embraced it so fully that they literally became American outsiders, living on the outer edge of American civilization. To Latter-day Saints, the Pentecostal message sounded like a generic version of Latter-day Saint identity—or as one observer put it, "an unconscious illapse [sic] into 'Mormonism.'"[11] And that is how most Latter-day Saints received it—a pale imitation of the true, full gospel already received by Latter-day Saint leaders almost a century before. When later in the twentieth century the charismatic renewal movement spread across Christianity, it did not affect the membership of the Church of Jesus Christ of Latter-day Saints as it affected Protestants and Catholics because Latter-day Saints were theological charismatics already. Latter-day Saints could point to the stories of Joseph Smith and their grandparents as examples of "true" charismatic experiences. They rarely spoke in unknown tongues any longer themselves, but the theology of charismatic expression was fully institutionalized within Latter-day Saint scripture and canon. Outside expressions could be viewed only as suspect and deceitful.[12]

Despite the difficulties in converting the Latter-day Saints, the historical narrative of Pentecostal growth in Utah illuminated the ignored fact that Utah is in fact religiously diverse. Most studies focus on the majority population of Latter-day Saints and misrepresent the lived religious reality. Religious diversity increased significantly from the late nineteenth to the early twenty-first centuries, from the state of Utah being approximately 70 percent Latter-day Saint in 1880 to roughly 55 percent in 2020.[13] Pentecostal churches helped fuel the growth of religious diversity in Utah during the twentieth century as they converted other Christians and religiously unaffiliated Utahns.[14] Early Pentecostal growth was different in Utah because it grew almost entirely through missionary transplants. Whereas in other parts of the country where many pastors read about the Pentecostal revival or visited the Apostolic Faith Mission at Azusa Street (or other early Pentecostal congregations), converted to the message, and carried their congregations into the movement, in Utah, no Utah pastors converted and no churches converted to Pentecostalism. Every Pentecostal church had to be built from the ground up. This delayed significant growth until later in the twentieth century. So even though Pentecostals failed to convert the Latter-day Saints en masse, they succeeded by other means in developing a vibrant Pentecostal community alongside the Latter-day Saint majority in Utah.

Pentecostal Christianity in the state of Utah provides three insights on religion in the American West. First, it reveals the historical narrative of the Pentecostal experience in Utah, from its origins in the early twentieth century to its struggles and growth in the twenty-first century. This narrative brings to light a variety of religious congregations previously ignored in the state's religious history, including the Assemblies of God, the Spanish Assemblies of God, the Church of God in Christ, United Pentecostal Church, Pentecostal Church of God, Asamblea Apostólica de la Fe en Cristo Jesús, the International Church of the Foursquare Gospel (ICFG), and various independent Pentecostal congregations. These religious groups share similar experiences, and their victories and struggles highlight a dimension of religious activity unfamiliar even to many lifelong residents of Utah.

Second, Pentecostal Christianity in Utah functions as a case study in the religious history of the American West. Discussing religion in the American West, Ferenc Szasz argued, "A completely secular interpretation of regional history is a lie about the West."[15] Very few historians of the American West consider religion a significant part of the analysis. Because of this oversight, Utah is commonly evaluated apart from the West due to its historical connection with the development of the Latter-day Saint people. This means, however, that Utah's history is conflated with Latter-day Saint history in an overwhelming way. There is a veritable mountain of historical works on the influence of the Church of Jesus Christ of Latter-day Saints on Utah, which might lead an individual to believe that Latter-day Saints are the only religious group in the state. Yet, as the story about signposts illustrates, many other religious groups struggle under the shadow of the Latter-day Saint community in Utah. It is a complicated network of religious interactions, often unseen by Utahns themselves and ignored by historians at large.

The religious interactions in Utah are demonstrative of the story of religion in the American West because they reveal how poorly western communities integrated outsiders. Instead of newly arrived citizens melding into the community, they felt cut off from the community because of their differences. Usually enough available land existed to allow these new westerners to create their own communities nearby, but as time passed and communities grew, conflicts arose. The history of the West is guided by these interactions, and the dynamics of western local communities are fleshed out by ways in which individuals sought to convert each other to their beliefs about culture and religion. It is a tale of conquest, as Patricia Limerick suggests, but not one of victory.[16] No one religious group came even close to conquering the West. Like the giants of Norse mythology, each institution sought to claim its own mountain, create its own space in the West, from whence it could stare suspiciously across the valleys at the other giants and plot its conquest. And the resulting factionalism prevented politically like-minded groups from working together for most of the twentieth century. Pentecostals and other evangelicals worried about voting for Mitt Romney in the 2012 presidential election entirely because of religious differences. As Neil J. Young points out in *We Gather Together,* religious concerns prevented political conservatives from working together for most of the twentieth and early twenty-first centuries.[17] Religion in Utah reinforces this claim, as does religious history in the American West generally.

Third, Pentecostal Christianity in Utah helps us explore the emerging American religious mainstream of the twenty-first century. As the religious identity of the United States undergoes important transformations in the twenty-first century, Pentecostal Christians and Latter-day Saints both maintain pivotal positions in the renegotiation of American Christianity. They are two of the fastest-growing religious groups of the twentieth century, and they emerged as significant counterparts to the fastest-growing religious group of the twenty-first century, the religiously unaffiliated. The growth of the religiously unaffiliated has directly affected the willingness of Pentecostals and Latter-day Saints to work with each other on national issues pertaining to religious liberty. Analyzing the ways in which Pentecostals and Latter-day Saints perceive each other may also shed light on the ways in which these institutions interact on national concerns.

RELIGION IN UTAH

It is difficult to situate Pentecostal history into the literature of Utah religion because there is yet to be written a decent volume on the subject. Most books focus only on Latter-day Saint history. Otherwise, three common types of books have been written about non-Latter-day Saint faiths in Utah: reminiscences/autobiographies, regional studies, and denominational studies. Reminiscences and autobiographies are helpful but do not always meet the standards of modern research. For example, Stanford Layton's edited volume *Being Different* and Eileen Hallet Stone's edited volume *A Homeland in the West* do offer historical experiences of religious pluralism in Utah as minorities or minority faiths.[18] However, they lack source citations and historical analysis. Other autobiographical accounts, such as Edmund W. Hunke's *Southern Baptists in the Mountain West* and

Carl Ballestero's Pentecostal autobiography *How High My Mountain* are similar in structure and style to the previous examples, but they also manage to offer insight into the experience of non-Latter-day Saint religious leaders living in Utah.[19] Then there are a few articles, like Martin Mitchell's "Gentile Impressions of Salt Lake City, Utah, 1849–1870," which help identify attitudes and tensions that existed historically between Latter-day Saints and outsiders.[20] These studies, even though they are less academically rigorous for the most part, still help to provide important details and therefore fill gaps in the missing literature about Utah religious pluralism.

Regional studies, while crucially important, do not always include much specific detail on religion. Around the time of the Utah statehood centennial (1996), the Utah State Historical Society commissioned a series titled the *Utah Centennial County History Series.* It includes twenty-nine books that catalog the culture, history, and, in some of the volumes, religion of each county.[21] The Works Progress Administration's *Directory of Churches,* Robert J. Dwyer's *The Gentile Comes to Utah,* Thomas G. Alexander and James B. Allen's *History of Salt Lake City,* and Jan Shipps and Mark Silk's *Religion and Public Life in the Mountain West* all focus on geographical regions and are representative of the regional approach to non-Latter-day Saint studies in Utah.[22] Religion is not usually the focus of a regional study, but it sometimes factors into it as part of the cultural, political, and historical elements of the region. And the few regional studies that do focus on religion are desperately outdated and need to be revised.[23] The comprehensive study *Utah's History,* helmed by Richard D. Poll as General Editor, remains the foundational work in regional studies for Utah. This large edited volume contains many references and statistics on Utah's religious pluralism, yet it fails to address Pentecostalism at all despite its detailed analysis of the twentieth century up to its publication date in the late 1980s.[24] Jesse Bushman, first working on behalf of James B. Allen and then on his own project, updated the general data on Utah religion in James B. Allen's *Still the Right Place.* Including an appendix on Utah religion, it updated available information on various non-Latter-day Saint traditions through the 1990s.[25] A few regional histories exist by ethnicity or race, such as Ronald Coleman's "A History of Blacks in Utah," Jorje Iber's *Hispanics in the Mormon Zion,* and Juanita Brooks's *The History of the Jews in Utah and Idaho.*[26] Similarly, these works focus more conceptually on the culture of the region, with a nod to that race or ethnicity's religious behavior. Although regional studies offer less information concerning Utah's religious pluralism, their insights on the relationships between culture, history, geography, and religion are invaluable and not to be ignored.

Denominational studies offer the greatest resource in understanding the history of religious pluralism in Utah. There are history monographs, dissertations, or articles for most major Christian denominations. These histories provide valuable information concerning the struggles, successes, and failures of religious outsiders as they attempted to cohabit the state. Edgar T. Lyon, Stanley Kimball, and Peggy Pascoe offer research concerning evangelical missionary movements in the nineteenth and early twentieth centuries.[27] The Presbyterian Church has the longest history in Utah (aside from the Church of Jesus Christ of Latter-day Saints and the Native Americans), and the recent works of Frederick G. Burton, R. Douglas Brackenridge, and Jana Kathryn Riess elucidate the long interaction between Latter-day Saints and Presbyterians.[28] Henry Merkel's *History of Methodism in Utah* was updated by the Utah Methodism Centennial Committee in 1970.[29] Bernice Maher Mooney's *Salt of the Earth* explicates Catholic history, Dee Richard Darling discusses Congregational history, France Davis and Maud Ditmars elaborate on Baptist history, and Frederick Quinn's *Building the "Goodly Fellowship of Faith"* stands alone for Episcopal history.[30] I am not aware of books or dissertations on other major non-Latter-day Saint denominations in Utah, though there are a few journal articles.[31]

Although it shares aspects of both a denominational study and a regional study, this work employs Pentecostal history in Utah as an avenue toward a more complete review of Utah religious pluralism. Pentecostal churches are a significant portion of the Utah Christian community that have not been represented in academic literature. It will complement and encourage a new compilation of updated religious history for the entire state. Furthermore, its implications about the changing nature of the American religious mainstream bring nuance to future studies involving Pentecostals, Latter-day Saints, and religion in the American West.

Several questions serve as broad guideposts in uncovering this history. First, in what way did Pentecostalism infiltrate the tight-knit Latter-day Saint community in Utah? Pentecostals, of course, were not the first Christian missionaries to test their mettle among Latter-day Saints.[32] How did their approach vary from the approach of other missionaries? Were their methods successful? Pentecostal missionary work in Utah spans most of the twentieth century, as individual missionaries sought to plant churches first in the major cities of Salt Lake City, Ogden, and Provo, followed by outreach into the more rural parts of the state. The creation of permanent congregations took decades of planting and failing during the first half of the twentieth century. And even early into the twenty-first century, some Utah communities remained flatly disinterested in outside religion.

Second, how was the Pentecostal message received? As storefront churches opened up, what kind of members of the community visited? Were some Pentecostal denominations more successful than others, and if so, why? The greatest difficulty noted by Pentecostal and other Christian missionaries dealt with the interconnectedness of Latter-day Saint religion and culture. Much like Judaism, Latter-day Saint theology forged religious directives, which affected great swathes of a Latter-day Saint's day-to-day activities, including dress, dietary restrictions, marital patterns, and economic relationships. This question addresses how Pentecostal denominations managed to gain a foothold in such a monolithic religious environment.

It also draws attention to the disdain that Pentecostalism received from all types of Christians in the early twentieth century. Latter-day Saints, despite what is inferred by most academic literature, were not the only religious people in Utah during the twentieth century. T. Edgar Lyon estimates that the percentage of Utah's total population that identifies as a Latter-day Saint has fluctuated around 60 to 70 percent since the 1890s, and Pew's "Religious Landscape" survey of 2014 estimated a low of 55 percent.[33] Among the non-Mormon Christians in Utah, Pentecostalism arrived as the newest form of Protestant Christianity. It was a Christianity neither mainline Protestants nor Catholics found any value in. So Pentecostal missionaries entered Utah with absolutely no safety nets. If the Latter-day Saint community rejected them, there would be no friendly Methodist or Catholic congregation with which to commiserate. Many Pentecostals would suffer and soldier on through this rejection and solitude for most of the first half of the twentieth century.

Third, how does one define the relationship between Pentecostals and Latter-day Saints? The themes of conquest and conversion frame the relationship. In terms of conversion, Pentecostals first sought to convert the "Mormons." So "Mormons" became the objects of Pentecostal evangelizing. When that proved far more difficult than expected, Pentecostals transitioned from the conversion of a people to the conquest of the land. They sought instead to create more room for themselves, and Utah itself became the object of Pentecostal evangelizing. They continued hoping for Latter-day Saints to convert but also laid claim to sacred space of their own amidst the deep roots of the Church of Jesus Christ of Latter-day Saints in Utah by planting small churches all across the state. Pentecostals engaged far-flung Latter-day Saint communities, some of which had never previously received any other religious options.

Pentecostals altered both the landscape of Utah and their relationship to Latter-day Saints through this conquest. They became the objects of Latter-day Saint exclusivism as they successfully developed small congregations around the state. Significant social isolation defined life in Utah for many Pentecostals—members of the community and not, involved in politics and not, living with Latter-day Saints and not. The exclusive nature of the Latter-day Saint community in Utah limited more than just religious conversation. It affected politics, economics, culture, and even the relationship between neighbors.

Finally, I ask how Pentecostalism in Utah differs from Pentecostalism in the rest of the United States. Utah is the only state in the United States where the Church of Jesus Christ of Latter-day Saints constitutes a large majority of the religious adherents. How is a Latter-day Saint majority different from a Protestant or Catholic majority? Did Pentecostalism in Utah change at all to survive in this unique religious context?

These questions examine Pentecostal history in Utah, but they also examine Latter-day Saint culture and history. Many Latter-day Saints perceive their history to be a story of intolerance and persecution at the hands of others, yet their cultural and religious dominance in the state of Utah reveals a surprising story of Latter-day Saint intolerance against Pentecostals. Framed as a narrative history of Pentecostals in Utah during the twentieth century, the answers to these questions enhance the study of Pentecostal history, Latter-day Saint history, and the history of the American West.

SPIRITUAL RIVALS AND REVIVALS

The Pentecostal revival of the twentieth century ignited a wave of missionary work and evangelizing across the globe. Millions of Christians claim connections to the movement. Approximately sixty-three million Pentecostal and Charismatic Christians reside in the United States alone, the vast majority of those being the latter.[34] Denominations and independent churches that adhere to aspects of Pentecostal theology or worship exist in almost every country. Many scholars consider it the future of world Christianity. Discussing the early origins of American Pentecostalism in the United States, Harvey Cox envisioned the movement as "a spiritual tsunami that would eventually engulf the entire globe."[35] As Pentecostalism enters into its second century of growth, it continues to be an immense religious force within modern Christianity.

The initial spread of Pentecostalism across North America leaped from Kansas to California and then back East across the continent. Classical Pentecostal denominations tracing back to Charles F. Parham, William J. Seymour, William H. Durham, and others formulated the theological relationship between spiritual gifts and Spirit Baptism. Within a few years of 1906, William Seymour's Apostolic Faith Mission, located in Los Angeles, California, flooded the Christian world with newsletters and missionaries. The Pentecostal belief in spiritual gifts, most notably the gift of tongues, emboldened missionaries to abandon the comfort of their homeland for distant shores, with the expectation that God had granted them the capacity to speak foreign languages to spread the Christian gospel to the heathen nations. Impressed by belief in a divine mandate and empowered for witnessing by the receipt of spiritual gifts, missionaries embarked on a quest to bring the experience of Christian rebirth to the entire world.[36]

But few Pentecostal missionaries ever stopped to preach their message among the Latter-day Saints as they crisscrossed back and forth over the Rocky Mountains in the United States. The so-called "Mormon corridor" ran from southern Canada to Mexico, and it included strong concentrations of Latter-day Saints in Wyoming, Idaho, Utah, Arizona, and Nevada. Many Pentecostal missionaries reported to newsletters about their travels through Salt Lake City and the majesty of the snow-capped mountains of Utah, but far fewer expended any efforts on spreading the fire of Pentecost among Latter-day Saints generally and in Utah specifically.

The history of Pentecostalism in Utah can be divided into three distinct periods over the last one hundred years. The first third of the century, beginning with the Azusa Street Revival in 1906, initiated several decades of tent revivals and failed church plants. The second third of the century, beginning in the 1940s, witnessed the first permanent Pentecostal congregations in Utah. From the 1940s to the late 1960s, members of Pentecostal churches dealt with rejection and persecution as they entrenched themselves in Utah and laid the groundwork for permanent congregations in the major urban centers of Salt Lake City, Provo, and Ogden, as well as a few rural locations. Finally, the last third of the twentieth century and early twenty-first century displayed the tensions and similarities that existed between Pentecostals and Latter-day Saints concerning their views on community, theology, interfaith dialogue, and politics.[37]

What must it have been like for a Pentecostal missionary to begin evangelizing among the rivers, mountains, and cities of the Salt Lake Valley? When Pentecostal missionaries first poured out from Los Angeles in 1906, Utah was a very different place from the present. The population in 1900 was 276,749 compared to 3,205,958 in 2019.[38] In 1914, there were 269,980 members of the Church of Jesus Christ of Latter-day Saints living in Utah compared to 2,109,578 in 2018.[39] In 1900, the federal government controlled very little inside the state compared to the many military holdings, recreation areas, national forests, and national parks now owned and operated by federal agencies. Despite federal interference in and prohibition of the Latter-day Saint practice of polygamy, the government more or less left the state alone once the church renounced its unusual marriage customs. The US Army maintained a small garrison east of Salt Lake City, but the first national park was not created in Utah until 1919.[40] The religion, culture, and politics of Utah convulsed as Utahns incorporated into the United States during the mid-twentieth century and found their footing in the national community. Labeled the "awkward" years of Utah's history by Charles S. Peterson and Brian Q. Cannon, early twentieth century Utah underwent a variety of changes as it transitioned from a religious colony to a permanent part of the United States.[41] So as the first Pentecostal missionaries entered Utah, they entered a community in flux, its religious and political institutions experimenting with the changes brought on by national attention, institutional introspection, and cultural progressivism.

The cultural makeup diversified dramatically during the early twentieth century. As mining and smelting companies invaded Utah, the need for cheap labor drove immigrants into the state as well. Italians, Greeks, Yugoslavians, Mexicans, and others all found jobs in the new mines across Utah.[42] They brought with them the faith and heritage of their homelands. Two World Wars brought military bases and defense industries, which in turn drew more outsiders to the state. Many of these new Utahns would become foundational to the formation of Pentecostal congregations.

Politics at the national and local level remained religiously charged during the first few decades of the new century. As Pentecostal missionaries first set foot in Utah, the Reed Smoot hearings continued in Washington. The federal government had already prevented the known polygamist B. H. Roberts from being seated in the House, and now Congress was conducting an investigation of the elected Utah senator Reed Smoot to determine whether he would also be removed from office.[43] T. Edgar Lyon and Glen M. Leonard note, "Utah has the distinction of being the only state in the Union that was founded primarily as a religious colony and in which the total population was all of one faith . . . in its first decade."[44] At the local level, as Latter-day Saint voters filtered into the Republican and Democratic national political parties, a third party called the American Party formed in Utah. Strongly supported by the Salt Lake Ministerial Association, the American Party supported Republican politics nationally and promoted the interests and concerns of non-Latter-day Saints locally. Although the American Party all but withered away by the start of the First World War, religion remained a controversial element of Utah politics throughout the twentieth century.

Into these chaotic circumstances, Pentecostal missionaries introduced the message and vibrancy of the full gospel to a religious group that already believed in rival spiritual gifts. Latter-day Saints shared a belief with Pentecostals in charismatic worship and spiritual gifts, albeit other Christians did not consider them within the Pentecostal umbrella because of their belief in the Book of Mormon and their rejection of the Trinity. Thus, the exciting charisma of the Pentecostal experience fell flat among the Latter-day Saints, who long believed in "the gift of tongues, prophecy, revelation, visions, healings, interpretation of tongues, and so forth."[45] Despite the practice of spiritual gifts dwindling among Latter-day Saints in the twentieth century, formal teachings placed spiritual gifts firmly within the purview of priesthood authority and practice. James E. Talmage, a leading apostle of the Church of Jesus Christ of Latter-day Saints, explained in 1931:

> Miracles, as the manifestations of such gifts are sometimes called, will not be done away as long as men are receptive to the operations of the Spirit of the Lord. . . . When the Christ came in person . . . , when he cast out unclean spirits that were afflicting men, there arose many who undertook to exorcise the demons, and to imitate the work of Christ. . . . And when the Gospel was again brought to earth, and the Priesthood restored in this, the last dispensation, there was a great revival and increase in the manifestations called spiritualistic phenomena, in the effort to put something forth that looked like the original and the genuine, and so lead people astray.[46]

Latter-day Saint leaders enshrined spiritual gifts within the purview of the "true church" of Jesus Christ. Spiritual manifestations outside of the church could be only imitations meant to "lead people astray." When Pentecostals suggested they too had access to such gifts, the historical narrative of charismatic gifts and worship among Latter-day Saints cast suspicion on the Pentecostal message, significantly increasing the difficulty for Pentecostal missionaries in Utah.

CONTINUALLY AT WAR WITH ITSELF

Because of its difficulties, the narrative of Pentecostal history in Utah illustrates the way in which religion influenced the creation of the American West. Many religious groups hoped to recast the frontier of the United States into sacred space uniquely all their own. None ultimately succeeded despite their best efforts. Some, like the Latter-day Saints, succeeded for a time and within a limited geographical region, but no single religious group conquered the American West. By the twenty-first century, many western states instead ranked among the most religiously diverse in the country.[47] Made up of religious forays, failed conquests, and factional realignments, religious pluralism played a creative role in the evolving narrative of all of the American West. As religious outsiders clashed with each other, the resulting American West of the twenty-first century became intensely factionalized into different religious and cultural groups. Instead of merely depicting Limerick's legacy of conquest, it seems to better represent an amalgamation of her theory with R. Laurence Moore's depiction of the model of religious growth sustained through the tension between religious insiders and outsiders. Many religious groups dreamed of being conquerors; instead, they simply fed the fire of religious pluralism.

Nineteenth-century academic debates about the American West focused on Frederick Jackson Turner's frontier thesis. Turner argued, "American social development has been continually beginning over again on the frontier," meaning that the history of America is best understood through a succession of frontier stories ending with the settlement of "the Great West."[48] Since his presentation of this thesis in 1893, studies of the American West invariably acknowledged the frontier as a historical process and conceptual tool for unpacking the particulars of American culture and life.

In the 1980s, several historians initiated a different approach to the American West in which they threw out the concept of frontier and replaced it with the West as a geographical region. Limerick, one of the core historians of the New Western History, complained how "Turner's frontier was a process, not a place. When 'civilization' had conquered 'savagery' at any one location, the process—and the historian's attention—moved on."[49] Studying the American West as a particular region allowed historians to extend the chronology in both directions. Limerick, along with Richard White, William Cronon, and Donald Worster, re-envisioned the West as a region filled with tragedy. The "legacy of conquest" left by the federal government as it explored and exploited the territory west of New England countered the traditional image of "independence, self-reliance, and individualism," which previous authors thought ferried white Americans to a more noble future among the western climes.[50] Instead, white Americans privileged by an increasingly powerful federal government raped the land and its inhabitants in the name of American capitalism and manifest destiny.

The New Western History received significant attention, but not all agreed. Other historians appreciated the introduction of race, gender, and ethnicity into regional studies of the West while pointing out that the New Western History reduced its ultimate interpretive capacity to a single geographical area. Turner's frontier thesis, or variations on that thesis, maintained stronger appeal among historians due to its greater capacity to make sense of trends broader than just the West. Robert Hine and John Mack Faragher authored *The American West* as an attempt to combine New Western history with Turner's thesis. They suggested, "The West is not only a modern region somewhere beyond the Mississippi but also the process of getting there."[51] They resurrected the frontier as "a unifying American theme, for every part of the country was once a frontier, every region was once a West."[52] Very much in the same vein as Turner, Hine and Faragher expanded the frontier to signify "what happens when cultures meet," and what comes from that interaction for better or worse. History, then, is a reconstruction of cultural interactions.

On the fringes of this historiography, a few attempted to synthesize religious history and history of the American West. Carl Guarneri and David Alvarez headed a conference in 1984 where they and colleagues identified religion in the American West as a mixture of "unusual flux and diffusion, innovation and plurality."[53] In 1994, Ferenc and Margaret Szasz surveyed the West as well, arguing that "Western religion was molded by both the historical moment of settlement and the vast spaces of the western landscape."[54] Ferenc expanded this introductory chapter into a monograph in 2000. He claimed, "The American West may well have set the stage for national religious life in the twenty-first century" because of its pluralism and lack of any religious mainstream. He also viewed twentieth-century Los Angeles culture as emblematic of twenty-first-century American religious culture, and also shifted his gaze toward California as the heart of the West.[55]

Perhaps most notably, Laurie Maffly-Kipp reoriented the academic perspective on religion in the American West. Writing in 1997, Maffly-Kipp noted, "All that most of us know and learn about American religion keeps us firmly moored in an east-to-west framework, and the farther west we go, the less important the religious events seem to become, in part because the vast majority of us know much less about them."[56] As outsiders made their way to the American West and established communities, they became widely forgotten or overlooked by their eastern counterparts and the catalog of American history. To understand the West, Maffly-Kipp argued that "ignoring other movements—northward from Mexico, southward from Canada, and especially eastward from Asia—as well as the history of the prior presence of those who never wanted to move at all, furnishes us not simply with an incomplete historical narrative, but with unsatisfying accounts of religious experience."[57] With a new perspective to view the migrations occurring in the American West, migrations coming from all directions, the religious history of the American West became even more pluralistic and diverse than before. Maffly-Kipp's reorientation of Western origins helped highlight many cultures and peoples in the West that history had previously ignored.

Questions of race, religion, and region guided more recent works. Fay Botham and Sara Patterson complicated the story by suggesting that "scholars need to investigate how the blending of racial and religious communities alters our understanding of western-American history."[58] Intertwining, race, religion, and region, they edited a volume of case studies intent on telling the religious stories not only of those "facing westward," but also "the perspectives of those who looked northward and eastward from places like Mexico and California."[59] Jan Shipps, through her extensive studies of Mormonism and the Intermountain West region, contended that historians "write Western history as if it were a doughnut, leaving historians of the Latter-day Saints to fill in the hole."[60] Yet Shipps identified the problem without fully identifying its scope; the doughnut is the American West, and religion in general is the hole. Nevertheless, Shipps's analysis of Mormonism, furthered recently by Paul Reeve's analysis of Mormon whiteness, also added dimensions of religion and ethnicity to the American West.

Todd Kerstetter's *Inspiration and Innovation*, the first survey of religion in the American West since Ferenc Szasz in 2000, drew on New Western history, Turner's thesis, and narratives within American religion. For Kerstetter, religion inspired the process of Americanizing the West, and the western region itself forced and shaped religious innovation unlike elsewhere in the United States. Whether religion "aided and abetted conquest" or offered "solace and strength to face the disruption and turmoil of conquest," religion brought light and life to the spirit of the American West.[61]

The narrative of Pentecostal history in Utah offers a case study of failed religious conquest and vibrant religious factionalism in the American West. As the New Western History suggests, Pentecostals invaded Utah with a vision of spiritual conquest. Yet after half a century of failure, they settled for the development of their own faction within the makeup of Utah culture. This religious competition highlights the significance religion played in the maturation of the culture of the American West. Sometimes the religious conquest of the West failed because of federal intervention, and sometimes it failed because of religious rivalries between outsiders, as in the case of Utah Pentecostals. Yet with every attempt at conquest, new factions formed, increasing both diversity and anxiety in various ways.

CHAPTER OUTLINE

The chapters in this book include both narrative history and topical analysis. The history of the various Pentecostal denominations in Utah is explored and analyzed in the first few chapters, followed by more in-depth discussions of particular points of interest in Utah and Pentecostal history. They are followed by an epilogue.

The first chapter delves into the history and activities of the predominantly white, English-speaking Assemblies of God churches in Utah. The Assemblies of God is the largest Pentecostal Christian denomination in Utah, and most of the early history of Pentecostal evangelism is under their aegis. The Assemblies of God in Utah is mostly white and middle class, much like the Church of Jesus Christ of Latter-day Saints. Assemblies of God missionaries and ministers came to Utah hoping to convert the Latter-day Saints. Initially hostile toward each other because of the differences in theology and the style and acceptance of spiritual expression and worship, the Assemblies of God managed to convert very few Latter-day Saints. Dividing the twentieth and early twentieth centuries into thirds, the chapter discusses three periods of development and growth within the largest Pentecostal denomination in Utah. Much of their success came from the endurance of lifelong missionaries and pastors that relocated to Utah and remained there for the rest of their lives.

The second chapter continues the narrative of Pentecostal history in Utah by exploring the other Pentecostal denominations and independent churches found around the state of Utah. Volatile and unstable, Pentecostal congregations within many of these smaller denominations underwent schisms, mergers, and transformations over the twentieth century. The creative energy and unpredictability of loose organizational structure resulted in a diverse expansion of the Pentecostal community in Utah over the twentieth century, and it modeled aspects of Pentecostal growth that exist on the fringes of the Pentecostal community at large.

Filled with vibrant, charismatic worship, these smaller denominations and independent churches are a vital part of the growth of Pentecostalism in the world today. In conjunction with the more stable, fixed denominations like the Assemblies of God, the Pentecostal movement overflows with variety as it expands in unique ways.

Since the early twentieth century, Utah's Latino community embraced the Pentecostal message. Chapter three discusses how the Latino Assemblies of God and the Apostolic Assembly of the Faith in Christ Jesus planted congregations early and remained a central part of the Spanish-speaking Christian churches in Utah. Navigating relationships with the Catholic Church and the Church of Jesus Christ of Latter-day Saints, Latino Pentecostals initially gained converts faster than the white Pentecostal churches. They struggled to build their churches without the resources of their white counterparts and maintained considerable autonomy over their congregations because of the language barrier. Latinos are the largest minority group in Utah and continue to grow rapidly into the twenty-first century.[62]

The history of the Church of God in Christ is explained in the fourth chapter. Pentecostalism was a significant part of the racial and ethnic experience in Utah. As a microscopic minority for much of the twentieth century, African American Pentecostal churches underwent unique challenges. Ignored and at times ostracized by the community, they suffered through racism and harassment as they struggled to build institutions that supported their members. Their stories help to contextualize the experience of not only ethnic and racial minorities but religious minorities as well. The uncomfortable status as double minorities defined and continues to define much of their existence in Utah.

The chapters become thematic beginning with an analysis of female Pentecostal pastors and evangelists in the state. Chapter five looks at how women negotiated their desire to serve within institutions that almost disparaged such desires. Their experiences reinforce the assertion by Estrelda Alexander and Amos Yong that Pentecostal "leaders willingly allowed them [women] to 'dig out' or plant new congregations and nurture them to the point of viability," but once achieved, men replaced women in those leadership positions.[63] Few women sought out leadership roles, and those who did understood the restraints placed on them by their institutions. Though Alexander and Yong accurately identify the gender bias, the attitudes of these historical women seem to fit better with Kathleen Cummings's conclusions concerning Catholic nuns in America; it is not always true that "women who were faithful members of a patriarchal church were largely incapable of genuine work on behalf of women."[64] Pentecostal women pioneered churches in Utah because they felt called by God to do so. By acting on those feelings, they paved the way for later women to have continued opportunities to do the same.

The local conflicts that Pentecostals faced as they sought converts and built churches expose the complicated relationship between religious outsiders. Unfamiliar with Pentecostal beliefs and practices and uninterested in learning more, many early Pentecostals in Utah dealt with prejudice, unequal treatment, and vandalism. The harassment from members of the Church of Jesus Christ of Latter-day Saints revealed an unsettling disregard for others who shared in the persecutions and entreaties for religious freedom found within Latter-day Saint history. Despite the Church of Jesus Christ of Latter-day Saints once being a persecuted religious outsider itself (or perhaps because of their history), Utahns also participated in the process of religious "othering." Chapter six discusses the local difficulties faced by Utah Pentecostals to evaluate the tensions that complicate the lives of religious minorities in the United States.

Finally, chapter seven analyzes the ways that Pentecostals and Latter-day Saints perceived of and engaged with each other over the twentieth and early twenty-first centuries. Neither Pentecostals nor Latter-day Saints placed much emphasis on the pursuit of interfaith dialogue until recent years. Prior to such institutional gestures of goodwill, Pentecostals and Latter-day Saints depicted one another as lost souls in desperate need of correction. Their perceptions of each other motivated the methods they employed to interact with each other and highlighted the reasons why these religious groups with very similar opinions on national politics and morality failed to cooperate for so many years.

These chapters illustrate a story of failures and successes, conversions and conquests, pioneering and pigheadedness, and a foray into the evolution of religious diversity in Utah. Yet looking beyond the academic arguments about religion and history, the narrative of Pentecostalism in Utah is richly layered with human experiences. The coming chapters are filled with details from individuals that lived simple, devoted lives. Very few gained any social prominence nor did they pursue it. Feeling called to religious work, they found meaning in the Pentecostal message of salvation and friendships found in Pentecostal congregations around the state. They endured feelings of loneliness, embarrassment, discrimination, and ridicule. They watched their children suffer through adolescence as religious misfits and societal outcasts. At times, they also rejoiced in surprising moments of interreligious goodwill, empathy, and solidarity.

As I pursued examples of differences between Pentecostals and Latter-day Saints, I found them easily enough. But along the way, I also found examples of kindness and love between people with irreconcilable theological differences. I hope in the chapters that follow, there is something good to be gleaned about what it means to be humans in close relationship with each other.

1

A BRIEF HISTORY OF THE ASSEMBLIES OF GOD IN UTAH

The *American Fork Citizen* announced on August 9, 1946, "The American Legion Hall has been rented Sunday afternoons and evenings as a temporary home for the religious services of the Assembly of God Church."[1] American Fork, a town founded by Latter-day Saints in central Utah and situated prominently on US Route 89, supported a thriving community of members of the Church of Jesus Christ of Latter-day Saints. Prior to Warren James and Dorothy Campbell opening Pentecostal services, only one other church, the Presbyterian Church established in 1877, existed in American Fork. These would be the only non-Latter-day Saint churches in American Fork through the 1970s.[2]

Pastor Campbell, a graduate of Central Bible Institute in Springfield, Missouri, and a veteran of the South Pacific in World War II, aggressively and enthusiastically engaged the citizenry of American Fork. Using the media, he posted Christmas greetings every December in the newspaper and initiated a radio program titled "Moments with the Master," which aired Tuesdays through Fridays on KCSU Provo. Campbell supported local associations like the American Fork Recreation Program and was the first Pentecostal pastor invited to lecture at Brigham Young University.[3]

The American Fork congregation also fervently evangelized Utah County. In 1951 Campbell wrote, "We have humbly sought to fulfill the Great Commission of the Lord Jesus when he said 'Go ye into all the World and preach the Gospel to every creature.'"[4] Their congregation held dozens of services at the Utah County jail, the Utah State Training School, the Utah State Mental Hospital, the Juvenile Home in Ogden, and the County Infirmary in Provo. He hosted guest evangelists as they passed through Utah and encouraged fellowship meetings with the few other Assemblies of God (AG) congregations around the state. His first fellowship meeting was held in November 1946, and Guy M. Heath, the AG pastor in Salt Lake City and Presbyter over the state of Utah, presided as the special preacher.[5] Changing their name to the Highway Gospel Tabernacle in 1948, they hoped to reach every person who passed through the roadside city of American Fork.

Despite such an influential splash into the quaint Latter-day Saint community of American Fork, the Highway Gospel Tabernacle struggled through the succeeding decades. Like many other early Pentecostal pastors, Warren and Dorothy Campbell felt called to move on from American Fork in 1955. The pastors who followed continued some things, like the annual Christmas greetings in the *American Fork Citizen*, but few managed to maintain the momentum originally provided by Pastor Campbell. From 1955 to 1977, nine pastors presided over the AG congregation, none remaining longer than four or five years before heading off to another field of labor. The congregation completed the building at 210 East 200 North, of which Warren Campbell placed the dedication stone in 1953, with the help of Pastor Lilly Strayer in 1958. By the 1980s, notices about the congregation diminished, and the building they labored and sacrificed to complete ended up being demolished soon after.

The history of the Highway Gospel Tabernacle in American Fork raises questions about how the Assemblies of God managed to become the largest Pentecostal denomination in Utah (as well as the second largest in the United States) by the end of the twentieth century. Despite increasing success, why did Campbell leave? And why did the church eventually close its doors? Not all Pentecostal churches closed their doors, obviously. So how did other congregations manage to persist through the mid-twentieth century and emerge in the early twenty-first century as significant non-Latter-day Saint churches in Utah?

Ultimately, it required several generations of Pentecostals to create a permanent and dynamic spiritual community in Utah. Over the course of the twentieth century, three unique generations of pastors helped spread the message of Pentecost, plant permanent congregations, and develop new ways of interacting with Utah and Latter-day Saint society. For the Assemblies of God to succeed in Utah, the culture of evangelism would need to evolve from a focus on the conversion of souls to the conquest of space. The Assemblies of God learned how to plant permanent congregations that survived the transition from founding to subsequent pastors by developing permanent infrastructure.

This chapter focuses solely on the history of white, English-speaking congregations of the Assemblies of God. In a later chapter, a rich, parallel history of the

Spanish-speaking Assemblies of God will be given. I have purposefully separated these stories because the histories unfold independently of one another. Therefore, this chapter is incomplete without its companion that follows in Chapter 3.

PLANTING THE ASSEMBLIES OF GOD IN UTAH

Despite many religious organizations in the United States losing members over the course of the twentieth and twenty-first centuries, the AG maintained steady growth over the last one hundred plus years. When various Pentecostal assemblies determined to come together in 1914, there were around 50,000 adherents within the new fellowship of assemblies. By 1955, they numbered around 400,000. The number continued to climb to 625,000 in 1971 and 1,629,000 in 1981.[6] The Assemblies of God reported their US membership at 2,577,560 in 2000, and it has steadily risen to 3,240,000 in 2016.[7] As a denomination, they have reported growth during all of the last twenty-seven years.

Denominational growth in Utah, however, took much longer to materialize. Of the 25,887 non-Latter-day Saint religious adherents surveyed in 1914, none readily identified as Pentecostals of any denomination. There were five hundred people listed in the "Others" category, but no direct mention of the Assemblies of God.[8] Nils Bloch-Hoell estimated there were approximately 23,000 members of Pentecostal denominations across all of the United States in 1916, with approximately forty Pentecostals residing in Utah.[9] A Salt Lake newspaper reported in 1939 there were three Pentecostal churches in Utah with a combined membership of one hundred.[10] By 1957, R. G. Fulford, district Superintendent for the AG Rocky Mountain district, reported twelve churches in Utah. The number remained static for some time, although by the early nineties it had increased to about twenty churches. By the year 2000, the AG reported fourteen congregations in Salt Lake County alone and forty-two congregations throughout the state, with 12,391 total adherents.[11] Figures grew slightly to include 13,688 total adherents by 2010.[12] To put that into perspective, in 2010 less than 1 percent of the Assemblies of God US membership resided in Utah.

Although numerically small, the Assemblies of God grew faster than almost any other religious denomination from 1980 to 2010. Examining data from the Association of Religion Data Archives (ARDA), in 1980, the Assemblies of God ranked as the tenth largest religious group in Utah, following behind Latter-day Saints, Catholics, Southern Baptists, Presbyterians, United Methodists,

Episcopalians, Missouri Synod Lutherans, Evangelical Lutherans, and American Baptists. By 1990, they matched the size of the Presbyterians, Methodists, and Lutherans, and by 2010, they rivaled Southern Baptists in size. The Assemblies of God, as well as other Pentecostal denominations, continued growing in Utah into the twenty-first century, despite growth stagnation and membership decline among most other Protestants.[13]

The 2014 Pew Religious Landscape Study reported that the Assemblies of God made up approximately 1 percent of Utah's population. Setting the Latter-day Saint population and the unaffiliated population aside (55 percent and 22 percent respectively), the Catholic community is now the only religious community in the state of Utah larger than the Assemblies of God. Although Baptists, Methodists, Seventh Day Adventists, and Presbyterians have a longer history among the Latter-day Saints, the Assemblies of God has grown more quickly and planted itself more firmly over the twentieth and early twenty-first centuries. Moreover, as the Pentecostal community continues to grow, their prominence in the state will likely increase as well.[14]

The Assemblies of God ran into similar problems as other religions did while they attempted to plant churches in Utah. Commenting on the small number of Pentecostals in Utah, Bloch-Hoell wrote suggestively, "The survey contains no surprises. It is not strange that the Pentecostal Movement found no favour [sic] in Utah."[15] The history of Utah is uniquely religious in nature. From the time that Brigham Young relocated the Church of Jesus Christ of Latter-day Saints to the Salt Lake Valley in 1847 to the Winter Olympics in 2002, the religious culture of the state affected almost every aspect of Utah society. As the members of the Church of Jesus Christ of Latter-day Saints spread out across the unincorporated lands of the West, they founded towns and cities that operated in lockstep with the tenets of the Latter-day Saint religion. Although not quite a theocracy, Thomas O'Dea aptly described Utah as a "near nation" under the control of the church.[16] Including parts of Utah, Idaho, Colorado, Wyoming, Nevada, and Arizona, the Mormon Culture Region shaped culture and society for the inhabitants in a quasi-theocratic community.[17]

As the American frontier shifted from the Midwest to the Pacific Ocean, the western lands once inhabited by only Latter-day Saints or Native American tribes became incorporated into the United States. Yet the state of Utah retained its idiosyncratic cultural, societal, and religious qualities, which inspired C. P. Lyford to declare it "a foreign mission field come to our own shores."[18] A missionary to Utah for four years in the late nineteenth century, Lyford worked for the Methodist

Episcopal Church attempting to establish Christian schools in Utah. He abandoned the effort, lamenting over Utah and how "as the light of our Christian land falls upon it, it reflects back no splendors."[19] Reporting on missionary progress decades after Lyford, R. G. Fulford reported to the *Pentecostal Evangel* in 1957 that "many missionaries who have worked in this state have told me they feel the same depressing spirit in Utah which they have felt in the heathen foreign fields."[20] Little seemed to change about the perspective of missionary work.

The relative fortunes of the Assemblies of God in Utah can be better understood through an evaluation of their denominational history. Edith Blumhofer's two-volume *The Assemblies of God: A Chapter in the Story of American Pentecostalism* argued that the denomination underwent significant changes from its first generation to its second. Written in 1989, her work divides AG history into two generations or historical periods: the first generation that lasted from 1914 to 1941, and the second generation from 1941 to the late 1980s. Founded among Christians with a strong "distrust of 'man-made organizations'" and a penchant for charismatic, revival-style worship, evangelists began infiltrating "independent missions, holiness associations, and other nondenominational settings to proclaim the full and final restoration of New Testament Christianity."[21] In 1914, Pentecostals from more than fifteen US states came together "to conserve the work, that we may all build up and not tear down, both in home and foreign lands."[22] They met in a general council in Hot Springs, Arkansas in the spring of 1914 and developed into a Pentecostal fellowship known as the Assemblies of God.

The first generation of Pentecostals thrived on the fringes of denominational Christianity. Disaffected Christians within the mainline denominations found in Pentecostal evangelists an escape from the confines of institutionalized worship and belief. They also found congregations that maintained the nexus of authority within the local assemblies themselves. Preachers acted more like the Methodist circuit riders of the previous century. They preached the exciting doctrines of salvation, Spirit baptism, and miraculous gifts, collected believers into new missions and congregations, and then headed off to preach the message in other locations.

From one generation to the next, however, the nature of the Assemblies of God transformed. "By 1941," claimed Blumhofer, "a movement shaped by a restorationist vision had become something its organizers in 1914 had repudiated—a new denomination."[23] According to Blumhofer, second generation members wanted a more grounded and predictable religious organization to which they could devote their time and energy in this life. Either unwilling or unable to keep up the pace of itinerancy and always remain on the move, second generation AG members began settling into more traditional, stationary congregations. Blumhofer concluded that "by 1941, a movement that had thrived on the preaching of itinerant evangelists" evolved, and the second generation "settled into pastorates."[24]

The history of the Assemblies of God in Utah can also be understood as a spiritual community inheriting tradition from previous generations and transforming it according to their own wants and needs. However, the resistance of the Latter-day Saint religious community in Utah to the message of Pentecostalism decelerated the transition to more permanent pastorates. Three generations helped to shape the Assemblies of God in Utah from the early twentieth century to the early twenty-first. The image of Utah Pentecost transitioned generationally from circuit riders and evangelists to permanent pioneers and finally to homegrown institution builders representative of the new twenty-first-century American Christian mainstream. Each generation of pastors and members evolved to meet the challenges of living within and eventually thriving among the monolithic Latter-day Saint culture of Utah.

Just as Blumhofer described the first generation of Assemblies of God leaders as itinerant evangelists, the first generation in Utah viewed Utah as "the largest open door in the United States, where this glorious Gospel has not been preached."[25] From 1914 to 1940, the Assemblies of God never quite managed to create a permanent community. Evangelists moved in with visions of converting a kingdom and oftentimes moved out leaving behind little more than a few advertisements in the Sunday paper. Others came to Utah for a time and left feeling as Herbert Buffum did on his departure. Famous for the many songs he composed over his life, Buffum wrote the song "I'm Going Through" as he rode a train away from the state of Utah. One of the verses of the song reads, "Many once started to run in this race, but with our Redeemer they could not keep pace; Others accepted because it was new, but not very many seem bound to go through."[26]

Utah proved a very difficult place for Pentecostal missionary work during the first half of the twentieth century. Very few Latter-day Saints converted, and the other Christian churches defended their flocks zealously from the excesses of the nascent Pentecostal revival. The earliest congregations commonly included little more than a few families connected by an evangelist and one of the many Pentecostal newsletters that circulated around the United States. Most were white transplants from other parts of the United States, although a few disaffected Latter-day Saints joined Pentecostal congregations as well. The newsletters included petitions for readers from anonymous, lone believers, to "pray for the spread of the full

Gospel" in little Utah towns.[27] The *Apostolic Faith*, *Christian Evangel*, and *Church of God Evangel* all counted Utahns among their subscribers in the early twentieth century.[28] But as evangelists felt the call to carry the Pentecostal message elsewhere, congregations withered and faded back into obscurity.

The second generation of the Assemblies of God in Utah should have mirrored Blumhofer's depiction of congregations comfortably settling into the forms of religious institutionalism, but no such institution yet existed among the Latter-day Saints. Instead, the second generation roared into Utah prepared to wage war with the seemingly impenetrable Latter-day Saint community. Some of the AG evangelists who made their way to Utah from 1940 to 1980 behaved exactly as the first generation. They reveled in the vision of Utah as the missionary opportunity next door. Yet their dreams of a mountainous wilderness filled with souls ripe for conversion devolved into consternation at a society willing to indulge in "demonic inspiration."[29] Others transferred to Utah expecting to find an established and financially supportive congregation over which they would preside. This too ended in disappointment and departure for many pastors in Utah. Those who stayed, however, learned that to establish AG congregations that would remain even after they were gone, they needed to change their focus from converting the Latter-day Saint people to creating Pentecostal sacred space. Purchasing or constructing physical worship buildings created stability unlike any previous methods. Those evangelists who planted themselves permanently in Utah looked after their congregations fiercely and built churches to carve sacred space of their own out of the mountainous landscape. Pioneers in their own right, the second generation of pastors accelerated the rate of growth in Utah exponentially.

Only once the third generation of leaders took the reins in Utah did the AG congregations begin to resemble Blumhofer's explanation of the AG's historical second generation. From 1980 to the present, the Assemblies of God in Utah fluctuated in defining itself having now gained a sure foothold in the state. Many of the concerns resembled those of the Assemblies of God in other parts of the United States. These congregations had to navigate the questions of practice concerning charismatic expression and the public display of glossolalia, or speaking in tongues.[30] Unlike many other locations in the United States, they also needed to decide how best to engage a community with a huge religious majority. Utah Assemblies of God churches chose to stop encouraging religious conversations about denominational differences and start engaging their communities politically and socially. Very few Assemblies of God pastors attacked the Church of

Jesus Christ of Latter-day Saints openly in this period. Some even reversed directions entirely and sought restitution. Now finding themselves among the largest Christian congregations in Utah apart from the Latter-day Saints, they worked to provide worship and support services for the communities in which they operated. They expanded their ministries to include immigrant and refugee populations. By cooperating politically and socially and avoiding religious confrontation, the Assemblies of God continued growing comfortably among the large Latter-day Saint majority of Utah.

Across three differing generations of Pentecostals, the Assemblies of God learned to adapt their styles of evangelism, worship, and church planting to create a vibrant and growing Pentecostal community among the Latter-day Saints in Utah. From initial expectations of quick acceptance and growth in the first generation, the second generation focused on institution building. They initiated annual camp meetings, built churches, and aggressively preached against Latter-day Saint religion. These tactics evolved again, as large, urban congregations sponsored satellite congregations in rural areas, using their resources to create a stronger network around the state. The evangelistic message turned inward as pastors preached less against others and more about their own path to salvation. The message also turned outward as they pursued greater influence on their community.

Although the community was small, the accommodations and innovations they developed to compete within a Latter-day Saint majority religious environment were unique to the region and lent themselves to further developing Pentecostal communities in other locations. Turning their focus from conversion of the majority of the community, many churches realigned the mission of their congregations with identifying unreached segments of society. Congregations reached out to immigrant populations and opened the use of their facilities to foreign language congregations. Others rebranded themselves as "church for people who don't do church" hoping to gain ground among "people that have been burnt out or disenfranchised with organized religion."[31] Some churches revised the nineteenth-century Protestant aim of establishing schools in Utah for the purpose of missionary work. Instead of focusing on biblical education, these schools modeled themselves as wholesome alternatives to public education. Through the process of redefining their institutional framework, many Assemblies of God churches no longer include "Assembly of God" in the name of their congregation. Creating an image that is open to all Christian believers, the Assemblies of God in Utah adopted a new image of their denomination in the state.

"THE LARGEST UNTOUCHED FIELD IN THE UNITED STATES": CIRCUIT RIDING EVANGELISTS AND THE FIRST GENERATION

The earliest pastors and evangelists affiliated with the Assemblies of God viewed Utah as another stop on the way to bringing the full gospel message to all the world. Unlike later generations, few preachers remained for very long, and the work in Utah suffered from their nomadic lifestyle of evangelizing.

Most initial Pentecostal congregations in the United States developed through the conversion of pastors and evangelists. Once the revival commenced under William J. Seymour at the Azusa Street Apostolic Faith Mission in Los Angeles, word spread quickly. Gastón Espinosa argued that Seymour's mission produced over 400,000 copies of the *Apostolic Faith* newspaper from 1906 to 1908, and it reached Christians around the world.[32] Curious observers poured in from across the United States, adopted Pentecostal theology and worship practices, and then carried it back to their home congregations. According to Espinosa, "many patterned their mission after Azusa," as they carried the Pentecostal revival to almost every major city in the country.[33] Many of these early congregations became the centers for emerging Pentecostal denominations. Others heard the new teachings from evangelists on their way home from Azusa Street. In Denver, Colorado, Gilbert E. Farr heard women evangelists from Los Angeles preach at a camp meeting about spiritual gifts including the gift of tongues. He adopted it, and their congregation, the Christian Assembly, joined the Pentecostal revival in 1907.[34] Similar events took place in towns across America.

The first wave of Pentecostal growth in the United States depended on the direction of adept leaders. Alongside theological claims that the Holy Spirit led the revival in lieu of human leadership, Grant Wacker argued, "The Pentecostal movement, like virtually all popular religious stirrings, required strong leadership if it was to survive at all."[35] Florence Crawford, William Durham, E. N. Bell, C. H. Mason, G. T. Haywood, Aimee Semple McPherson, and A. J. Tomlinson all employed their organizational skills to develop strong Pentecostal institutions. Churches like Reverend Farr's Christian Assembly in Denver joined Pentecostal networks developed by these early leaders. As evangelists traveled east from Seymour's Apostolic Faith Mission, they planted seeds predominantly among independent Christian churches and Holiness churches. The Pentecostal revival thrived on the conversion of Christian leaders dissatisfied with traditional worship.

Even Salt Lake City contained a Pentecostal mission by 1914, but the lack of converted leaders or interested congregations left Utah a complicated place for

Pentecostal growth generally. Holiness churches tended to be more receptive to the Pentecostal message, like the Church of God (Anderson) and the Salvation Army. Both groups had small missions in Salt Lake by 1914, but numbering fewer than twenty individuals.[36] There are no records of any Utahn attending the Azusa Street revival and no Utah congregations that would have been receptive to the message anyway. No native leaders or interested congregations contributed to the difficulties of evangelizing in Utah.

Nevertheless, the Assemblies of God tried to plant congregations in the state from the time of its inception. The minutes from the first General Council of the Assemblies of God held in April 1914 included among the list of missionaries a woman named Mrs. Olive H. Walker.[37] Walker opened a Pentecostal mission at 371 East 400 South in Salt Lake City on August 10, 1914 with the hopes of drawing together any other believers in the state. She ran an ad in *The Christian Evangel* on October 24, 1914 promoting the new mission as fulfilling a long overlooked need: "Many hungry souls had been praying for years for such a mission, as it is such a Mormon center."[38] The mission hoped to open a rescue home for fallen girls and continue spreading the Holy Ghost message to outlying Utah communities. Such parachurch organizations thrived in the early twentieth century, and a few even existed in Utah, such as the Salt Lake City Industrial Christian Home, founded in 1886 by Angie Newman. Walker's mission, however, was the first Pentecostal mission in Salt Lake.[39]

The mission truly took off in 1916 when the nationally acclaimed evangelist Maria Woodworth-Etter held a revival in the city. Newspapers reported on meetings during 1914 and 1915, but the revival created a significant amount of publicity for the nascent Assemblies of God.[40] Robert Harry Lowe, the new pastor of the AG mission, organized the event in the hope for "an ingathering of the saints from many quarters during this meeting. The assembly here is small and but newly established, so come praying, and help us make this campaign for souls successful."[41] Lowe, like many others after him, found Salt Lake to be geographically important for church growth. "The inter-mountain country is practically an untouched field," he declared. "Salt Lake City is situated about equa-distant [sic] from Denver, San Francisco, Portland, and Los Angeles, like the hub of a wheel—the logical place for the establishment of a strong assembly, and work."[42] The congregation (likely no more than a handful) rented the Grand Theater in downtown Salt Lake and prepared for an outpouring of the Spirit "in this darkened city."[43]

The revival made news throughout the month of October and firmly established the work already begun by the Assemblies of God in Salt Lake. Woodworth-Etter delivered her unique variety of ecstatic preaching and healing, offered twice a day Tuesday through Saturday and three times a day on Sundays.[44] From October 6 to October 29, August Feick recalled how "on the same mat, where prize fights are staged—stained with blood—sinners weep their way through to God, and saints receive their baptism."[45] Fred Eiting, who also attended the revivals, reported how "God has been adding souls each week, and hungry souls are being filled."[46] The report to *The Weekly Evangel* described a most spectacular revival:

> Last night the glory of God filled the theatre mostly all through the meeting. Sister Etter was held like a statue a good part of the time by the power of God. At the close of the meeting, about a half a dozen of the most spiritual young saints made inquiries about the peculiar mist in the building. They did not know that it was God's glory, or that any one else saw and felt it. Jesus was seen on the platform. A report just came to me through a sister saying she knows of outside people who testify that they saw angels while the meeting was going on. Marvelous messages in tongues with interpretations come continually. Some Mormons have received their baptism already, others are seeking. The work that God does in the way of healing is drawing many people.[47]

For weeks, Woodworth-Etter continued to preach, heal, and impress her audiences. The Salt Lake Tribune reported, "While now more than seventy-two years of age, Mrs. Etter displays remarkable endurance, tiring out her assistants of less than half her years in the continuous round of meetings to which she addresses her energies."[48]

Only a few details emerge about who attended the revival. They hoped to draw people from Utah and elsewhere to support the small congregation in Salt Lake, and many did come from outside. Describing the attendance, Fred Eiting reported that "a number of the people are living here, and quite a number who came—some to be saved, others to be healed and to be filled with the fullness of God—have returned to the different states."[50] The newspapers reported on "considerable interest . . . being manifested" in the revival but shared no details about attendees.[51] At least a few Latter-day Saints converted during the revival according to August Feick, but the congregation remained quite small.

Despite its size, the momentum of the revival carried over to the work of planting a permanent congregation. Fred Eiting, a traveling evangelist, traveled to Salt Lake for the revival and decided to remain with Pastor Lowe to strengthen the fledgling assembly. Eiting encouraged other evangelists to come and stake a claim in "the largest untouched field in the United States," listing Utah, Nevada, Wyoming, and Arizona as places without an "established Pentecostal work in them, that I know of."[52] No doubt in part thanks to the popularity of Woodworth-Etter, the mission managed to secure an old Lutheran church building to hold their meetings. Thomas Griffin, an evangelist who called himself "the converted gambler," sought out permission from the city and commenced a prison ministry.[53] By April 1917, Lowe indicated that "a number have received the baptism of the Holy Spirit, ten or twelve baptized in water, and about sixteen seeking the baptism of the Spirit at the present time."[54] Things continued to improve through 1917, with Griffin counting seven more spirit baptisms in the month of May.[55]

Yet labor as they might, the assembly suffered in its growth. Geographically it made sense to plant a Pentecostal congregation in Salt Lake, but the constant flow of evangelists passing through Utah made leadership and stability confusing for the small congregation. Pastor Lowe continued leading the little Salt Lake congregation on and off again into the mid-1920s while other evangelists tried their hand at the wheel. Philip (sometimes listed as P. M. Stokely) and Catherine Stokely and Samuel and Sadie Finley all worked cooperatively with Lowe during 1917 and 1918.[56] A pastor named P. D. McCabe introduced his work in Utah in 1919, announcing that "we have a nice hall, and are sending our first missionary offering with our love and prayers."[57] His name did not appear again in Salt Lake. Several other evangelists appeared in newspaper columns as they visited the Salt Lake congregation for weeks or months at a time, but only Pastor Lowe remained. Even Thomas Griffin abandoned his prison ministry and headed for Santa Barbara, California in early 1918.[58] When the Assemblies of God filed official papers of incorporation in 1921 through the state of Utah, Lowe filled the position of pastor.

A man named J. D. Wells demonstrated the problematic nature of an evangelistic ministry always in flux. By 1923, Pastor Lowe had retired, although he "consented to help in the work to such an extent as demands upon his time and the state of his health permitted, so long as the assembly needed his assistance."[59] Lowe left the congregation to its deacons as they prepared to build a church on their new land at 57 East 1300 South in Salt Lake City. J. D. Wells arrived in April and assumed leadership of the congregation. "Utah and Nevada," Wells preached, "lie sleeping in awful ignorance of the fact that these are the last days, waiting for someone to come and awaken them with the Spirit of God." He called for workers from crowded missions in the eastern United States to make their way to the virgin lands of Utah, and he promised them masses of willing souls to heed their call:

> There are eleven cities of 5,000 to 118,000 without a Pentecostal preacher or mission. There are altogether over a half million people and only three Pentecostal preachers: W. L. Thompson at Reno, Nevada, J. D. Wells and Mrs. Lillian Wells at Salt Lake City, Utah. Mormonism is losing its hold on this generation and the people are hungry for the real power of God.

Wells reveled in the great opportunity of Utah and its surrounding environs. "Can you realize a stretch of 1100 miles between Sacramento, California, and Denver, Colorado, with only one mission," Wells marveled.[60]

Wells's estimation of a weakening Latter-day Saint community reflected the beliefs of other early twentieth century Protestant ministers and newspaper writers in Utah. David Utter, a Methodist, and Dr. Paden, a Presbyterian, both noted fewer public expressions of charismatic gifts. "A few years ago," wrote David Utter, "it might have been truly said that there was nothing more distinctively Mormon than their belief in the gift of tongues, prophecy, healing, etc."[61] The *Salt Lake Tribune* claimed in an editorial in 1910 "that a large section of the young people of the Mormon church are breaking away from the old superstition that characterized almost every utterance and movement having to do with the inception of that organization."[62] Statistically, the proportion of Latter-day Saints to non-Latter-day Saints decreased through the early twentieth century dramatically, from around 97 percent in 1890 to 70 percent in 1940.[63] The Church of Jesus Christ of Latter-day Saints continued to grow rapidly in Utah, but the outsider population grew quickly right alongside it.

Unfortunately, Wells's ambition overshadowed the congregation he presumed to lead. In the summer of 1923, he headed to Denver where he encouraged and organized the inclusion of Utah and Wyoming with Colorado to form a new regional district of the Assemblies of God. They called it the Intermountain District Council, with William H. Boyles as chairman and offices in Denver.[64] Wells managed to land himself the position of State Presbyter over all of Utah. Before the redistricting could be finalized, members of the Salt Lake Assembly intervened. Pastor Lowe questioned Wells's credentials and warned against his aspirations: "This man, coming in here simply as an evangelist and with the welfare and advancement of the work as his primary interest, as we supposed, has conducted himself in a high-handed, arbitrary, overbearing manner and his self-elevation into a position of authority over the work in this state, which he seeks to assume, is going to be disastrous." A month later two deacons of the congregation also wrote to the office of the General Superintendent, expressing the unanimous opinion of the Salt Lake congregation against joining the Intermountain District. They too condemned Brother Wells. "The assembly at Salt Lake," they recounted, "has experienced such a flight of difficulties and setbacks throughout its existence, and more particularly of late, at the hands of itinerant preachers, traveling evangelists and others of that class as to have seriously shaken their faith in the capacity and judgment of such men and to have created a very disturbed condition."[65] They accused Wells and his associates of depleting the congregation's finances and alienating members of the assembly.

The revolving door of itinerants meddling with the Salt Lake Assembly factored into the congregation's decline. Instead of evangelists rolling through Utah leaving behind converts in the wake of full gospel preaching and spirit baptisms, itinerant preachers damaged the work of a small and struggling congregation. While not uncommon in the early years of the Pentecostal revival, AG congregations outside of Utah managed to weather the difficulties of the first generation of whirlwind itinerancy because they continually gained new, local converts. This did not happen in Utah. The excitement of the Woodworth-Etter revival and the first wave of Utah Pentecostals through the Assemblies of God achieved an estimated "group of more than 200" members, according to a brief history printed in the *Pentecostal Evangel* in 1954.[66] Yet when Mrs. G. W. Wagner reported on the work in Salt Lake in June 1924, the number of members "in dark Utah" had shrunk to only seven. Mrs. Wagner plead with her readers to "pray through that God may send someone to us for a mighty revival, it is so needed; pray also for a pastor."[67] The *Evangel* history, written much later, insinuated the decline occurred when "moral corruption common to the area gained inroads" to the Salt Lake Assembly.[68] But in this particular case, the very nature of Pentecostal itinerancy failed to take root in a highly religious Latter-day Saint community, leaving nothing to blame for its failure but the mode of Pentecostal evangelism itself.

The state of Utah struggled with modernization in the 1920s and 1930s, and very few people made their way to Utah during these decades, including Latter-day Saints. Since the mid-nineteenth century, leaders encouraged new converts to gather at the church's headquarters. In 1921, apostle Orson F. Whitney wrote an editorial titled "Stay Where You Are!," reversing the longstanding encouragement of migration. "The counsel of the General Authorities to the yet ungathered saints, is not to flock Zionward under existing conditions," wrote Whitney.[69] Instead, church members began expanding congregations elsewhere. Shortly following the end of World War I, only 400 Latter-day Saints lived in Los Angeles; by 1927, more than 8,000 resided in the LA area. They moved to California from many locations, including Utah and Idaho, because it offered better employment opportunities. [70] Whitney cited "abnormal industrial conditions" as one of the reasons in his editorial to end the migration: "Many of our people are out of work and cannot find employment, and those who go there now, hoping to better their lot, are liable to be disappointed and to become disheartened."[71] Perhaps slowed migration assisted Utah's economy because the standard of living rose slowly and steadily through the 1920s.

Yet the state suffered devastating losses in the Great Depression. Charles S. Peterson and Brian Q. Cannon note how "Utah's economic plight exceeded that of the nation at large by 1932–33."[72] One-third of Utah's banks closed, the value of manufactured goods fell 50 percent, farm incomes fell 57 percent, and mineral production sank 80 percent. Utahns abandoned the state in pursuit of work elsewhere. The immigrant population also pursued work in other locations. From 1930 to 1940, the number of Mexican immigrants living in Utah dropped from 4,000 to 1,000, and the Japanese population fell by half. By the end of the 1930s, Utah experienced a net outward migration of almost 92,000 people.[73]

Very few non-Latter-day Saints entered Utah either over the 1920s and 1930s, resulting in almost no Pentecostal growth over the same period.[74] Those pastors and evangelists who did weather the economic storm came and went leaving similar stories behind. L. Vere Elliott, a seasoned missionary to Jerusalem and India made an attempt at evangelization in Utah in 1926. He inherited a floundering Pentecostal mission located at 44½ South Main Street in Salt Lake and immediately affiliated it with the Assemblies of God. As quickly as he descended on Salt Lake, Pastor Elliott was gone. The mission at 44½ South Main Street resurfaced in 1927 as an independent Pentecostal mission called the Full Gospel Mission under the direction of a different pastor.[75] Paul Kienel pastored a mission at 64 Richards Street, which later moved to 430 South 200 West. Notices of his meetings appear from 1929 to 1930, but then he fades from Utah and only reappears in AG records as a pastor in Florida in 1934.[76] Benjamin Caudle spent 1933 in Ogden, Gilbert T. Thompson preached in Monticello in 1937, and Joe Clapper evangelized in San Juan County from 1938–1939.[77] No pastor saw fit nor could afford to remain in Utah, and likely very few congregation members stayed either. Leading into the 1930s, the Assemblies of God annual report listed Utah as the second lowest state in recorded offerings, with only Vermont lower than it. By 1930, Utah settled in comfortably at the very bottom.[78]

PIONEERS IN THEIR OWN RIGHT: THE SECOND GENERATION

For the Assemblies of God to become a fixed part of Utah culture, the second generation of pastors needed to claim sacred space of their own. The first generation preached the old-time religion from storefront churches, but they garnered very little success among the Latter-day Saints. The integration of religious, social, and communal life made it very complicated to disentangle individuals and convert them to Pentecostalism.[79] Evangelists like Dwight C. Ritchie tried to contend with Mormonism through tracts and street meetings, hoping to demonstrate the flaws within Latter-day Saint theology and draw families to the theology of Pentecost. Instead, most new members came from the unchurched population or migration into the state; very few converted among the Latter-day Saints. The pastors of the second generation who succeeded in planting permanent congregations in Utah sought to conquer space over souls. Through the building of Pentecostal churches, the Assemblies of God managed to create geographical and spiritual spaces, which nurtured fledgling congregations and provided them with the confidence to grow.[80]

In the mid-1940s, Sunnyside, Utah, flourished as a coal-mining town. Since the creation of the Carbon County railway in 1899, the scattered mining towns of eastern Utah experienced booms and busts, just like other parts of the United States. Because of the wars fought in Europe and Asia, Utah's coal country surged with business and miners received good wages. The work would eventually dry up, and the Carbon County Railway would cease operations in 1984, but during the boom years, Carbon County attracted families of all faiths. Robert Smith found himself living in Sunnyside and East Carbon for that very reason; his father worked in the mines while Robert learned to play steel and rhythm guitar at a local Pentecostal church.[81]

Robert Smith entered the Pentecostal community for social purposes before finding himself and the Lord in their meetings. Impressed by the worship music, Smith enjoyed performing with La Veda Francis, the daughter of Lee and Lola Francis. When Lee Francis, the Assembly of God pastor in the area began the construction of a new church building, Smith volunteered his time to the task. By the time the building was completed, Smith's conversion to Pentecost was completed as well. He witnessed miracles in the mining towns and felt Lee Francis's sincere concern for his well-being, which inspired in him a pioneering spirit.

Robert Smith heard a "Macedonian call" to create sacred Pentecostal space across the great expanse of Utah.[82] After pastoring a church in Meeker, Colorado, for five years, Robert and his wife pastored the AG church in Moab, Utah, from 1961 to 1967. They shepherded a congregation excited by the prospect of making a place to call their own, and once more Smith found himself building a sanctuary for his flock. When in 1967 they took over the pastorate of the Kearns Assembly of God (later renamed the Valley Assembly of God and then Life Church Utah), they planned to build again. Their exuberance for evangelism inspired more members of their congregation to spread the message of Pentecost in Utah. In total, Robert Smith supervised or assisted in the construction of fourteen churches in places as far-reaching as Moab, Richfield, Cedar City, St. George, and Fredonia, Arizona, to the south, and Tooele, Roosevelt, Brigham City, and Logan in the north. Over the 1970s and 1980s, Willard Coleman, Vern Fink, Phil Smith, Ray Smith, and Alex Lucero all found their footings in the ministry with Robert Smith. And with each new building, the Assemblies of God created permanent homes for congregations, which would last through the rest of the twentieth century.[83]

Pastors like Robert Smith may not have found their way to Utah if not for the considerable economic and cultural changes occurring in Utah during the 1930s and 1940s. Peterson and Cannon argue that "defense spending during the 1940s expanded Utah's industrial base, generated thousands of jobs at defense installations, and transformed Utah into an economic satellite of Washington, DC."[84] The federal government spent millions of dollars in Utah building air bases, army installations, and small-arms plants. The wartime economy reinvigorated agriculture, mining, and steel. Tens of thousands of jobs brought new life to the Utah economy and attracted outsiders to the state, including African Americans and other minorities. The flow of soldiers through the newly constructed military installations diversified the predominantly Latter-day Saint culture of Utah. This affected the religious diversity of Utah as well. The *Ogden Standard-Examiner* reported, "At the many places of worship provided in Ogden, attendance is generally reported to be excellent."[85] The influx of people from all walks of life meant greater opportunities for starting new churches. Although many people left Utah at the war's end, others stayed and transformed the makeup of cities like Salt Lake City and Ogden.

The earliest permanent congregations of the Assemblies of God managed to plant themselves firmly in Utah thanks to the wartime economy, but also in great part thanks to the work of pioneering pastors. James Summerton and Elmer "Ted" French Chopper arrived in Utah early in 1940. Acting as co-pastors, they re-established Salt Lake Assembly of God meetings in March and Ogden assembly meetings in August.[86] They quickly organized tent meetings and fellowship meetings, both of which would become important staples in creating a community of Pentecostals in the state.[87] At the first fellowship meeting held in October, Summerton reported how "some who had lived in Utah for many years, having been saved elsewhere, told how they had prayed God to send in some workers to open some assemblies, and that they were now privileged to behold the answer to their prayers and to have a part in the work."[88]

The Ogden Assembly garnered more attention and success in the early part of the 1940s. Long considered an intersection for national railroad commerce, the construction of what would eventually become Hill Air Force Base added to the diversity of the Ogden area. Despite the commercial relationship Ogden shared with the rest of the nation, most Pentecostal missions of the early twentieth century focused their evangelistic efforts on Salt Lake City. Perhaps unaware of Ogden's religious diversity dating back to the influx of outside rail workers and passengers following the completion of the railroad in 1869, Pentecostals overlooked Ogden as a welcome location for growth.[89] Only Benjamin Caudle sought to plant a congregation in Ogden. Holding revivals at the old Weber theatre on Twenty-Fifth Street, Caudle planned to establish a regular congregation and meeting place following his 1933 revival. He opened a mission on Twenty-Seventh Street in October 1933, but the endeavor failed to take root.[90]

E. F. Chopper enlisted the help of local brothers Alpha and Nathan Padgett and Clarence Hirschy to formally organize an AG congregation in Ogden.[91] Hirschy pastored the congregation from 1941 to 1945, moving from a rented location on Wall Avenue to an old Seventh Day Adventist church, which they purchased in early 1942. As the congregation grew, they received visits often from members of the Rocky Mountain district leadership including district superintendent J. E. Austell. Having established a safe place to congregate and worship, the Assemblies of God established their first firm foothold in Utah.

The assembly in Salt Lake followed closely behind Ogden, but the creation of sacred space took several years longer in the busy downtown streets of the state capitol. James Summerton operated out of a storefront church on State Street until Dwight C. Ritchie assumed the pastorate in late 1941. They moved to an old church building at 226 West 300 North.[92] Pastor Robert Lowe had purchased land in the 1920s near State Street on 1300 South but never managed to make any improvements. Advertising the Assembly of God as a "nonsectarian church," both "Pentecostal" and "Fundamental," Ritchie pursued the goal of raising enough funds to build a meeting house on the church-owned land.[93]

Pastor Hirschy in Ogden sought to make all people welcome at his church. Styling his church as "a friendly place to worship," Hirschy ran ads in the paper and invited all to join him in "an old-fashioned revival for a new-fashioned world."[94] He encouraged charismatic expressions of the gifts of the Spirit and pressed "Uncle Sam's army to attend church."[95] "This church is not a lecture platform, not a moving picture theatre, not a center for socials and suppers," declared Hirschy, "but a place to worship God. A place where God is manifested, a place where Jesus Christ is preeminent, a place where the Holy Spirit is Lord, a place where the sick are healed, a place where souls are baptized in the Spirit."[96]

In contrast to Hirschy, Pastor Ritchie aggressively confronted the theological views of the dominant Latter-day Saint culture, impugning "Mormon doctrine" as false and misleading. He produced stacks of Sunday School lessons in rhyme and tracts concerning Latter-day Saint history and beliefs. A clever writer, Ritchie explained his intent with the following verse: "These words were written not to make of error merchandise, but to reprove an evil work and to inform the wise. Accept the truth which they convey, and from all error turn; then pass them on that others may these facts important learn."[97] Ritchie believed that by exposing the errors in Mormonism, he might draw more Latter-day Saints to the Assemblies of God. And he did find some success with his approach. Reporting on a revival meeting held in late 1944, Leona Bryant described how "one lady who had been a teacher in the Mormon church, had traveled abroad, and speaks five languages, was wonderfully saved and filled with the Holy Ghost. Her husband is a high priest in the Mormon church and his grandfather was one of the twelve apostles (of the Mormons)."[98] Yet compared to Hirschy's more compassionate approach, Ritchie's leadership in Salt Lake did not meet with the same immediate success as the assembly in Ogden. So long as the focus remained on converting souls over converting space, the congregation would struggle to grow.

During this second generation of pastors, preachers also made efforts to reach out to the Native American populations of Utah as they spread further across the state. Most of the Home Missions work of the Assemblies of God occurred in New Mexico among the Navajo in the first half of the twentieth century. Angela Tarango argued that these evangelists and missionaries "outwardly encouraged Native conversion but faltered in nurturing the development of local indigenous churches and national indigenous leadership."[99] Leadership problems slowed growth among

Native American congregations. Very few missionaries worked among the Native Americans in Utah, but a similar pattern of white leadership existed among those who did. By 1960, Addie Croasmun had planted congregations in the southeastern Utah towns of Monticello, Blanding, and Mexican Hat. The small congregation in Mexican Hat, a little town on the Navajo reservation, was completely Native American except for Addie and her husband Grant. They eventually shifted their focus entirely to the Native Americans and moved from Utah to New Mexico. Their work on the reservation in Utah lasted only a few years, until Addie's death in 1968.[100]

At least one Native American born in Utah became a licensed pastor for the Assemblies of God. Samuel Antes was born in 1902 near Aneth, Utah. Aneth existed in southeastern Utah near the Four Corners area. In 1895, Howard Ray Antes moved to the area and opened the Navajo Faith mission. Previously a Methodist minister, Antes became an independent Holiness preacher so that he could be "entirely free to wholly follow Jesus."[101] Howard and his wife adopted a two-year-old Navajo boy named Da-he-ya in 1904 after his parents died. They renamed the boy Samuel Antes. Samuel grew up on Christian missions around Utah and Colorado. In 1944, he decided to become a minister himself for the Assemblies of God. He attended the Bible Institute of Los Angeles (BIOLA) and served as assistant pastor of the Dove Creek Assembly of God in Colorado, but he spent much of his time in the 1940s and 1950s as a traveling evangelist. He played the piano and violin, and he would tell his life and conversion story to congregations. Telling his life story entitled "From Sagebrush to the Pulpit," Antes assisted Pastor Guy Heath with revivals in Salt Lake on a few occasions.[102]

The AG congregations of the mid-twentieth century developed important cultural institutions that diminished the geographical distance between nascent missionary efforts around the state and abated the pressure of social isolation. New congregations in Provo and the Price area consisted of little more than a few families meeting together. Left to their own devices, these churches might have withered and closed their doors like others before them. Two practices in particular, however, sustained the faith of Utah Pentecostals: the annual state camp meetings and local fellowship meetings.

Guy M. Heath and his wife Mary organized and hosted the first annual state camp meeting in August 1945. As evangelists, the Heaths participated in a Salt Lake tent meeting around 1941, but they returned as permanent fixtures of the Utah Pentecostal community in April 1945. By 1945, the various assemblies in Utah had all held revivals, sometimes even in tents, but the annual camp meeting marked a concerted effort to bring all of the AG congregations in Utah together in worship. Pastor Heath announced that churches from Utah, Colorado, Wyoming, and Idaho would all participate for a week of worship meetings in August.[103] They erected the tent, sixty feet by ninety feet, on the property at 1300 South and invited additional evangelists from around the country to participate before and after the six-day annual meeting. Reports listed six AG congregations in Utah at the time of the meeting. In his report of the event, Rocky Mountain District Superintendent J. E. Austell listed in attendance pastors Guy M. Heath of Salt Lake, John J. Ridge of Ogden, Vern A. Harris of Provo, Lee Francis of Helper, and Vidal Enriquez of the Salt Lake Spanish congregation.[104] "Everyone felt that the Camp was a real success due to the great interest shown by the Mormon people of the city," glowed Austell, and he proudly reported that "several seekers were filled with the Holy Spirit as an outward witness to the many curious onlookers."[105]

The annual state camp meetings reinforced the importance of public worship to Pentecostal Christianity. Oliver McMahan observed that Pentecostal "spirituality is frequently defined within the context of a church service more than a devotional closet."[106] Private devotion to God, exhibited through particular beliefs and behaviors, was absolutely necessary in Pentecostalism, but the encounter with the sacred occurred more commonly in the rituals of public worship. Pentecostal meetings in the United States followed a similar style as some other Protestant Christians, with meetings usually beginning with worship, followed with the sermon or receipt of the Word, and ending with an altar call. Within such meetings among Pentecostals, they encounter opportunities to interact with the movements of the Holy Spirit in unique forms. It is a time for "doing business with God," according to Daniel E. Albrecht and Evan B. Howard.[107] Ranging from speaking in tongues, dancing in the Spirit, receiving words of prophecy, or being slain in the Spirit, the public worship meeting becomes the place where Pentecostals most commonly engage the divine. That engagement occurs most comfortably within a community of believers. The Pentecostal practices of tongues, interpretation of tongues, words of prophecy, healing, and other rituals operate more fluidly within congregations, as opposed to experiences among individuals privately. Developing within the context of American religious revivalism, Pentecostals felt the influence of the Holy Spirit more often together than apart.

And the annual state camp meetings provided plenty of opportunity for Pentecostals and onlookers to engage with the charismatic expression of the Spirit. Year after year, newspapers and pastors reported increased turnout for the daily services under the tent. The location of the event moved around, sometimes meeting in halls or auditoriums, to accommodate the growing congregations outside of Salt Lake City.[108] Columns shared stories of healings and conversions as evidence of the Pentecostal message. Whenever they occurred, witnesses made certain to report Latter-day Saint conversions. "We rejoice," declared Guy Heath, "in the real triumphs of God's grace in the hearts of these Mormon converts who have freely renounced their superstition and ritual, removing their temple garments, and have found salvation and Pentecostal fullness."[109] In 1952, Pastor Heath told of "an entire Mormon family of five" who were "converted, filled with the Holy Spirit, and baptized in water. They were brought in through the remarkable healing of the husband."[110] Reports of healings and the "gracious infilling of the Holy Spirit" underscored the power of the Pentecostal message in the minds of the growing Utah community.

The annual camp meetings used American revivalism to reinforce member worship and inclusion while also creating a vehicle of evangelism around the state of Utah. Though the Church of Jesus Christ of Latter-day Saints had arisen during the Second Great Awakening, tent revivals had never been an important part of Latter-day Saint practice. This particular form of the old-time religion style, therefore, became a religious curiosity to the Utah community. As a religious event, Pentecostals developed this very public opportunity to participate in Pentecostal worship and evangelize the Pentecostal theology at the same time.

The fellowship meetings of the 1940s–1960s existed for the same worship purposes, but they focused more specifically on the social dimensions of the Utah Pentecostal community. Fellowship meetings provided various activities for the youth to socialize and make friends within their own faith. Most local community activities revolved around the social network of the Church of Jesus Christ of Latter-day Saints. As such, the Assemblies of God planned rallies and campouts with their youth group called Christ's Ambassadors. They also brought congregations together to participate in worship together. From the 1940s through the 1960s, monthly fellowship meetings occurred at various locations throughout the state of Utah. They met together in Salt Lake, Ogden, Provo, American Fork, Moab, Price, Dragerton, Vernal, and Bountiful. Many youth found friends and eventually spouses thanks to the interactions they shared in fellowship meetings. Like the camp meetings, they worshipped together, but in the fellowship meetings, they also socialized and ate meals together. They developed a support network for smaller congregations to find the strength to continue struggling in the more rural areas of Utah. These social meetings, combined with the public worship in the annual camp meetings, effectively nurtured the Assemblies of God in Utah from infancy to adolescence during the mid-twentieth century. They helped fulfill the basic needs of individual members and congregations alike as they planted churches in places like Provo, Bountiful, Vernal, Layton, Moab, and elsewhere.[111]

Efforts at creating Pentecostal space and networks did not always go unnoticed or happen without opposition. In most cases, communities welcomed Pentecostal congregations, but not in all cases. As Guy Heath endeavored to build a prominent structure in the heart of Salt Lake City, he described how "legal technicalities delayed it for nineteen months and then only by supreme pressure from the State Bar Association was the difficulty settled."[112] Once they managed to get the building erected and services started, hecklers disturbed worship meetings and interrupted preaching. "Six times the front doors of the church have been destroyed or badly damaged; windows have been broken; and tools have been stolen."[113] In smaller communities, pastors sometimes struggled with local municipalities to gain legal rights to build meetinghouses and hold services. Occasionally the creation of sacred space required a willingness to fight for their place in these communities. Viewed as barbarian invaders by some communities, Pentecostal Christians persevered despite such intolerances.[114]

Ultimately, Pentecostal congregations required their own sacred space and support networks to thrive in Utah. Like pioneers, they built sanctuaries with their own hands. Pastors rarely received enough support from church offerings to be able to focus solely on ministry. Instead, they developed the skills, which enabled them to carve out their own homes along the canyons and valleys of Utah. Despite being outsiders to Utah, they managed to plant churches in most parts of the state by the late 1970s. Pastors like Guy Heath, Kenneth Brethouwer, Peter Pilot, Jasper Weaver, and Robert Smith needed both a pioneering spirit and an iron will to cultivate new territory to create the kind of Pentecostal community that would eventually stack up against and outperform most other religious minorities within the religious society of Utah during the twentieth century.

LANDING ON THE MOON: THE THIRD GENERATION

The 1980s and 1990s functioned as a period of incubation for the Assemblies of God in Utah. Children in congregations that achieved stability mid-century spent their entire adolescence engaged in church worship and activities. Born in Utah, they intended to remain in Utah. Many of the third generation of pastors attended grade school through the late 1970s and early 1980s and began careers in ministry shortly thereafter. Plenty of others continued to come to Utah because of the pull of a mission call to the area, but these homegrown pastors maintained the successes of the previous generations by innovating their ministries in the state.

One method of innovation included the creation of private schools or academies to promote Bible fundamentals in education. Burdette Leikvoll pastored the Logan Assembly of God in the early 1980s. During that time they created the Cache Valley Christian Academy as an alternative to public schools and education. It operated throughout the decade until closing its doors in 1987. Around the same time, Pastor Stanley Arias of the World Vision Assembly of God in Vernal opened a Christian day school, which enrolled sixty children in its courses before an economic downturn in 1985 depleted its funds.[115] Also in the mid-1980s, the Layton First Assembly of God purchased prime real estate near Hill Air Force Base and built a modern building on the land. The congregation continued growing to several hundred, and Pastor Myke Crowder felt directed to open a school on the premises. Named the Layton Christian Academy, it opened as an elementary school in 1993. Since that time, it has grown into a preschool through twelfth-grade campus, with over 600 students from a wide variety of religious backgrounds.[116] Myke Crowder continues as pastor of the Christian Life Center in Layton. Beginning as an at-home church pastored by Lillian Strayer in 1952, the Christian Life Center has grown into a respected community center and school.[117] To compete with the local Latter-day Saint seminary program offered as release time study to Latter-day Saint junior high- and high school-aged students, several churches including the Vernal Assembly of God collaborated on a Christian seminary for non-Latter-day Saints. Beginning in the early 2000s, they created a Bible-based curriculum available to any interested students.[118]

The idea for religious schools was only innovative in that no other churches were currently operating religious schools in Utah. The Presbyterians and Episcopalians operated a network of schools and academies in the late nineteenth and early twentieth centuries but eventually closed them as the public school system emerged in Utah.[119] Pentecostals joined the charter school movement in the 1980s and developed their schools to provide Christian alternatives to public education. Even though many attempts to open and maintain schools did not succeed, those that did provided additional social services to minority groups in Utah looking for an alternative from the options provided within the general community. These programs assisted Pentecostal families in providing programs for their children that did not have the assumed cultural influence of the majority religious faith dominating the agenda through the informal influence of local school boards, community centers, and other municipal services.

The end of the twentieth century witnessed several other innovations among Utah Assemblies of God churches, which increased their visibility and prosperity. Assemblies developed methods to include growing international communities into their programs. As of 2017, over 60,000 refugees lived in the Salt Lake metropolitan area and more are arriving every year.[120] The Salt Lake Christian Center under the leadership of Ray Smith opened its doors to the spiritual needs of Pentecostal minority groups from around the world. They began working with minority groups to create a network of congregations at the church. As of 2017, fourteen different international congregations existed in conjunction with Smith's church, from Chinese and Ethiopian to Navajo and Brazilian.[121] These congregations share facilities with the original Utah congregation, and they also interact in charitable work and social activities. The intuitive leadership of the seventy-five-year-old congregation demonstrated its ability to find new ways of reaching the Salt Lake community.

The decision to include international communities partially stemmed from the very low conversion rate to Pentecostalism from the Church of Jesus Christ of Latter-day Saints. Since the second generation of Pentecostals in Utah, pastors and congregations began recognizing that Latter-day Saint conversion would not be as simple as they hoped. While the second generation developed sacred space of their own, the third generation developed ways of including other minority groups within the Utah community.[122]

Other assemblies began reaching out directly to the unchurched population of Utah. The religious "Nones" make up 22 percent of Utah's population, which dwarfs every religious group in the state except Latter-day Saints.[123] As a statistical category, the Nones are not easily understood. Generally stereotyped as secular or non-religious, the Nones also include those that identify as spiritual but not religious. Elizabeth Drescher observed, "While Nones are characterized by the fact that they do not claim formal, membership-based affiliation with institutional religious groups, many of those I interviewed periodically—indeed, in some cases quite regularly—attended services in one or more church, sangha, synagogue, temple, or other religious community."[124] While 3 percent and 2 percent of Utahns identified as Atheists and Agnostics respectively, the remaining 17 percent of the Nones constitute a major interest to denominational evangelism.

Several churches, including the Assemblies of God, began in the early 2000s to develop church congregations focused on the new demographic of Nones. Non-denominational churches like the Alpine Church and K2 first began developing worship styles more centered on the anti-institutional attitudes of Nones. On K2's website, they explain, "Don't like church? Perfect. This is a church for people who don't like church."[125] Alpine Church advertised itself with the slogan "Church can be different."[126] The Genesis Project's multiple campuses in Utah focused ministry on the unchurched population as well.[127] Emphasizing community over theology, these churches have been successful in gaining younger members that might be somewhat reticent to affiliate with traditional denominations. Hoping to reflect greater inclusivity, many Assemblies of God in Utah adopted new names that do not include the name of the denomination. The inheritors of the Salt Lake Assembly of God developed into congregations called the Life Church Utah and the Salt Lake Christian Center. The distinctive charismatic practices are less visible in their services, but they continue representing the denomination in creative new ways.

Finally, the Assemblies of God began interacting directly with the Church of Jesus Christ of Latter-day Saints in the early twenty-first century. Through the organization created by Greg Johnson known as Standing Together, Pentecostals and Latter-day Saints established a series of dialogues with each other, to improve denominational relationships.[128] For the Assemblies of God, this dialogue peaked with a formal visit to Brigham Young University in 2013 from George O. Wood, the General Superintendent of the Assemblies of God. Although theologically very distinct and separate, Pentecostals and Latter-day Saints realized they could help shoulder the burden of shared cultural and political concerns. These specific interactions will be unpacked in later chapters, but this kind of institutional interaction did not exist prior to the third generation of Pentecostal history in Utah.[129]

In January 2018, the Canyon Road Assembly of God Church installed a new pastor named Dan Gilboy. Although Ogden now has several Assembly of God churches, the congregation at Canyon Road descends from the church established in the 1940s by Elmer Chopper, Clarence Hirschy, and the Padgett brothers. It celebrated its seventy-fifth anniversary in 2016. Alex Lucero, Assistant District Superintendent of the Rocky Mountain District, installed Dan Gilboy as pastor. During his welcome to the new pastor, Alex said to Pastor Gilboy, "Welcome to Utah. There will come a time in the near future where you will wonder if you landed on the moon."[130] Lucero, born and raised in Utah, recognized that to an outsider like Pastor Gilboy, the religious culture of Utah might in some ways resemble that of a foreign planet. At 55 percent of the state's population, the Church of Jesus Christ of Latter-day Saints retains a strong majority over other faith groups in the state. Other than the Catholic Church at 5 percent, no other religious denomination makes up more than approximately 1 percent of the population.[131] Since the 1940s, the Assemblies of God have grown more than many other denominations in Utah, but they remain a significant minority. For Pastor Gilboy, that meant he would need some time to adjust to life in the Latter-day Saint society.

For homegrown pastors like Alex Lucero, Ray Smith, Dane Wead, and many others, expanding the Assemblies of God in Utah meant experimenting with new ways to improve the spiritual life of extant congregations. Their cultural and social expertise of the religious environment in Utah enabled them to interact with the nuances of associating with both the Church of Jesus Christ of Latter-day Saints as a religious entity and Utah culture as a societal entity. The third generation of Assemblies of God pastors learned how to survive on the surface of the moon by reaching out to immigrant and unchurched populations and developing a new network of Pentecostal congregations.

CONCLUSION

Over three successive generations of Pentecostal pastors and congregations, the Assemblies of God successfully carried the full gospel message to Utah, created sacred spaces for Pentecostal worship, and developed dynamic institutions that are continuing to grow into the twenty-first century. A survey of the Assemblies of God in Utah today shows very little of the struggle that it went through over the last one hundred years to make its mark on the desert and mountain landscape. Men and women, from the birth of the denomination to its modern incarnation, felt called to preach the Pentecostal message among the Latter-day Saints. Early missionaries thought establishing congregations would occur as easily in Salt Lake as in Chicago, New York, and other large American cities. They left disheartened, feeling like strangers in a strange land, unaccustomed to the religion and culture of Utah people. Missionary families sacrificed lucrative jobs and burgeoning congregations elsewhere to suffer isolation and poverty in farming and mining towns. Occasional moments of interfaith friendship and community joined Pentecostals and Latter-day Saints together, but for the better part of the twentieth century, neither tradition understood how to work with, communicate with, or coexist with the other. Yet through the sweat, perseverance, and faith of a few, the Assemblies of God left their own signature in the mountains of the Beehive state.

The Assemblies of God did not convert all Utahns as they had hoped, but by the early twenty-first century, they prevailed in becoming the largest Protestant denomination in the state. That success came in great part through the efforts of pastors and congregations willing to settle into Utah for the long haul. They built the church literally with their own hands, and they repeated the process in communities across the state. Their outreach to the ignored or unchurched populations of the state expanded their membership and enabled further growth into rural areas. They may not have converted the kingdom, but the sacred spaces they constructed provided more than enough room to care for those Pentecostals who chose to remain in Utah.

2

UNDERNEATH THE RADAR

Less Represented and Independent Pentecostal Denominations in Utah

Forrest Leslie Stinson grew up in Clayton, New Mexico. Born on December 15, 1909, Stinson worked as a meat cutter in his early life and moved around the southwest. He married Juanita Merle Chester in 1929, and together they organized a Pentecostal church in East Los Angeles. They made their way to Ogden in 1948, where Forrest operated the Courtesy Market grocery store for many years.[1]

Stinson became known throughout Ogden for his decades of ministerial service. He pastored the Ogden Assembly of God church briefly when he arrived in 1948. Then in 1949, he opened the Full Gospel Assembly at 3028 Grant Avenue, which moved to 2168 Lincoln Avenue shortly thereafter. He converted an old meat market into a church building for the growing congregation. The Full Gospel Assembly functioned as an Independent Pentecostal congregation, holding revivals and preaching salvation through Jesus and the outpourings of Pentecost.[2]

By 1953, the Full Gospel Assembly affiliated with the Pentecostal Church of God. Leo Waggoner took over Stinson's church on Lincoln Avenue, and Stinson headed to Sunset, Utah, just outside of Ogden. Preaching "the old-time Gospel, A Gospel of Deliverance," Forrest opened a Pentecostal Church of God at 25 East Center Street in Sunset.[3] Like other Utah pastors of the period, he used radio broadcasts and hosted "Moments with the Master" Sunday mornings at 8:00 AM.[4] No longer independent, Stinson remained passionate about the expansion of the Pentecostal message. He preached with the Pentecostal Church of God for most of the 1950s.

Yet once again, Stinson embarked on a fresh work under a different affiliation. The *Ogden Standard-Examiner* reported in 1961 that Forrest Stinson began conducting services for the Church of the Foursquare Gospel in Brigham City.

"The name means Jesus Christ," Stinson explained to the newspaper, "as our savior, our healer, our baptizer with the Holy Spirit, and as our coming king."[5] Forrest and Juanita, along with their children, made the commute to Brigham City to pioneer the first mission for the International Church of the Foursquare Gospel in Utah. They remained there during most of the early 1960s.

Always on the move, Forrest took his next assignment with the International Union of Gospel Missions.[6] The Stinsons took over the Ogden Rescue Mission shortly after it opened in 1966 and relocated the mission to 28th Street and Wall Avenue. From 1966 until December 1973, they directed one of the most charitable organizations in Weber County, Utah. During the first year of operations, they opened a facility with housing accommodations for around thirty people, assisted hundreds in job placement, and held spiritual services twice a day at the mission.[7] Over the next several years, the Stinsons helped collect and donate literally tons of clothing and food to various communities inside and outside of Utah. They worked with Utah Governor Calvin Rampton and Ogden Mayor Bart Wolthuis to meet the needs of thousands in Ogden through meals and rehabilitation programs. "We tell them to look up and trust the Lord," Forrest explained in 1969.[8] With the help of Hill Air Force Base, the Rescue Mission sent 9,200 pounds of aid to Mississippi after Hurricane Camille devastated several communities and provided approximately 5,000 pounds of basic necessities to a program called Project Navajo which brought relief to the Navajo reservation.[9] They held annual Thanksgiving suppers for hundreds and encouraged all members of the community to support the effort with donations of time and commodities.[10] By the time Forrest and Juanita Stinson resigned as superintendents of the Ogden Rescue Mission in December 1973, thousands had benefited from their constant efforts to relieve suffering.[11]

His concern for others continued until the day he died in February 1974. "The gospel can comfort the tired and lonely," believed Stinson, describing how he sought to "move men and women into a new life that can bring them new hope."[12] His vision rubbed off on his children, as well. David Stinson followed his father into the ministry, becoming a pastor for the Assemblies of God and ministering at the Canyon Road Assembly of God in Ogden and the Vernal Assembly of God.[13] Sharon Stinson worked with the Wycliffe Bible Translators in Brazil, translating the Bible into native dialects.[14] Spanning three decades and operating through various organizations, Forrest Stinson and his family bolstered the Ogden community with their Pentecostal convictions.

Many smaller denominations and independent Pentecostal churches in Utah experienced significant fluidity in their institutional affiliations as they formed, merged, split, and transformed congregations within the Pentecostal community. Forrest Stinson is an example of the transitions, starts, and stops, experienced by minor denominations during the twentieth century. Pastoring for three different denominations, as well as opening an independent church and operating a rescue mission, Stinson embodied the passion and volatility with which Pentecostal pastors made their way through Utah.

Over the course of the 1900s, very few Pentecostal denominations in Utah managed the same kind of permanency as the Assemblies of God. More often, independent pastors initiated works across the state, petitioned denominations for support, and struggled to keep their organizations afloat. Success required permanency, and many pastors within smaller denominations planted roots in Utah, only to wrench them from the soil again as they felt the call to other fields beyond the Beehive state. Some independent Pentecostal congregations fared better than many smaller denominations because, much like the second generation of Assembly of God pastors in Utah, they dug into the community for the long haul and created sacred spaces of their own. When they failed to create such space, these communities often transformed in personality and transgressed denominational boundaries as they sought to remain a part of Utah culture.

The various schisms between denominations and the creation of independent congregations continue to add vibrancy to the Pentecostal community in Utah specifically and the United States generally. It might seem counterintuitive for chaotic institutional arrangements to promote growth, but this seems to be the case among Pentecostals. The minor Pentecostal denominations and independent churches of Utah demonstrate the kind of growth that continues on the fringes of Pentecostalism across the United States today. This chapter looks at many different Pentecostal denominations and congregations and how they have fared over the years in the state. The sporadic, unpredictable ways that these congregations evolved models the ways that Pentecostal congregations continue to transform as Pentecostalism grows generally throughout the United States. The early years of classical Pentecostal denominations in the United States were filled with mergers and leadership changes. The denominations also split apart and rebranded. Several major denominations emerged, but many smaller congregations continued practicing independently. This process continued throughout the twentieth and early twenty-first centuries. Not only leaders, but followers traded denominational labels for various reasons. Pentecostal loyalty became more associated with the Pentecostal experience than the denominational appearance, and Pentecostal Christians continue to add an element of uncertainty and spontaneity to the growth and variety of Christianity in the United States today.

Grant Wacker, Gastón Espinosa, and others argue concerning the reasons for Pentecostalism's continued growth in the contemporary religious world. Wacker writes that Pentecostals balanced primitive impulses of the afterlife and powerful spirituality formed from an intense connection with God, with pragmatic impulses of the need to engage oneself in the commercial world and participate in the necessities of everyday life. Despite tensions pulling them toward one or the other impulse, "the genius of the Pentecostal movement lay in its ability to hold two seemingly incompatible impulses in productive tension," enabling them to grow and expand throughout the world.[15]

Gastón Espinosa argues that the growth of Pentecostalism is better understood through the movement's failure to find balance. Espinosa explains how contrary to Grant Wacker's primitive/pragmatic balance, the movement keeps growing "precisely because of its leaders' inability to balance these competing impulses." Wacker viewed Pentecostals as miraculously managing to contain lightning in a bottle, whereas Espinosa replied that every time Pentecostals tried to contain the lightning, the bottle would crack and fragment, resulting in denominational fracturing and new identities within the larger Pentecostal movement.[16]

Many Pentecostal congregations in Utah experienced this sort of fracturing and restructuring. Sometimes congregations dissolved and members joined other congregations. Sometimes congregations chose to depart from one denomination and join a different one or even become an independent congregation. Throughout it all, the Pentecostal community in Utah continued to grow.

CHURCH OF GOD, CLEVELAND

Beginning as a Holiness church in 1886, the Church of God transformed into one of the earliest Pentecostal churches in the United States. Under the guidance and leadership of R. G. Spurling and A. J. Tomlinson, the church moved its headquarters to Cleveland, Tennessee, and embraced the Pentecostal message. Congregation members experienced spiritual gifts including speaking in tongues prior to the Azusa Street mission in 1906, but they did not publicize it. When the 1906

Pentecostal revival became national news, the Church of God took note. They would eventually become part of the growing movement.[17]

The Church of God, Cleveland, engaged the question of Mormonism earlier than any other Pentecostal denomination, but they arrived in Utah shortly after missionaries for the Assemblies of God.[18] In March 1921, A. J. Tomlinson, the editor of the *Church of God Evangel*, urged his readers to spread the *Evangel* to every state in the United States where it had not yet gained subscribers. He called for "a thousand men and women to carry the printed pages and go from house to house and talk and pray with the people and leave the silent messengers to preach after they are gone."[19] Included among the states without subscribers, he petitioned individuals to go to Utah, for "every foot of ground must be covered."[20]

By June of that same year, Tomlinson recapped how he "made a note in the paper that there were four states that had no subscribers, but since that time some one [sic] helped us start it into Utah." To the Church of God, distributing the journal mattered because "the paper has preceded the Church in many states where the Church is now flourishing, and in most cases it opened the way for the Church to be established." "If we can only get a start," believed Tomlinson, "get a seed planted, it is sure to commence multiplying."[21] Thus, the *Church of God Evangel* preceded any actual ministers as the first representative of the Church of God in the state of Utah.

The *Church of God Evangel* first received word of a growing congregation in Utah in 1929.[22] Loretta Boyd and Grace Hall wrote to the periodical to share gratitude for the revival held in Summit Point and led by Jess W. Kinsey and his wife, Ella.[23] Located in southeastern Utah about thirty miles northeast of Monticello, the city of Summit Point had little more than a post office, school, and general store. Grace Hall explained how in the summer of 1929, she and others in Summit Point began seeking an experience with the Holy Spirit in response to the miraculous healing of Grace's sister Ethel. Remembering that her other sister Ella married a "Holy Ghost preacher," they wrote to the Kinseys and asked them to come to Summit Point. The Kinseys came in fall 1929. "In a very short time," recalled Mrs. Hall, "I was talking in other tongues and could not speak English."[24]

A formal establishment of the Church of God in Utah took place on Monday, October 6, 1930.[25] The Kinseys asked E. L. Moore to come and formally organize the congregations into a part of the denomination. He did so, and shortly thereafter S. W. Latimer, General Overseer of the Church of God, named E. L. Simmons to be the first Utah State Overseer.[26] E. L. Moore reported the organization to the Annual Assembly of the Church of God.[27] With only nine members, the small congregation in Summit Point became the first Pentecostal congregation of any denomination in southern Utah.

The congregation struggled during the first few years. "We are out entirely on faith," declared E. L. Moore, "and are not able to purchase for the encouragement of the work or our advancement. Many times we can't buy stamps to write our friends."[28] Summit Point sat a few miles outside of Monticello, Utah, and Monticello itself was a small town along the road which traveled down through Utah toward the Navajo reservation in the Four Corners area of the Southwestern United States. "Many people came into the county to build corrals, homes, fences, and brought farming equipment," described Elizabeth Summers, "only to leave and give up the venture and go elsewhere to begin again."[29] Because of the remote location, few people moved to and remained living in San Juan County, Utah. A family affiliated with the Assembly of God joined the congregation in early 1932, but the total size remained around ten people, according to E. L. Simmons.[30]

The church enjoyed very few converts from the predominantly Latter-day Saint community. Ethel Perry moved from Summit Point to Monticello and opened a "church house" near the post office, to be able to reach more people.[31] Yet the style of worship created considerable opposition. Frank Silvey described the congregation in 1936 for a historical survey of San Juan County:

> A small group (about twelve) at Summit Point San Juan County, who call themselves "Church of God" people, but seem to have an individual religion to us westerners as they radically believe in "Hell fire and brimstones" everlasting punishment for those who do not believe in their special brand of religion, teach fear to children, who today are timid and fear all strangers and outsiders, have little rise for schools but are teaching their members young and old to be preachers. They are utterly opposed to dancing, and all other amusements and have succeeded to date in partially breaking up dances and amusements. They hold revivals sometimes lasting for days or rather nights and do not go home until morning. They shout, "talk in tongues," (each member has his own language) and causes a babel of voices, roll on the floor, etc. Their emotions are so aroused they seem to forget time and the world. Some members declare: We get drunk on the "Wine of God," and are very happy.[32]

Silvey also mentioned a "roving band of Mexican singers and players of a faith similar to the Summit Point branch," which came and converted around fifteen people to their religion. Almost certainly referring to José Marez and the Gallegos family, the community did not have a very high opinion of Pentecostal belief and worship.[33] Most often those who did join these congregations came from outside Utah, looking for work in the area. The Monticello community, predominantly made up of Latter-day Saints, allowed the little congregation to worship but kept their distance from these "radical" Christians.

Nevertheless, through the perseverance of the women who formed the foundation of the Church of God mission in Monticello, the congregation managed to grow and expand into other areas.[34] Grace Hall kept the community aware of their revivals as the correspondent for Summit Point news in the *San Juan Record*.[35] A ten-day sermon and revival series held by Overseer S. J. Wood in 1938 "addressed full houses every night" at Ethel Perry's mission south of the post office in Monticello.[36] They reported eight converts during the 1938 revivals.[37] There is no information available about who attended the revivals. The only records of the revivals come from the reviews written by the pastors in charge, and unfortunately, they rarely reported on the characteristics of those in attendance.

The Church of God and the Assembly of God shared members and activities in the late 1930s. The Gallegos family affiliated with the Latino district of the Assemblies of God, but the Church of God supported their revival efforts in Monticello, shutting down their own services during the activities.[38] And when the Church of God held a Bible trivia contest, two of the prizes went to Vidal Enriquez and Romana Gallegos, members of the Assembly of God.[39] The separate congregations worked together to support the evangelizing endeavors of the Pentecostal community. This cooperation, however, appeared to taper off by the mid-1940s, after Vidal Enriquez relocated his ministry to Salt Lake City.

The lack of business opportunities in the area and the death of foundational members resulted in the eventual dissolution of the congregation. Elizabeth Prickett died in late 1940, and others moved away to find work.[40] H. E. Ramsey, the Utah overseer from 1940 to 1942, worked to spread the work to Moab. He reported "seventeen baptized in water" during revivals there in May and June 1942, but no record of the congregation continued past the early 1940s.[41] "We found Sister Ethel Perry at Moab still on fire," Rev. Ramsey noted in July 1942, but he also admitted that "many of the Church of God members left the church." Hoping to improve conditions, Ramsey pleaded for support: "Oh, how we need some God-called ministers out here in Utah and Colorado, who are not afraid of hard places."[42]

Just as was the case with Forrest Stinson, the Church of God mission depended heavily on a few devoted individuals. Recalling the event which drew her and her sisters to Pentecostalism, Ethel Perry recounted in 1945 her miraculous healing which occurred in 1928. "We had a sister [referring to Jess Kinsey] who had gone into the Deep South and had become very religious. She had joined a church quite strange to us," Ethel recalled.[43] Over the two decades which followed, Ethel Perry, Grace Hall, Loretta Boyd, and Elizabeth Prickett carried the work. Like many other Pentecostal pioneers, women directed the early work of the Church of God in Utah. Unfortunately, as they aged or moved away, denominational administrators were unable to sustain the congregations from a distance. Utah shifted around within the hierarchy of the Church of God, beginning as a part of the Utah, Colorado, and New Mexico district, until later being lumped into the Western district, which included California, Oregon, Washington, Idaho, Utah, Arizona, and Nevada.[44] Despite reports of "a Sunday School in Utah with an average attendance of forty" in 1948, news of the church went quiet by 1950.[45]

The Church of God lost much of its presence in the mid-twentieth century. Missions opened in Salt Lake, and a few congregations existed in the 1980s, but no congregations maintained continuous services over the years.[46] It is probable that some converts to the Church of God made their way to the Assembly of God congregations which began gaining strength in the 1940s and 1950s. Within the state of Utah, as one denomination lost strength, its members often found a home within another Pentecostal work somewhere nearby.[47] Yet many new congregations, especially within the growing Spanish-speaking community, established themselves around Utah in the twenty-first century. In 2020, the Church of God online directory reported eight Spanish congregations and four English congregations around the state. These churches and missions are following in the footsteps of the many evangelists before them.[48]

INTERNATIONAL CHURCH OF THE FOURSQUARE GOSPEL (ICFG)

Although the completion of Aimee Semple McPherson's Angelus Temple made the news in Salt Lake in 1923, the movement did not come to Utah until the 1960s.[49] Founded by McPherson in January of 1923, it crafted a Pentecostal theology centered on Jesus Christ as savior, baptizer with the Holy Spirit, healer, and coming king. Yet McPherson's embrace of baptism in the Holy Spirit was broader than some Pentecostal denominations, and she never heavily focused on speaking in tongues as essential evidence of Holy Spirit baptism. By the time the denomination arrived in Utah, the Foursquare gospel had taken its place within the wider evangelical community. As Matthew Sutton argued, "while Pentecostalism remained the core of McPherson's theological identity, the exploding fundamentalist-modernist controversy had a greater influence on her throughout the 1920s."[50] McPherson did return to her more Pentecostal roots later in her life, but her incredible success and very public life may have altered American Pentecostalism generally, pushing it toward a more socially acceptable, politically conservative Christian movement.[51]

In Utah, the International Church of the Foursquare Gospel has a relatively short history. After Forrest Stinson opened a Foursquare mission in the 1960s, a few others followed. Pastor Rollan Morgan opened the Community Bible Church in Granger, Utah in 1976.[52] Through the rest of the century ministers appeared sporadically, planting churches often nondenominational in their approach to missionary work. By the mid-1990s, Pastor Steve Mullen reported that roughly 700 people congregated in ten churches around Utah.[53] In 2018, there were approximately 264,000 members of the denomination across the United States, with nine congregations in Utah.[54] Even though the number of congregations has remained about the same, they are not all the same congregations historically. Some, like the True Life Center pastored by Pete Akins (which opened its doors in 2003), replaced other congregations now defunct.[55]

The types of Foursquare congregations in Utah vary widely and participate with each other only loosely. Three of the present congregations are located around the Ogden area. Pastor Craig Wyjack's church, the North Park Foursquare Church, is as functionally different from Pastor Robert Guiller's Crossroads Christian Fellowship as night is from day. Located ten minutes apart from each other, the North Park Foursquare caters to a small, local congregation, which describes itself as a "spirit-filled" church, whereas the Crossroads Christian Fellowship seeks to "present the Gospel of Jesus Christ in such a way that turns non-Christians into converts."[56] The North Park Foursquare Church has a much older demographic and a much smaller membership, while the Crossroads Christian Fellowship maintains a younger congregation with more children and youth.

Even though they are both affiliated with the International Church of the Foursquare Gospel, it is a loose fellowship that gives individual churches significant independence. This also means, as it does in this case, that some churches rarely associate with the other. Despite being affiliated with the same denomination, older congregations lost more youthful members to congregations with contemporary worship styles. Newer Foursquare congregations in Utah resemble nondenominational churches in their branding and ministering, which is not as attractive to some long-time members. But most traditional congregations are no longer able to support programs and resources for families, so these younger members find a more suitable congregation elsewhere. In the case of the North Park Foursquare Church and the Crossroads Christian Fellowship, the difference in traditional and contemporary worship style is significant enough to keep congregations of the same denomination from fellowshipping together on the one hand. Yet both churches continue operating, on the other hand, maintaining diversity in the Pentecostal community.[57]

PENTECOSTAL CHURCH OF GOD (PCG)

Following the success of the Azusa Street revival, Chicago emerged as an influential center of Pentecostal activity. Larry Martin argued two main reasons for Chicago's significance to the Pentecostal movement: Chicago was a major transportation hub in the early twentieth century, and it was also relatively close to John Alexander Dowie's Zion City in Zion, Illinois. Many Pentecostals first experienced the movement through the various churches that organized in the Chicago area.[58]

The Pentecostal Church of God first took root in Chicago through the work of George Brinkman and others. George Brinkman created the *Pentecostal Herald* in 1915. It quickly became one of the most distributed Pentecostal periodicals in the early twentieth century. After controversy between Brinkman and the newly organized General Council of the Assemblies of God over control of the *Pentecostal Herald,* Brinkman left the Assemblies of God altogether. On December 29 and 30, 1919, he met with various ministers in Chicago to form a new organization called the Pentecostal Assemblies of the United States. The organization altered its name to the Pentecostal Church of God in 1922. As of 2015, the Pentecostal Church of God reported approximately 90,000 members in the United States. Only a few hundred reside in Utah, spread among five congregations.[59]

The Pentecostal Church of God may have influenced Pentecostals in Utah as early as 1917 because of the wide distribution of the *Pentecostal Herald*. From 1917 to 1922, the *Herald* listed R. R. Lowe as a field representative located in Salt Lake City.[60] Robert H. Lowe pastored a mission that affiliated itself with the Assemblies of God during this same time in Salt Lake, and he may be the same person listed in the *Herald*.[61] Just like Forrest Stinson, some early Pentecostal pastors maintained connections with various denominations. Larry Martin explained,

"Many of Brinkman's subscribers, both individual and bulk, were Assemblies of God ministers and adherents."[62] It is probable that Pastor Lowe at least functioned as a representative for the *Herald,* if not also the Pentecostal Assemblies of the United States of America.

The *Salt Lake Herald* and the *Salt Lake Telegram* both ran advertisements in early 1920 for a Pentecostal Church of God. Evangelist McCabe held meetings at the Masonic Temple on Second Street, preaching on the subjects of the second coming of Christ and "the Baptist [sic] with the Holy Ghost with Speaking in Tongues."[63] Although the Pentecostal Assemblies of the United States of America would not reorganize themselves under the name "Pentecostal Church of God" until 1922, McCabe's mission may have been associated with the denomination.

Another mission appeared in the early 1950s under the direction of the Reverend A. C. Pope. Listed at 517 2nd East in Salt Lake City, the mission began running ads in late 1950. Pope, along with district superintendent Harold Laster, petitioned "ministers of other churches in the city to attend a series of Saturday services . . . in the interests of greater church unity in the work of God."[64] They worked to promote ties between Pentecostal congregations and held meetings with independent Pentecostals, including the Greek Pentecostal Church called the Full Gospel Assembly.[65] Although ads continued for this mission through 1953, very little information is available detailing the work done by these men in the state of Utah.[66]

In the mining town of Sunnyside, John Wonder established an independent Pentecostal Church in the 1940s. As early as 1946, Wonder preached and participated in the KOAL radio station's Gospel Hour with other pastors in Carbon County.[67] Initially an independent congregation, Reverend Wonder began fellowshipping with the Pentecostal Church of God in the early 1950s. They held meetings at the old Greek Church in Sunnyside for several years. J. R. Davenport and Elmer Overstreet pastored the Sunnyside congregation after the Reverend Wonder.[68]

Leo Waggoner initiated the first significant movement within the Pentecostal Church of God in the state of Utah. Waggoner became District Superintendent for the Rocky Mountain District on July 19, 1950. It included Colorado, Utah, and Wyoming at that time. He and his wife Ethyl lived in Colorado, but they began working with John Wonder's independent church in Sunnyside and Forrest Stinson's independent church in Ogden. As the two congregations grew, Forrest L. Stinson hosted joint revivals in Ogden. "The group from Sunnyside church will visit the assembly," announced Stinson in March 1951.[69] Still known as the Full Gospel Assembly located in Ogden, Stinson eventually turned over the church at 2168 Lincoln Avenue to Leo Waggoner in 1954.[70] By 1955, Waggoner pastored the Full Gospel Tabernacle (formerly the Full Gospel Assembly), Stanley E. Swanson pastored the church Stinson established in Sunset, and another church opened its doors at 340 East 500 South in Salt Lake City.[71] Under the direction of Waggoner, the legal incorporation for the Pentecostal Church of God in the state of Utah took place on Friday, October 21, 1955. The Reverend Waggoner became the District Superintendent for the state of Utah when it split away from the Rocky Mountain District in 1955. Many of the early church buildings were built by Waggoner himself with little to no monetary support from the denomination.

The years following the incorporation were turbulent as the denomination struggled to maintain a presence in the state. Congregations grew during the 1950s. John Nickerson pastored a Spanish congregation in Ogden and L. A. Barbee opened a revival center with healing services and "'old-time' Bible preaching."[72] Most growth occurred in the Ogden area as the denomination engaged the community through youth activities and media events, although congregations did soldier on elsewhere. Pastor Waggoner's congregation in East Carbon remained active into the twenty-first century, but the congregation in Salt Lake did not. Pastors Robert Norman and Zeff Burks worked in Salt Lake over the years, but the congregation eventually dissolved.[73]

Despite retaining very few members in present day Utah, the Pentecostal Church of God continues evolving new methods of engaging the community. In Ogden, Harley Boyles and Ed Jones pastored congregations during the 1980s and 1990s.[74] Fred Lopez pastors the Hope Resurrected congregation. They work closely with the city in offering a food pantry and other services to the vulnerable populations of the Ogden area. Just outside Roosevelt in a town called Fort Duchesne, Burnell Hammonds spent several decades constructing a church and growing a congregation on the Uintah Native American reservation. Hammonds organized the mission in 1972. Fred Smith took over the work in 2000 and redirected the work to focus on the development of "First Nation" ministries. He continues to promote the message of Pentecost through the Community Pentecostal Church of God, and he also trains Native leaders and operates schools in locations across North America. He and his wife also run the Oasis Christian Center in Fort Duchesne, which is an elementary school attended predominantly by members of the Ute Native American tribe.

UNITED PENTECOSTAL CHURCH INCORPORATED (UPCI)

Theological and institutional controversies and realignments gave rise to the United Pentecostal Church, Incorporated. Theological developments in the early years of the Pentecostal revival fractured the movement. Many Pentecostals believed that three works of grace constituted the process of salvation: conversion, sanctification, and baptism in the Holy Spirit. The concepts of sanctification and baptism in the Holy Spirit came from the Holiness tradition, and they took on new meaning in the Pentecostal revival. William H. Durham argued in 1910, however, that the process was needlessly complex. He collapsed the experiences of sanctification and baptism in the Holy Spirit into one event, which occurred subsequent to conversion. Known as the Finished Work of Calvary (or Finished Work Theology), the change divided Pentecostals. Then in April 1913, at a major Pentecostal camp meeting held at Arroyo Seco just outside Los Angeles, R. E. McAlister argued that baptism should be in the name of Jesus only. He abandoned the traditional triune formula of baptizing in the name of the Father, the Son, and the Holy Ghost. Frank Ewart and G. T. Haywood preached it openly and adamantly, developing a theology that understood the trinity to be a "threefold 'manifestation' or revelation of the one God."[75] This redefinition of the trinity became known in the Pentecostal movement as the New Issue.[76]

The controversy ushered in a decade of Pentecostal institutionalization as groups defined themselves by their theological beliefs. In 1916, the Assemblies of God adopted the "Statement of Fundamental Truths," which drew a proverbial line in the sand for many members of the Pentecostal community; most Pentecostals would adhere to belief in the trinity. G. T. Haywood, Howard Goss, Frank Ewart, Juan Navarro Martinez, and all those who rejected a Trinitarian view of the godhead forged a new Pentecostal identity under the banner of Oneness Pentecostalism. Various denominations adopted the Oneness theology, including the Pentecostal Assemblies of the World (PAW). Organized in 1907, it reorganized as a Oneness Pentecostal church in 1915 under G. T. Haywood, an African American man, as presiding bishop.[77]

Racial tensions fractured the denomination, resulting in various divisions during the 1920s to the 1940s. William J. Seymour's desire to use Pentecost to create racial harmony continued within the Pentecostal Assemblies of the World, but by 1924 it was no longer sustainable. The white members left the PAW and created the Apostolic Churches of Jesus Christ. African American members, despite their best efforts at maintaining unity in the denomination, lamented the separation. Various mergers within the Oneness movement resulted in the creation of the United Pentecostal Church, Incorporated. Beginning in 1945, it became the largest Oneness Pentecostal denomination. The Pentecostal Assemblies of the World, the predominantly African American denomination, remains the second largest. There are currently eight UPCI churches in the state of Utah, and most of them are in the Salt Lake City metropolitan area.[78]

The first United Pentecostal Church in Utah still operates today, but its institutional affiliation changed over time. Pastor Covey began mission work in East Carbon in the early 1950s, at the same time as other Pentecostal denominations made their way to the small mining community.[79] He soon relocated to Salt Lake City and opened a church there. Known as the First Pentecostal Church of Salt Lake, the UPCI officially recognized it as part of the denomination on September 12, 1957.

Initially meeting at 740 South 700 East in Salt Lake City, Brother Covey established the congregation and Fred Neiderheiser pastored during the 1960s, followed by George Eades, Carl Ballestero, and Dewey Duplissey. William Fitzgerel took over the church in 1973, and under his ministry, it eventually became an independent apostolic church. Fitzgerel purchased an old Latter-day Saint meetinghouse, remodeled it, and moved the congregation to 1680 East Stratford Avenue. Known as the First Apostolic Church, it is currently pastored by Mark Lareau.[80]

Other pastors sprouted from the original Salt Lake congregation and planted churches elsewhere in the state. Ivan Johnson, a Utah native, converted to Pentecostalism in 1962 while living in California. He and his wife moved back to Salt Lake in 1964 and then relocated to Moab. They pastored a congregation in Moab until 1971, when they decided to relocate to Ogden.[81] From 1971 to 2001, Johnson pastored the Gospel Tabernacle on E Avenue. Ivan's son Erik took over the church in 2001. Although the church is now an independent Pentecostal congregation, it functioned with the United Pentecostal Church for thirty years.[82] Harry D. Thurston opened another church in Kearns, Utah. Requesting additional "tentmakers" and "door knockers," Thurston reported that "the harvest is very ripe here."[83] These churches maintained a small presence throughout the 1960s.

Additional congregations took root in Utah, often in association with the decision by the United Pentecostal Church to hold their annual general conference in Salt Lake City. Conferences would gather at the Salt Palace and Delta Center six times, including the years 1973, 1979, 1982, 1988, 1992, and 2004. The conferences intentionally targeted mission areas. Before and after conferences, the Home Missions department worked to plant new congregations. "One of the major objectives of the Salt Lake City Crusade was the establishment of a brand new church in the city," explained J. T. Pugh, director of Home Missions in 1973.[84] Pastors Paul Russell and Keith Clark established a church in 1973, alongside another Salt Lake church pastored by Harold Davies and later Daniel Gill.[85] Eugene Guerrero pioneered a church following the conference in 1979, and another church opened after the conference in 2004, pioneered by Frank Bounds and Ronald Rice.[86]

The United Pentecostal Church is the largest Oneness Pentecostal Church in the state of Utah. Its unique theology and charismatic worship style help it to cultivate a religious experience all its own. While there are a few independent churches in Utah with similar theologies, it is the largest denomination, and it continues to grow in the twenty-first century. Most growth is among Spanish-speaking Utahns and minority populations. Churches in the Salt Lake metropolitan area include large numbers of international members; many are refugees who have found a new home in the Salt Lake area. As Salt Lake City continues to become more diverse, the United Pentecostal Church will likely continue to grow in urban centers throughout the state.

GOING SOLO: INDEPENDENT PENTECOSTALS

Independent Pentecostal churches exist all around the state of Utah, as they do across the United States and the rest of the world. They fill in the gaps between the charismatic fringes and formal denominations of the Pentecostal movement. In Utah, various independent churches added to the growth and variety of Pentecostalism. The Full Gospel Assembly, the Faith Temple, and the First Apostolic Church demonstrate the kinds of independent Pentecostal churches that managed to leave a long imprint in the history of Pentecostalism in the Beehive State.

Greek immigrants began relocating to Utah in the early twentieth century. Helen Zeese Papanikolas detailed the motivations of the Greek people as they fled their bankrupt and battered homeland, subjugated for centuries by the Ottoman Empire and Turkish nation, and found a new home in the Salt Lake Valley. Greek culture and religion would carve out their own space in Salt Lake City and Carbon County as men found jobs in the city and the mines. The Greek Orthodox Church of the Holy Trinity was established in 1905 and remains one of the largest Greek Orthodox communities in the Western United States.[87]

Not all those that migrated from Greece joined the Greek Orthodox church in Utah. Constantine A. Nicholas, born at Tripoli, Greece in 1884, became a preacher in 1912 while living in Cairo, Egypt, and then moved to Salt Lake in 1917. He established a Pentecostal mission in 1917 from a home near North Temple and 300 West. Through the 1920s and 1930s, they moved around from 44½ South Main Street to 517 South 200 East, and Pastor Nicholas dedicated his time to preaching the full gospel, not only to the Greek community but to all willing to hear him. He held "open-air religious meetings," preached Sunday sermons, and conducted religious services at the Utah state prison, county jail, and county hospital.[88] Nicholas worked until his death in 1946 to build up his church, eventually known as the Full Gospel Assembly.[89]

The congregation continued to grow through most of the twentieth century. Brothers Chris and William Christopulos pastored the church following Pastor Nicholas. They continued performing street meetings at intersections and parks around the Salt Lake area. They also purchased a church from the Seventh Day Adventists at 1840 South 800 East in 1957. Advertising their church as a place where "we preach the whole Bible," the brothers encouraged the gifts of "healing, faith, miracles, diverse tongues, interpretation of tongues, discerning of spirits, words of wisdom and knowledge and prophecy."[90] They remained at the building on 800 East until 1993 when they relocated to West Valley City.[91]

The affiliation of the Full Gospel Assembly varied over the decades that the congregation existed. Pastor Nicholas identified the affiliation of the church as a part of the Hellenic Protogonos Apostolic Ecclesia, also known as the Greek Original Apostolic Church.[92] Headquartered in Oakland, California, the network united various Greek churches that supported the Pentecostal message, including the Full Gospel Assembly in Salt Lake. As early as 1951, they fellowshipped with Assemblies of God congregations in Utah.[93] The Apostolic Ecclesia became an ethnic branch of the Assemblies of God in 1953, but it eventually disbanded in 1968. According to Pentecostal historian Darrin Rodgers, as the children of members of ethnic branches "Americanized and learned English, the churches founded by immigrants joined geographic districts and most language branches dissolved."[94] The Full Gospel Assembly, however, did not appear to become absorbed by the Assemblies of God. In 1968, the year the Greek branch was dissolved by the Assemblies of God, pastor William Christopulos described the congregation in Salt Lake as "independent, sovereign, evangelistic and Pentecostal." They believed in speaking in tongues as the initial evidence of the baptism of the Holy Ghost, but Christopulos explained that "membership is not stressed because each person who attends the church is a member, regardless of religious affiliation, if he financially supports the church, attends all functions faithfully and upholds the church standards."[95]

The Full Gospel Assembly, like Forrest Stinson's congregation in Ogden by the same name, exemplified how independent churches often maintained themselves in Utah. As they grew, they flirted with denominational ties and sometimes dissolved into larger bodies. At other times, however, the Pentecostal urge away from institutional structure kept them on the fringes, and their congregational style often attracted a unique facet of society underrepresented by other Pentecostals in the area. By the mid-1990s, the Full Gospel Assembly seemed to fade away from the Salt Lake metropolitan church scene, but it remained active through most of the twentieth century as one of the oldest continuously operating Pentecostal congregations in the state of Utah.[96]

Another significant, independent Pentecostal church received most of its support from a different minority group in the Salt Lake area. Despite the Church of God in Christ operating several churches in and around Salt Lake and Ogden, some African Americans chose to attend an independent church instead. In an editorial for the *Park Record*, an individual named Teri Orr recounted when the performing group known as the Faith Temple Pentecostal Choir performed at the Park City Community Church in 1992:

> Members of what has been referred to as the Ralph Lauren church (Park City Community Church) saw the rafters shake and the windows rattle and the altar move back and forth. The more than fifty members of that choir, in addition to their three keyboards, drums, guitar, and sax player, made a joyful noise unto the Lord. Simply put, they were rockin'.
>
> The hour service stretched to almost two but nobody seemed to mind. The congregation was standing and clapping and waving like a revival meeting. . . . It was one of those moments that you can't duplicate or easily even try to write about. But I gotta tell you, no one who was there Sunday could deny the energy in that room and the connection that was made, even for just a few short hours.[97]

Beloved by many, the Faith Temple Pentecostal Church Choir held concerts all around Utah in the late twentieth century. Directed and founded by Rosemary Radford Cosby, the church and choir functioned as influential components of the Utah African American community as well as the Pentecostal community.

Raised in Indianapolis, Cosby dropped out of school in ninth grade, got married, and had four children. Shortly after her husband left her, she joined the Christ Temple Church and was baptized. "I had a vision while I was at my church," she explained, which left her feeling called to Salt Lake City despite not even knowing where it was. "When I asked the bus company what the fare was," Cosby recounted in an interview, "it turned out to be a fortune, so I knew it was a long way away." With her four children in tow, Cosby traveled across Missouri, Kansas, and Colorado, sometimes on foot, sometimes receiving assistance from churches they attended along the way until arriving in Salt Lake City in 1961. Cosby received ordination through the Pentecostal Churches of the Apostolic Faith Inc. in 1964 and opened an independent church called the Faith Temple Pentecostal Church in 1967.[98]

In addition to Faith Temple No. 1 in Salt Lake City, Rosemary Radford Cosby built a small empire aimed at assisting underprivileged communities in Salt Lake and Indianapolis. Faith Temple No. 2 opened its doors in Indianapolis in 1984. From there, Rosemary and her second husband Robert C. Cosby worked to open a school, a restaurant, a beauty salon, a real estate company, and a gospel radio station listed as KLLB 1510 AM. Fondly called "Mama" by her parishioners, Cosby ran a daily program called "The Voice of God's Ministry, Back to the Foundation." By the time she died in 1997, Mama Cosby's ministry and community outreach significantly impacted the African American community in the Salt Lake area. Despite a schism in the church following her death, the Faith Temple Pentecostal church continues to operate in Salt Lake City into the present.[99]

Many Pentecostal churches' legacies in Utah cemented themselves in the community through the outreach they provided to various special interest or minority groups. Forrest Stinson's Rescue Mission in Ogden, the Full Gospel Assembly's focus on the Greek community, and Mama Cosby's work within the African American community all demonstrated how throughout the twentieth century Pentecostal churches developed spaces of their own around the majority religious community. The Church of Jesus Christ of Latter-day Saints reached out to all residents of Utah through its expansive missionary program, but Pentecostal churches managed to successfully and independently develop ministries that sometimes responded more effectively to the unique needs of Utah's minority communities. Certainly, some Latinos, Greeks, and African Americans converted to the Church of Jesus Christ of Latter-day Saints, but many others felt more comfortable in small, independent churches.

Occasionally churches became independent as denominational leadership and congregational leadership changed over time. Instilling the longstanding aversion to institutional hierarchies and organizational bureaucracies, various Pentecostal congregations in Utah broke away from larger denominations. The

Pentecostal movement itself materialized in part as Holiness preachers in the late nineteenth century ventured to the fringes of acceptability within their own Protestant denominations and eventually broke away to form new movements. The First Apostolic Church in West Valley City broke away from the United Pentecostal Church in 1967. Pastors Carl Ballestero, William Fitzgerel, and Mark Lareau adhered to an understanding of Pentecost free from denominational ties, and the church continues to operate as an independent church in the present. Erik Johnson's Gospel Tabernacle in Ogden similarly became an independent congregation centered around an independent Pentecostal experience. These churches, while typically smaller than the denominational congregations, permeate the Pentecostal community in Utah (just as they do elsewhere) and encourage a spirit of independence and revival that influences new ideas and directions within the Pentecostal movement in the twenty-first century.[100]

The fluidity and flux described within the history of the smaller Pentecostal denominations and congregations in Utah reinforce Gastón Espinosa's argument concerning the nature of Pentecostal growth addressed at the beginning of the chapter. As congregations achieved some degree of balance between the pragmatic demands of life and the primitive impulses of spirituality, those that felt comfortable in that balance established congregations that joined larger denominations like the Assemblies of God. Yet many times parts of or whole congregations failed to find such balance and reinvented themselves through schism or dissolution. New congregations developed, increasing the size of the Pentecostal community. Margaret M. Poloma and John C. Green analyzed the charismatic behavior within the Assemblies of God and argued, "The most vital sectors of the Pentecostal movement are likely to be loosely coupled or decoupled from traditional Pentecostal denominations like the AG."[101] Utah provides some examples that reinforce this explanation.

Fracture and schism explain only part of Pentecostal growth, however. By far the largest Pentecostal denomination in Utah is the Assemblies of God. New Pentecostal churches continue to appear, but significant growth occurred within a single denomination. It may be that both Wacker and Espinosa recognized characteristics of Pentecostal growth that provide only part of the complete explanation. They use the analogy of catching lightning in a bottle to explain the tension between pragmatic and primitive impulses. Instead of finding balance every time or the bottle cracking every time, it seems the real problem is that there is no stopper for the bottle to contain the primitive impulse within a pragmatic institution. Institutions like the Assemblies of God will permit charismatic expression only to a certain point. Anyone wishing to go beyond that point is either removed from the community or chooses to remove themselves. The result is continued growth both within the more pragmatic denominations and among the more primitive or spiritually charismatic denominations and independent congregations. It is not that the bottle cracks under the tension of these two impulses; there is just no way to put a stopper in the bottle when it is full. Those individuals interested in a more charismatic spiritual experience flow out from recognizable Pentecostal denominations to smaller denominations or independent congregations.

In this way, growth continues in the various types of Pentecostal congregations in Utah and the United States. Despite the transitory affiliations of members and impermanence of congregations within Pentecostal communities in Utah during the twentieth and twenty-first centuries, the community continues to grow and expand, even within a geographical space dominated by the presence of the Church of Jesus Christ of Latter-day Saints. From forty Pentecostals in 1916 out of Utah's population of approximately 400,000, to approximately 35,000 Pentecostals in 2018 out of Utah's population of about 3.1 million, it is growth spread unevenly among various denominations and independent congregations, but the aggregate continues to rise.[102]

3

STRUGGLING ON THE FRINGES

The Latino Assemblies of God and the Asamblea Apostólica de la Fe en Cristo Jesús in Utah

Pastor Guy Heath beamed with enthusiasm in 1950 as he reported to the *Pentecostal Evangel* on another successful revival in Salt Lake City. They ended their program with the "Cooperative Utah Baptismal Service," which included thirty-six Holy Ghost Baptisms and thirty-four water baptisms into assemblies around the state. Reveling in the "Pentecostal downpour," Heath noted, "The largest Pentecostal gathering in Utah history was recorded during this revival when 217 attended the night service of the December Fellowship Meeting to hear Brother Ketner."[1]

Approximately six months earlier in August 1949, another Utah pastor by the name of Néstor Bazán also eagerly shared a revival experience. Published in the Spanish language periodical *La Luz Apostolica*, Bazán recalled the meeting: "The worship for the evening was a Pentecostal worship. There were more than 300 souls on this occasion, and the power of God fell upon us in such a way that our Brother Joaquin could not preach."[2] Prior to the evening worship, approximately two hundred people gathered together as pastors Leví Medina and Néstor Bazán baptized twenty-six more into their assemblies. These combined meetings among the Spanish-speaking Assemblies of God in Utah outshined Pastor Heath's estimation of "the largest Pentecostal gathering in Utah history" by over 50 percent.

Utah Pentecostalism suffered from the same racial and cultural maladies as Pentecostalism did elsewhere. Even though minorities participated in some of the earliest

Note: I have chosen to use the term *Latino* to represent the discussion in this chapter about the growth of the Latino Pentecostal community in the state of Utah. The Latino community in Utah over the twentieth century predominantly included Mexicans and Mexican Americans born in Utah, Colorado, and New Mexico. The term *Latino* seeks to include these different backgrounds, as well as the smaller groups of individuals from Latin America that also converted to Pentecostalism in Utah.

Utah Pentecostal congregations, as the movement grew it excluded non-whites from the main fellowship and relegated them to the fringes. Latino congregations grew early and quickly but rarely made the printed news in the larger urban centers of Utah. African American congregations planted themselves firmly in Salt Lake City and Ogden as well.[3] Yet when the monthly fellowship meetings rolled around or churches reached out to one another through interfaith activities, most often these congregations found themselves without invitations. They shared ethnic and racial struggles with other minorities as non-whites, but their beliefs about Pentecostal worship and theology sometimes separated them from their racial and ethnic communities. Becoming double minorities because of their religious views, Latino and African American Pentecostals encountered opposition from almost all directions.

Latino Pentecostal communities developed lonely but vibrant histories of their own that highlighted the changes occurring within Utah religion and the American religious mainstream during the twentieth century. As minorities relocated to Utah, they brought non-Latter-day Saint beliefs with them, increasing the religious diversity of the state. Although Latino Pentecostal churches did not grow as large as their white counterparts, they remained part of the Utah community since the early twentieth century and established permanent congregations despite the lack of support from their denominational institutions. As Utah's demographics became less white in the twenty-first century, these groups developed into significant religious fixtures in Utah.

Latinos and African Americans also highlighted the racial and ethnic changes transforming the larger American religious mainstream. In 1976, 81 percent of Americans identified themselves as white Christians; only 43 percent of Americans identified this way in 2016. Many white Americans are shifting their views away from denominational affiliations, increasing the number of religiously unaffiliated individuals.[4] As Christian denominations become increasingly non-white, racial and ethnic congregations are becoming a larger part of the Christian base of the American religious mainstream. Latino and African American Pentecostal churches may achieve serious gains in the twenty-first century.

"HASTA AQUÍ JEHOVÁ NOS HA AYUDADO": THE LATINO ASSEMBLIES OF GOD IN UTAH[5]

Although there are centuries of Latino history in Utah, the history of Latino presence in Utah under United States jurisdiction began around 1900.[6] According to

Paul Morgan and Vincent Mayer, census data acknowledged approximately 40 people of Mexican birth in Utah in 1900, 160 people in 1910, 1,200 people in 1920, and 4,000 people in 1930.[7] Many of these early migrants to Utah relocated for work in the cattle, sheep, railroad, and mining industries emerging in Utah. The earliest Latino families relocated from New Mexico to southern Utah near Monticello during the first few decades of the twentieth century, while many workers spread across the labor fields of the state. More often than not, single men came to Utah, or else married men left families behind and worked seasonally, which created a very uneven distribution of men and women. In 1930, there were 1,200 single males and only 100 or so single females in the Latino communities of Utah. The Bracero Labor program, developed by the United States and Mexico to improve working conditions and increase contract workers from Mexico, drew many more Latinos to the country for work during the war effort of the 1940s. When it ended in 1964, statistics became more complicated with the increase in illegal immigration. The data also suffers because the US Census Bureau did not include a Hispanic category until 1970. Once included in the questionnaire, census data reported 33,911 Hispanics residing in Utah in 1970, 60,302 in 1980, 84,597 in 1990, and 201,559 in 2000. The population continued to grow rapidly into the twenty-first century with 358,340 in 2010 and 492,912 in 2020. By the early twenty-first century, the Latino population became the largest minority in Utah by a large margin, making up 15 percent of Utah's population in 2020, compared to roughly 3 percent in 1970.[8]

The Latino Pentecostal movement originated right alongside the global Pentecostal movement. After experiencing charismatic worship under William J. Seymour at the Apostolic Faith Mission in Los Angeles, Abundio L. López received ministerial credentials from Pastor Seymour and opened the "Spanish Apostolic Faith Mission" around 1909. The contingent of Spanish-speaking, predominantly Mexican worshipers at Seymour's mission followed Pastor López to his sister mission in Los Angeles.[9] In Texas, independent congregations of Latino Pentecostals formed through the work of Antonio Ríos Morin, Arnulfo M. López, and others familiar with the preaching of Seymour and Charles Fox Parham. These congregations operated entirely independently and autonomously until Henry C. Ball began the process of organizing them into the fold of the Assemblies of God. Despite over a decade of Latino leadership, Ball believed these congregations needed to be shepherded by more experienced, white Euro-American leaders. Ball worked to publish Spanish language materials to increase the audience among Latinos in the American Southwest. His publication, *La Luz Apostólica*, would eventually reach thousands of readers in the early to mid-twentieth century.

By 1920, congregations of the Latino Assemblies of God existed in Texas, New Mexico, Arizona, and Colorado. And they continued expanding to new areas in search of opportunities for new congregations.[10]

The first Latino Pentecostals in Utah made their way to the state with the first wave of Mexican workers who settled in the southern town of Monticello. Narciso Gallegos was born in Albuquerque, New Mexico in 1886. He moved to Monticello in 1898. Near the same time, Ramón González moved his family to Monticello as well. He and his wife Guadalupe arrived in 1900 with their daughter Romana and their son Prudencio. The Gallegos and González families worked as shepherds, and Narciso met and married Romana in 1904. They would eventually have ten children together.[11]

Narciso and Romana converted from the small Catholic community in Monticello to the Assemblies of God when José Facundo Marez visited from Colorado. Marez converted to the Assemblies of God in 1929 under the preaching of Carlos Trujillo.[12] Marez immediately entered the ministry himself, working in cities across western Colorado and eventually becoming presbyter of the western conference of Colorado (within what was known as the Latin district of the Assemblies of God). From the assembly in Dove Creek, Colorado, Marez branched out into Utah and became acquainted with the Gallegos family in 1933: "The acts of adoration were accompanied with the power of God and soon there were results. Sister Romana Gallegos and her children, and they opened their doors so that others also in Monticello accepted Christ and His great salvation."[13] Monticello offered few religious options in the early twentieth century. The Church of Jesus Christ of Latter-day Saints constructed a log cabin chapel in 1888, followed by a brick building in 1912. St. Joseph's Catholic Church was not completed until 1935. Baptists and Presbyterians made attempts to plant churches, but they failed to maintain a presence in the town. At the time of their conversion, the Gallegos family became the first Spanish-speaking Pentecostal Christians in the state of Utah.[14]

Through the rest of the 1930s, Romana Gallegos led the effort to create a congregation around her family. Gallegos actively participated in her new faith, attending conferences in Carlsbad, New Mexico, El Paso, Texas, and Salida, Colorado.[15] In January 1935, they announced in the local newspaper that "the public is cordially invited to the regular Pentecostal services held at the Gallegos home every Sunday, Wednesday, and Friday evening at 7:30."[16] They printed the ad in English and occasionally held services in English when it benefited visitors. Although the Gallegos family spoke both Spanish and English, the revival meetings held with Joe Clapper of Dove Creek were advertised in the paper as meetings "in English only" but held at the "Spanish Assembly of God Church."[17] They would hold Sunday School in Spanish, followed by English preaching sometimes provided by visiting evangelists or pastors.[18] By 1937, the congregation grew large enough to organize Christ's Ambassadors, the youth organization of the Assemblies of God. Led by Eduard Gallegos, Max Archuleta, and Irene Gallegos, they totaled eighteen youth.[19]

When the Church of God opened a Pentecostal mission in Monticello around 1935, they formed a working relationship with the Spanish Assembly of God to share the Pentecostal message together instead of battling each other for adherents.[20] "Since the Assembly of God Church teachings and mode of worship so nearly parallel the Church of God principles and rituals," the *San Juan Record* reported, "Mrs. Perry has discontinued services at her house of worship for the duration of these revival services."[21] This kind of cooperation proved the rare exception for Latino Pentecostals, however, and likely occurred only when English-speaking evangelists came to town. The rest of the time, they pursued denominationally separate congregations.

The extensive repatriation of Mexicans in the 1930s made Pentecostal growth nearly impossible for the young congregation. From 1930 to 1940, almost 75 percent of all Mexicans in Utah left the state.[22] Approximately one million Mexicans in the United States returned to Mexico, and Daniel Ramírez estimated that the repatriation took nearly one-third of Spanish-speaking Pentecostals from the country.[23] While Utah did not hold any large-scale repatriation programs, newspaper reports of Mexican deportations appeared regularly throughout the 1930s.[24]

The first Spanish-speaking congregation in Salt Lake City emerged from the congregation in Monticello. A few evangelists including Carlos Trujillo made efforts to preach in Salt Lake City in the 1930s, but with very little success. A. T. Salazar recalled when the inspiration for a permanent Salt Lake congregation came to a young man living in Monticello in 1935: "In the church in Monticello, Utah, this same year, Bonifacio Hernández continued as pastor of the new church and a young man by the name of Vidal Enriquez received his call to go to these places."[25] Born in 1913, Vidal's family moved to Monticello for work. He married Elizabeth Gallegos, a daughter of Narciso and Romana Gallegos, and began preparing himself for ministry. By 1940, *La Luz Apostólica* included Pastor Enriquez as the head of the church in Salt Lake City.[26] They opened a small mission at 470 West 200 South. Vidal and Elizabeth Enriquez and the Archuleta family constituted the original membership.[27]

The work commenced slowly and coincidentally right alongside the return of white Assemblies of God pastors to the city of Salt Lake.[28] Pastor Enriquez struggled to gain new members beyond his immediate family and friends who relocated to Salt Lake for wartime jobs. When three individuals received the baptism of the Holy Spirit in February 1942, he declared the event a "veritable triumph for the work."[29] A few months later he explained to readers of *La Luz Apostólica* the difficulty of planting a church in Salt Lake City: "We have been here for two years working in this city. The first year we did not see any encouraging results."[30]

In the early 1940s, they competed heatedly for members with Catholics and Latter-day Saints. As a demographic, Jorge Iber writes, "By the onset of the Great Depression, Hispanics represented the largest minority group in the state," living predominantly on the west side of Salt Lake City and in the Wall Avenue area of Ogden. In these areas, they shared space with "large numbers of Italians, Greeks, Japanese, Syrians, and Koreans."[31] By 1940, the Catholic Church had already opened the Spanish convent-chapel of Our Lady of Guadalupe on the west side of Salt Lake to meet the needs of the Latino community. The Mexican branch of the Church of Jesus Christ of Latter-day Saints, called the Rama Mexicana, opened its doors in 1923. Between the Catholics and the Latter-day Saints, very few Latinos manifested interest in Pentecostalism. It offered no support during the dire economic reality of the Great Depression and the complications of the Mexican repatriation. From 1930 to 1940, over two-thirds of all the Spanish speakers in Utah left, many by choice and some by deportation, to find better circumstances elsewhere. Those who remained did so because they joined the support networks offered first and foremost by the Church of Jesus Christ of Latter-day Saints and then second by the Catholic Church.[32]

Yet by the 1940s, more Utah Hispanics in Salt Lake began converting to Pentecostalism than to other Protestant churches in the area. Joseph Allen surveyed 491 Mexicans in Salt Lake City in 1947 about their religious affiliation.[33] Four hundred and thirteen identified as Catholics, 38 identified as Latter-day Saints, and 29 identified as AG members. The remaining few included six Methodists, three Seventh Day Adventists, one Unitarian, and one Baptist. The fast growth of the Assemblies of God among the Latino community differed significantly from the slow growth of the white assemblies in the state of Utah during the first half of the twentieth century.

Most Latino converts in the Southwest came from the ranks of the Catholic Church. Gastón Espinosa described the struggles and persecutions of early Pentecostal leaders in Arizona, Colorado, and New Mexico, in his book *Latino Pentecostals in America*. Latinos who became "aleluyas" (a term used to identify Latino Pentecostals) lost homes from arson and loved ones from violent attacks in the 1930s.[34] The Gallegos, Enriquez, and Bazán families moved to Utah from New Mexico and Colorado, along with many other Latinos looking for work in the 1940s. There are no recorded accounts of similar violence against Pentecostal converts in Utah. Joseph Allen reported in 1947 that "the general consensus of opinion is that there is much less anti-Mexican feeling in Salt Lake City than in most of the large towns or cities from which these people have come."[35] Because many of their conversion stories originated from within a Catholic context, perhaps the much smaller Catholic population in Utah decreased the persecution of Latinos who converted to Pentecostalism. It may also be the case that Salt Lake City felt friendlier to Latinos because the Latter-day Saints established colonies in Mexico in the late 1800s, increasing the cultural connections between Mexico and Utah.[36]

The federal government pumped new life into the Salt Lake Valley through the various wartime industries it funded in Utah, and Pastor Enriquez gloried over the opportunity to convert souls where he could. The new industries brought back Latino workers to the state through the federally negotiated Bracero Labor program. He thanked God for six spirit baptisms that occurred in May 1942.[37] Vidal and his family worked almost entirely alone preaching among the minorities on the West side of Salt Lake until José Marez, presbyter of the Western Colorado Conference of the Latino Assemblies of God, formally organized the congregation in March of 1943.[38] They moved locations a few times, ending up at 155 South 500 West by 1948.

As the Latino population grew in Utah, Spanish Assemblies of God congregations expanded as well. Demetrio Bazán, superintendent of the Latin District, visited Salt Lake in 1946 and left feeling that "the work in the Mormon capital promises much."[39] Carlos Trujillo returned to Ogden in 1943, where he remained for decades building the Spanish congregation. Miguel Salazar headed another congregation in Price, Utah. Romana Gallegos maintained the congregation in Monticello until her husband Narciso died in 1944. Then, she relocated to the Salt Lake congregation. Eugenio Girón cared for a small group of twelve in Dragerton, Utah.[40] Congregations in nearby areas made it possible for monthly fellowship meetings, and the first meeting occurred in late 1946. Vidal Enriquez hosted an exciting gathering: "The atmosphere was light and glorious in the midst of the congregation, and there were precious and unique manifestations of the power of the Holy Spirit among us. While we were under the waves of blessings from above, some cried, others danced in the Spirit, others prayed and still others shouted of the celestial joy that filled their hearts."[41]

For several decades, there was only one Spanish-speaking congregation for the Assemblies of God in Salt Lake City. Alfonso G. Vigil replaced Vidal Enriquez as pastor in 1949. Alfonso and his wife Virginia graduated from the Bible Institute in Saspamco, Texas in 1944. They pastored in New Mexico a few years before taking over in Salt Lake City. They remained in the pastorate until 1954. They would move back to New Mexico and Texas before eventually returning to Utah.

Néstor Bazán followed Pastor Vigil as the third pastor of the Salt Lake Assembly of God. Born in Tampico, Tamaulipas, Mexico, Néstor worked for the military academy until feeling called to the ministry. Perhaps through the encouragement of his uncle, Demetrio Bazán, Néstor and his wife Célia pastored first in Dragerton, Utah, beginning around 1948.[42] The federal government allocated development funds through the Defense Plant Corporation in 1943 to build the city to increase the production of coal for the war effort.[43] Many outsiders moved there to mine coal for the Geneva Steel mill, and Bazán's church benefited in the process. By April 1949, the Dragerton Sunday School exceeded one hundred members.[44] Working alongside Leví Medina, the Spanish pastor in Price, their congregations experienced phenomenal growth during the beginning of the 1950s. Alberto Medina described how when he moved to Price in 1943, "There was no work nor a church here." Through spring 1950, however, "Each Sunday our number exceeds 100 . . . 104, 108, and even 120, in attendance."[45]

During this period, the Latino assemblies grew more quickly than the white assemblies. United within the Assemblies of God denomination, these separate assemblies very rarely met together. A notice in the *Ogden Standard-Examiner* reported on an upcoming meeting in 1943 and explained, "Spanish people from Salt Lake City are expected to be here for this meeting."[46] Virginia Vigil remembered attending some of the English revivals in the late 1940s and early 1950s, but the monthly fellowship meetings for the English and Spanish assemblies were separate affairs.[47] Latino Pentecostals may have attended the annual state camp meetings held by Pastor Guy Heath, but there is no record of it, and very few Utah Pentecostals recalled any shared activities.[48]

The dissociation between assemblies inhibited opportunities for growth across the state and demonstrated unequal distribution of funds and concerns for Assemblies of God congregations. English-speaking congregations often relied on the financial support of the denominational institution to fund building projects. Guy Heath, Robert Smith, and others all received funds to purchase land and materials for the construction of chapels. When Néstor Bazán took over the Salt Lake pastorate in 1954, the congregation had outgrown their rented location again. He announced to the readership of *La Luz Apostólica* their intention to construct a building because their Sunday school surpassed two hundred individuals. The process of purchasing and constructing the building took three years. When Pastor Bazán announced the building's completion in 1957, he offered thanks only to God. Located at 116 South 900 West, the Spanish congregation used their own hands and money to construct the new chapel.[49] Despite the financial poverty of the Latino community, they continued to outpace the early efforts of white assemblies in Utah.

"EN EL NOMBRE DE CRISTO JESUS": THE APOSTOLIC ASSEMBLY OF THE FAITH IN CHRIST JESUS[50]

Another Latino Pentecostal church arrived in Utah during the 1950s, called the Asamblea Apostólica de la Fe en Cristo Jesús.[51] Like the Latino Assemblies of God, the Apostolic Assembly of the Faith in Christ Jesus also grew out of the Azusa Street Revival in California. Juan Navarro and Genaro Valenzuela attended the revival under William J. Seymour and converted to the Pentecostal message in Los Angeles. By 1912, they had established their own Apostolic Faith Mission in the home of Genaro Valenzuela. After the camp meeting at Arroyo Seco, Navarro and Valenzuela adopted the Oneness theological view about the nature of Jesus Christ. They eventually connected with other Oneness Pentecostals and associated themselves with the Pentecostal Assemblies of the World.

Under the direction of converts Francisco Llorente, Marcial de la Cruz, and Antonio Castañeda Nava, the Latino churches functioned as the Mexican group of the Pentecostal Assemblies of the World (PAW). They received ministerial licenses through the PAW, but many early Latino members felt they received "no other type of help from that organization."[52] Separated by geography and culture, most Latino congregations left in 1925 and eventually incorporated in 1930 as the Apostolic Assembly of the Faith in Christ Jesus.[53]

The first Apostolic Assembly congregation in Utah began in the late 1950s. Harold Vigil converted to the Apostolic Assembly under Bishop Richard Ochoa in Colorado. Vigil and his wife moved to Utah when Harold found work at the airbase near Ogden. At first, they worshipped with Pastor Paul Thomas at the United Pentecostal Church on Lake street, but Harold felt called to establish a Spanish-speaking church in the area. He began evangelizing around 1957 and became friends with a man named Mr. Gomez. Gomez owned a passenger train car on his property on 26th Street near the railroad tracks in Ogden, and in 1959, Harold Vigil began holding church meetings in Mr. Gomez' train car.[54]

Theological differences made it nearly impossible for the Apostolic Assembly and the Latino Assemblies of God to fellowship together. The longstanding disputes between Oneness Pentecostals and Trinitarian Pentecostals created rifts within the Pentecostal community at large that separated denominations theologically and socially. At times, Trinitarian Pentecostals (the majority of Pentecostals are Trinitarians) and Evangelical Christians would even label Oneness Pentecostals as "pseudo-Christian" heretics because of their views on the godhead.[55] So Paul Thomas's United Pentecostal Church was the only place the Apostolic Assembly could find fellowship.

The church grew slowly through the next decade as it established a more permanent home. Harold Vigil became an ordained pastor around 1961 or 1962, and he moved the congregation from the train car to an addition constructed onto the Vigil's home. The congregation had outgrown the train car, and it soon outgrew the addition as well. They purchased the building of an old car wash, moved it to the Vigil's property, and remodeled it for church services. Services were held in Spanish, and most members of the congregation were Mexican Americans. Many members worked for the government at military installations, for local farmers as harvesters in the fields, or for the railroad companies.

As the church in Ogden grew, the Apostolic Assembly expanded into other parts of the region. When the Vigils opened the church in Ogden, they fellowshipped with churches in New Mexico and Colorado. As churches developed in Idaho and Oregon, they also made trips to churches in those states. Eventually, they formed the district of Utah and Idaho. Missionary work from the Ogden church allowed for ministers to plant churches in Brigham City, Clearfield, Layton, and Logan.

GROWING UP IN AMERICA—SECOND AND THIRD GENERATION LATINOS

By the 1960s, the Latino community in Utah had become a multigenerational ethnicity struggling to establish itself as American. The racial stress and violence of the 1950s and 1960s affected Latinos also. In the late 1940s, Elena Martinez explained how she had to "stick on a whole box of powder every time I go out so somebody won't think I'm a 'nigger' or something. Just because I'm dark they think they can push me around."[56] Latinos moved to Utah at a much higher rate than African Americans. And Latinos like Elena understood that social climbing required distancing themselves from other minority groups.

It also meant developing community centers and organizations to meet the needs of Latinos. As second and third generation Americans, they created the Utah Spanish-Speaking Organization for Community, Integrity, and Opportunity (SOCIO). With at least 50,000 Latinos living in Utah by 1960, they made up the largest minority group by far. And the SOCIO "served as the most important, though not the only, voice representing the concerns, complaints, and hopes of the Spanish-surnamed people of Utah to political, business, educational, and religious leaders."[57] Through the 1960s and 1970s, Latinos like the members of the Assemblies of God and the Apostolic Assembly worked within the Latino community to improve social conditions with a strong emphasis on education.[58]

The Latino Assemblies of God filled the church they built together. The photo displayed as Figure 8 in the image gallery is emblematic in many ways of the Utah Latino experience in the later twentieth century. The American and Christian flags framing the congregation showed pride in their country and desire to assimilate. After the repatriation, Latinos worked hard to become model citizens and upstanding members of the American Christian community. The neat simplicity of the building exemplified the characteristics of meekness and hard work. Most members of the Utah Latino community labored long hours at difficult jobs and garnered meager wages. Yet despite these difficulties, they managed to construct beautiful physical spaces of their own, representative of the strength within their growing communities. And the multigenerational congregation itself displayed the familial structure within Latin society. Families stayed close and worked together. Romana Gallegos, the matriarch of the Latino Pentecostal movement in Utah, continued supporting the church and encouraging her children and grandchildren to remain faithful members.

Occasionally the Latino Pentecostal experience in Utah had far-reaching effects on Pentecostals elsewhere. David Velasquez's musical career is an example of this. David was born in 1940 in Youngsville, New Mexico. His father Ed Velasquez moved to Dragerton, Utah, in 1944 to work in the coal mines. The Velasquez family converted to Pentecostalism through the Latino Assemblies of God in New Mexico prior to their move. Now in Dragerton, they joined the fledgling congregation in the mining community.

Ed Velasquez loved music and believed it to be an important part of Pentecostal worship. He had nine children, and Ed and his wife taught all of them to sing and play instruments. David Velasquez recalled how he and his two sisters, ages six, four, and eight respectively, performed a live music radio show every Sunday morning. Singing in harmony and playing guitar, they provided music at KOAL radio in Price for the pastor's sabbath radio broadcast. David's love for musical worship cemented him and his family as an integral part of their congregation. "During that time in the Pentecostal church," remembered David, "it was kind of like bring your instruments and let's worship. Let's sing and have a good time. Sometimes there were more musicians on the platform than in the congregation."[59]

David Velasquez found his call to ministry through his musical gifts. He attended the Latin American Bible Institute from 1961 to 1963. After graduation, Velasquez accepted a pastorate in Gallina, New Mexico, near his hometown. During his stay at the Bible Institute in El Paso, he met Paul De La Torre and Danny Ramos. Together, they formed the Kings Three Trio in 1963. They recorded a self-titled album in San Antonio, Texas made up of familiar Pentecostal songs and a few original works. Appreciation for their music spread, and the Kings Three Trio were invited to perform at the General Council of the Assemblies of God in 1964 and again in 1965. They were then asked to provide a weeklong musical revival at the Assemblies of God headquarters in 1965.

Following their revivals for the General Council, interest in their ministry spread rapidly. David Velasquez noted that the United States had very few Latino traveling musical groups at that time. After the early success of the Kings Three Trio, David Velasquez returned home to Dragerton, Utah, because he hoped to perform music with his brothers and sisters. They became the Four Latinos in 1966, comprised of David, Eddie, and Mike Velasquez, and a friend named Vince Montano. Occasionally Anita Velasquez also performed with them.

The configuration of the band and name would change, adding other Velasquez family members and friends, until they settled on the name Los Latinos. Through the 1970s and 1980s, Los Latinos released half a dozen albums, performed in churches across the country, and went on international tours. David Velasquez went on to form The Amigos, The Galileans, and he continued performing with his children in the 1990s.[60]

After over fifty years in music and ministry, David Velasquez' influence through music and ministry had spread far beyond the borders of Utah. He performed in every state in the United States except Alaska and toured in thirty-eight countries around the world. He and his family, raised in a Latino Assembly of God church in Dragerton, Utah, helped spread Pentecostal worship to countless locations. "Christian music should be more of a worship type of thing," explained David. "It's not about us; it's about Him."[61]

Still, growth and change within Utah were almost inevitable given the increasing size of the Latino population. Within the Apostolic Assembly, Harold Vigil oversaw the ministry until 1972. His brother Jim Vigil moved to Salt Lake City and opened a church there in the late 1970s. Other family members pastored after Harold, and his son Tommy Vigil became pastor of the church around 1980. From Ogden and Salt Lake, additional churches opened further south in West Valley City, Sandy, and Provo.[62] At the Salt Lake Latino Assemblies of God, several pastors followed after Néstor Bazán, including Fidel and Eva Valdez and Danny and Connie Manchaka. Most notably, Frank Trevino pastored from 1966 to 1979. Luis Enriquez, son of Vidal Enriquez, and his wife Inez also pastored at the church in the 1980s.

Language became a barrier to the process of social assimilation and internal community building for Utah Latinos. Like many immigrants to the United States, each subsequent generation adopted more of the culture of American life. Thus, many older Latinos still struggled to speak English while many younger generations that grew up in Utah primarily spoke English and spoke Spanish as more of a second language. Younger pastors like Tommy Vigil at the Apostolic Assembly and Luis Enriquez and Roy Cazares at the Assemblies of God worried the younger generations of Latinos might miss some of the message and experience if the churches only offered services in Spanish. They began offering English services. Growth and social preferences led to a split in the Salt Lake Assemblies of God. Luis Enriquez created a new congregation under the name Mount Calvary Assembly of God (now known as the Mount Calvary Worship Center), and in 1985, Roy Cazares became pastor of the Salt Lake Latino Assembly of God.

The dynamics of growth within these congregations reflected the dynamics of growth within the larger Utah Latino community over the end of the twentieth century. When Roy Cazares became pastor of the Latino Assembly of God in 1985, he and his wife Becky began preaching and holding services in English. The congregation grew through the 1980s, and a fortuitous conflict with the Mountain Fuel Company over land contamination resulted in the funds to purchase a temporary building and eventually construct a new building in the Salt Lake suburb of Rose Park.[63] During these physical transitions in the 1990s, the makeup of the Utah Latino community transitioned as well. From 1990 to 2000, the Latino population in Utah grew by 140 percent. About half of the growth came from Mexico, while the other half came from various other Latin American countries. The Latino Assemblies of God felt these changes, as their congregations became infused with Latinos from El Salvador, Guatemala, Nicaragua, Argentina, Brazil, Colombia, and elsewhere. The Salt Lake Latino Assembly of God changed its name to the Centro de Vida Christiana (Christian Life Center) and returned to Spanish worship services around 1995.[64]

Through the early twenty-first century, growth continued within the Utah Latino Pentecostal community. Both the Centro de Vida Christiana and the Mount Calvary Family Worship Center offer services in Spanish, and there are many other Latino Assemblies of God churches spread around the state. Over the second half of the twentieth century, the English Assemblies of God congregations did overtake the Spanish congregations in size and number, but many of the older churches now also offer Spanish-speaking services.

Congregations of the Apostolic Assembly continue to expand in Utah. At present, Brigham City, Logan, Provo, Sandy, Taylorsville, Layton, Ogden, Salt Lake City, Washington City, and West Valley have congregations. Ogden is the largest with over 200 members divided between Spanish and English services. The other churches offer services in Spanish, with a few of them providing an English translation. The churches range in sizes from thirty to eighty members. There are three congregations of the Apostolic Church of the Faith in Christ Jesus (Iglesia Apostólica de la Fe en Cristo Jesús), which shares its historical and denominational origins with the Apostolic Assembly but originated as a sister denomination in Mexico.

Utah Latino Pentecostals have many more options in the twenty-first century, and as the Latino community continues to grow, so do their options.[65] Nearly a century since the work initiated in Monticello by Romana Gallegos, many Latino churches large and small dot the rugged Utah landscape. As Pastor Roy Cazares reflected on the history of Latino Pentecostalism in Utah, he said, "This church was built not by any people who have money—no lawyers, no doctors, no people with a lot of money. That to me is a miracle . . . , and God had blessed them."[66]

4

"TAKING US HIGHER"

Church of God in Christ History in Utah

On September 29, 1989, Pastor David Franklin Griffin passed away. Many civic and religious leaders from across the community attended his funeral services. He was a stalwart pillar in Ogden's community, having pastored the Griffin Temple Church of God in Christ since 1946. A few years earlier in February 1985, the Ogden Christian community awarded Griffin the honor of Pastor of the Year for his service to his church and city. Bishop Nathaniel Jones Jr., Jurisdictional Bishop for the Church of God in Christ in Utah, gave Pastor Griffin the nickname "Mr. Church of God in Christ" because he "eats, sleeps, wakes up, walks and talks and possibly dreams about the people of this 'Grand Old Church.'"[1]

Pastor Griffin's devotion to preaching proved itself to a miraculous degree on one occasion. Elder Roland E. Hurrington, pastor of the Mount Zion Church of God in Christ, had invited Elder Griffin to give a sermon at his Salt Lake City church. Then in his later years, Elder Griffin suffered from a few ailments but never turned down an opportunity to preach. While in the middle of his sermon,

Note: For decades, Pastor Henry McAllister of the Church of God in Christ has carefully collected historical information on the COGIC congregations in Utah. I am indebted to his labor of love and history in the writing of this chapter. He assisted me throughout the writing process, providing critical feedback and revisions. I also extend my great gratitude to the congregations of the Church of God in Christ in Utah for generously sharing their community records. The photos and history have been collected by church members over the years and kept together primarily through the efforts of Pastor Henry McAllister. But many others in the community also deserve credit for preserving and sharing their history. A version of this chapter was previously published as Alan J. Clark and Henry McAllister, "Led to the Mountains: The Church of God in Christ Comes to Utah," *Utah Historical Quarterly* 90, no. 1 (Winter 2022): 41–56.

Elder Griffin stopped breathing and collapsed to the floor. Fortunately, a nurse was present among the members of the congregation and rushed to his assistance, eventually resuscitating him. Elder Griffin, knowing no limits on the importance of preaching, got up and finished his sermon to the astonishment of the congregation. Not even the specter of death kept him from his calling.[2]

Despite his lifetime of service, very few Utahns knew about Pastor Griffin or the Church of God in Christ, to which he devoted his life. This chapter seeks to remedy this oversight by outlining the history of the Church of God in Christ (COGIC) in the state of Utah. Since the 1930s, African Americans began migrating to Utah and establishing COGIC congregations in various cities. Their Pentecostal theology and worship separated them from the tiny group of African American churches already operating in the state and required church members like David and Daisy Griffin to devote years of service organizing churches and developing their own social networks within the African American community that existed in Utah for much of the twentieth century. Their resilience and endurance in forging a home in the West enrich the history, diversity, and heritage of Utah.

THE CHURCH OF GOD IN CHRIST IN UTAH

Although a few Black individuals colonized Utah with the Latter-day Saints in the nineteenth century, the African American community was very small in the early territorial years; the 1850 territorial census counted twenty-four free and twenty-six enslaved Black people in Utah.[3] The ending of slavery in the United States and the coming of the railroad to the West allowed for increased migration, and the 1900 census listed 672 Black people residing in Utah. By 1910 the Black community in Utah nearly doubled to 1,144 African Americans in the state, with most residing in Salt Lake City. Around two hundred Black people lived in Ogden. During the Great Depression and the Great Migration of African Americans from the South, more men and women headed west in search of work, but few picked Utah. The population barely changed by 1940, with 1,235 African Americans in Utah. Yet, as with other minority populations, the massive amount of military and federal industrial growth in Utah during the 1940s and 1950s dramatically increased the size of the community. Known as the Second Great Migration, beginning around 1941 many African Americans left the South to pursue employment opportunities elsewhere. Their population in Utah doubled by 1950 and nearly doubled again by 1960, arriving at 4,148 (about 0.5 percent of the state population).[4]

The community grew steadily through the second half of the twentieth century, numbering 17,657 people in 2000, followed by another surge in growth to approximately 43,000 by 2014. Growth was not evenly distributed across the state, however. According to a study of the 1990 census, African American households were only found in 40 percent of Utah's cities.[5] Most of the demographic growth occurred in urban areas in and around Salt Lake City and Ogden. Despite rapid growth in the early twenty-first century, the African American population remains one of the smallest demographic minorities at about 1.1 percent of the statewide population—smaller than the Hispanic and Asian populations in the state (15.1 percent and 2.4 percent respectively).[6]

The same racial segregation and Jim Crow–era discrimination that plagued the rest of the country existed in Utah, but it manifested itself in different ways. Opportunities for work primarily determined where African Americans lived in Salt Lake City, Ogden, and elsewhere in the state. Railroad companies employed large numbers of African Americans during the late nineteenth and early twentieth centuries, and correspondingly the segregated areas of Salt Lake City and Ogden included the neighborhoods adjacent to the train stations.[7] Although Utah did not have the same kind of state-sponsored segregation as existed in the South, municipalities and residents employed their own methods to keep communities apart. Real estate covenants and private businesses excluded Blacks from living in certain neighborhoods or frequenting certain business establishments. Ogden in particular, because of the large Black community that worked for the railroad, used these mechanisms to segregate the city. Anna Belle Weakley, who owned and operated the Porters and Waiters Club on Ogden's 25th Street, described the social segregation of Ogden as "unannounced segregation."[8] Because segregation was not mandated by law, African Americans had to intuit the social rules. A few businesses catered to everyone, but most did not. As Eric Stene pointed out in his discussion of the 1940s, "Ogden's Twenty-fifth Street was segregated; Whites stuck to the north side of the street, and Blacks stayed on the south side, along with Italians, Asians, and Hispanics through the decades."[9] Even after the passage of Civil Rights legislation in the 1960s, the climate of segregation continued, most forcefully in real estate. As late as the 1990s, 60 percent of Utah's cities still had no Black residents.[10] Even after restrictive covenants were removed, a cultural desire to maintain segregation seemed to remain and made it complicated for African Americans to purchase homes outside of traditionally Black neighborhoods.[11]

Despite these racial barriers, the lure of work and a better life continued to draw people to Utah from the east. For most of the new arrivals, religion guided their day-to-day activities and functioned as the center of community life. This had been the case since the 1880s and 1890s when African Americans began organizing churches in Salt Lake City and Ogden. Reverend James Saunders led the organization of the Trinity African Methodist Episcopal Church in 1890.[12] Emma Jackson began holding prayer meetings for Baptists in her home in 1892, and the Reverend A. E. Reynolds became the first permanent leader of the Calvary Baptist Church.[13] African American churches proliferated in the early twentieth century with the addition of several more Baptist churches and the Liberty Park Seventh Day Adventist Church.[14]

With very small congregations and slow population growth, Black churchgoers struggled greatly to develop their own communities in the state, but their struggle resulted in increased diversity and vivacity within the Utah African American community. Churches functioned as worship centers as well as social centers. They provided individuals opportunities for leadership roles and allowed them to make work connections. The churches also provided relief and economic support to their members.

The Church of God in Christ emerged in the late nineteenth century out of the Holiness movement among African American Baptists in the South. The Holiness movement grew out of the established Protestant churches with an emphasis on the doctrine of sanctification. Many Protestants felt that the denominational churches had strayed from the path of Christian devotion and instead pursued social status and acceptability. The Holiness movement forcefully reemphasized the Wesleyan doctrine of Christian perfectionism. The movement created contention during the nineteenth century among Protestants, and many individuals left the established denominations in pursuit of a Christian experience centered around a sanctified Christian life.

Originally organized as a holiness church in 1895 by Charles Price Jones and Charles Harrison Mason, the Church of God in Christ split over the importance of William J. Seymour's Azusa Street Revival and the foundation of Pentecostal worship and theology.[15] Upon visiting Seymour's Los Angeles revival in March 1907, according to Mason's biographer, Mason "experienced a radical ideological upheaval, ultimately resulting in a doctrinal reformation of the Church of God in Christ."[16] When Mason shared his Pentecostal experience with Jones, Jones rejected the Pentecostal view of speaking in tongues as the initial evidence of the baptism of the Holy Spirit. They parted ways, and in August 1907, C. H. Mason became the first "Chief Apostle" and leader of the Church of God in Christ, newly transformed into one of the most prominent Pentecostal churches in the United

States.[17] With a strong emphasis on evangelism and an intensely charismatic worship style, COGIC has grown into one of the largest predominantly African American churches in the United States. The denomination estimates there are 6.5 million members, rivaling the membership of the National Baptist Convention, USA Inc.[18] It is also arguably the largest Pentecostal denomination in the United States.[19]

Because of its foundation in Pentecostal theology, members of COGIC do not usually worship with other African American churches.[20] Their numbers are among the smaller in Utah, with approximately two to three hundred strong.[21] With very few members and no initial support from the surrounding churches or general population, individuals like David and Daisy Griffin worked tirelessly establishing COGIC congregations among other Protestant and Pentecostal churches in Salt Lake City and Ogden. COGIC did not often establish strong ties with other Pentecostal churches and congregations—though connections were sometimes made, as evidenced by the interfaith meeting between Pastor Griffin's and Pastor Leo Waggoner's congregations. More often, when the monthly fellowship meetings rolled around or churches reached out to one another through interfaith activities, COGIC congregations found themselves without invitations. They shared ethnic and racial struggles with other minoritized groups as non-whites, but their beliefs about Pentecostal worship and theology separated them from their racial and ethnic communities. Living in Utah as double minorities because of their religious views, African American Pentecostals encountered opposition from almost every direction. They faced the opposition with endurance and resolve, laying the foundation for some of the oldest continuously operating Pentecostal churches in Utah. As Pastor Griffin said in his daily prayer, "Lord don't let me die until I finish my work, for no man can do my work for me."[22]

No one deserves more credit in establishing the Church of God in Christ in Utah than Alberta Harris Jennings. Born around 1902 in Lake Charles, Louisiana, her family worshiped with the Baptist church. As an adult living in Beaumont, Texas, Harris (not yet Jennings) heard the teachings of the Church of God in Christ and felt called to the work of evangelism. Bishop C. H. Mason believed increased national evangelism would not only preserve "the best features of Slave Religion but also a commitment to replicating the nonracist early church and [creating] a just society."[23] COGIC missionaries fanned out across the country. Feeling the call, Harris uprooted in 1938 and sought out a place without any COGIC congregations. Through the inspiration of the Spirit and the encouragement of her local leader, Bishop D. M. Paige, she decided on Salt Lake City.[24]

During the first few years of her Utah ministry, Harris struggled not only to hold services but also to make a living.[25] She came to Utah with no contacts and joined a segregated community of about seven hundred African Americans in Salt Lake City. Despite having attended Texas A&M College, Harris could only find domestic work. Her preaching drew few listeners beyond concerned members of the Salt Lake City Council. Although COGIC did not recognize women as preachers, Harris could hold street meetings at Pioneer Park in Salt Lake City and revivals at churches willing to host her. When Harris began holding outdoor services, the Salt Lake City Council investigated the outdoor meetings due to concerns of public disturbance but ultimately allowed them to continue.[26] Reportedly her favorite worship song was "God's got a hold of my hand and He's leading me." She felt led to Salt Lake City, despite not knowing anyone or having ever visited. Her evangelizing style, spontaneous and unconventional, contributed to the Pentecostal revivalism in the state.[27] A few other Pentecostal churches existed at this time in Utah, including the Assemblies of God and the Church of God, Cleveland, but these denominations evangelized primarily to white audiences. The Assemblies of God in particular, having decided to break away from COGIC in 1914, did not evangelize among the African American community in Utah. In her outdoor services, Harris did not place any limitations on who could participate together.

Women played important roles within COGIC during the early twentieth century. Bishop Mason saw women's value within the community and as evangelists. He established a women's department in 1911 and often sent husbands and wives together into the "mission field" to establish congregations.[28] Anthea Butler explained how Church of God in Christ women "appropriated the southern revivalist traditions of outdoor preaching and canvassing from door to door for converts, and these techniques bore fruit in the urban locales to which they migrated."[29] Marrying home mission work with home life, "church mothers" performed the important work of community building, caring for both the spiritual and the temporal needs of those around them. According to Ithiel Clemmons, "They were unashamed to have street worship services, to approach and talk to gangs of roving, idle youth."[30] The combination of preaching and caregiving helped women confront the difficulties of urban life.

The role of "church mothers" transformed into a formal title for COGIC, reflecting the role of women as "mothers in Zion." Anthea Butler argued that "COGIC church mothers' quest for spiritual empowerment by means of 'the sanctified life' provided the moral, spiritual, and physical fuel that enabled them to negotiate for and obtain power both within the denomination and outside it."[31] In the early twentieth century, Black women faced many impediments to social mobility and leadership. Harris exemplified the willingness of Black Pentecostal women to engage societies that sought to limit and ignore them by means of her spirituality.

Fueled by her resolve to establish a church, Harris managed to earn enough money to purchase property at 552 West 300 South near the Rio Grande train station in Salt Lake City around 1939.[32] She and her husband Jack built a small home and meetinghouse on the property. They named it the Mount Zion Church of God in Christ. Elder W. C. Caldwell became its first pastor.[33]

With a church secured, Harris provided a platform for other evangelists to launch additional missions around the state. She also prompted the establishment of a new geographical jurisdiction in the western United States for COGIC. Around this time, an evangelist named Isaac Finley was preaching in Oregon and Washington. He subsequently traveled around the West extensively, considering where to start new churches. He preached in Reno and Las Vegas, Nevada, and then made his way to Pocatello, Idaho. Finally feeling the call to preach in Utah, Finley connected with Harris in Salt Lake City and offered his support. This led COGIC to appoint in 1938 Finley to the position of overseer in 1938 for Utah, Idaho, and Nevada.[34]

Racism in the mid-twentieth century complicated COGIC growth in Utah. Racial aggression had surged in the 1920s, including the brutal lynching of Robert Marshall in Price, Utah. The Salt Lake Branch of the National Association for the Advancement of Colored People (NAACP), organized in 1919, held an "antilynching mass meeting" to protest the acquittal of Marshall's lynchers.[35] The Ku Klux Klan operated briefly in the state, appearing in 1921 and seemingly disappearing by 1926, but according to Larry Gerlach failed to take root due to opposition from high-ranking Latter-day Saint church leaders.[36]

The racism that African Americans dealt with in Utah was often more covert. In other parts of the country, communities faced racism in public disputes, protests, and violent encounters. In Utah, racism typically emanated from systemic stereotypes and infrequent interactions with diverse populations. Doris Fry moved to Salt Lake in 1913 at the age of six. She recalled bitterly the discrimination she suffered as a child in Salt Lake:

> Well, the children were prejudiced. They called us names. They didn't take kindly to Black people. We were called negroes then. We call ourselves

> Black now. But the negroes were discriminated against. In fact this was predominantly a Mormon city. A Mormon state and the Mormons did not believe Blacks were quite human. We're not supposed to have souls. We were never supposed to go to heaven. If they were Mormons they could belong to the Mormon Church but they could never enter and hold a priesthood because they were cursed by their Blackness and that was taught to their children and they used that against us.[37]

Because of the very small minority populations, Utah never segregated schools or colleges. Children like Doris suffered discrimination in the classroom on a regular basis. Danny Burnett recounted when a friend of his visited Brigham Young University (BYU) and attended a football game in the 1950s:

> He says, "I went to a football game down at BYU, and they were playing this team that had three or four Black players on it, and almost every time they jumped up, they'd always say tackle that Nigger, this [sic], that Nigger that, Nigger that and that's where it's at in racism." He says, "They really throw that word Nigger around." And I said, "The Mormons do that?" and he says, "Yeah, that's a part of their everyday vocabulary."

Burnett explained his dislike for Salt Lake, saying, "I felt they were too conservative, and . . . there was just a lot of things you couldn't do, and then there was a lot of racism among the Mormons."[38] Howard Browne recalled a trip with his mother and brothers to southern Utah in the 1940s. As they purchased gasoline at a station, lots of children gathered to watch Browne and his family. Curious why they kept walking behind him, he asked his mother, "What's the matter with them kids? What are they looking at?" She replied, "Well, the Mormons teach that Black people have got tails. They're descended from the monkey and they've got tails and they've got horns. And they're trying to see where your tail is."[39]

These incidents recounted by African Americans in the twentieth century exemplified what Doris Fry described as racism "in a more subtle form."[40] James Gillespie, an African American who relocated to Ogden from Mississippi stated that "in Mississippi they'll kill you, in Utah they just starve you to death."[41] Thomas G. Alexander argued, "In Utah as in most of the West, African Americans, Native Americans, Latinos, and others suffered formal discrimination, but most anti-minority sentiment appeared more insidiously cloaked in the dressing gown of the protection of private property."[42] He meant that most urban areas in

Utah incorporated real estate covenants that prevented African Americans from purchasing or even renting property. Joan and Charles Nabors struggled to find anyone who would rent to them when they moved to Utah in the early 1960s.[43] On one particular occasion, they responded to an ad for an apartment and were turned down only to find the ad in the paper again later that week. It had been revised to state the apartment was available for rent to someone "white and LDS." Outraged by the simple difficulty of finding a place to rent, Joan vented, "I had really never had a lot of discriminatory situations after I left the South, other than one in Illinois. . . . But by 1961, you're thinking, what is going on? And you're realizing that Utah is way behind the times."[44]

Members of the Church of God in Christ struggled with this kind of racism throughout the 1940s and 1950s. Alberta Harris dealt with opposition to her outdoor services from various municipal and church organizations. Utah members of COGIC recall that even the Church of Jesus Christ of Latter-day Saints requested Harris explain to the Quorum of the Twelve Apostles the brand of Christianity she preached.[45] In Salt Lake City, W. C. Caldwell became the first pastor of Harris's newly organized Mount Zion Church of God in Christ. The *Salt Lake Tribune* reported on March 25, 1943, "A revocable permit to conduct religious services in a tent . . . was granted by city commissioners to the Rev. W. C. Caldwell of the Church of God in Christ." When the same paper reported on the permission granted to the Assemblies of God for a tent revival, they apparently had no need to emphasize the "revocable" nature of the permit.[46] But it served as a reminder to Elder Caldwell to preach with caution. Without formal segregation laws, municipal courts could use the acceptance or rejection of city permits as mechanisms of discrimination.

Elder Brealey B. Mike also faced such cultural opposition, but with far less subtlety, in establishing a congregation in Ogden. Mike moved to Utah for work in the late 1930s. Initially, he met with Alberta Harris Jennings at her street meetings in Salt Lake City. When Bishop Isaac Finley and Mother Jennings encouraged Elder Mike and his wife to begin a church in Ogden, they relocated. Prentiss Jones opened his home for meetings to Elder Mike around 1938. In 1941, Elder Mike purchased a lot at 28th Street and Wall Avenue in Ogden where he built a small home and held tent meetings with Elder Caldwell of Salt Lake City.[47] In the winter, Mike and Caldwell held meetings in the "Little House" as they called it. They would carry the beds out to make space for the service. Elder Ralph R. Girley and his wife attended meetings with Elder Mike until starting their own church in Ogden. It took several more years to complete the church building on the property because every time they tried to begin work, white neighbors would complain, which led the city to put a temporary stop to the construction. The building was finally dedicated in October 1948 as the 28th & Wall Avenue Church of God in Christ.[48]

Church growth proceeded more quickly in Ogden than in Salt Lake City despite the former's smaller African American population. Elder Mike died in 1956 after pastoring the Wall Avenue church for fifteen years. Elder John Parker succeeded him in the pastorate and continued until 1971. Nearby in Ogden, Elder David Franklin Griffin felt called to the ministry. Griffin's parents had joined the Church of God in Christ in Arkansas in 1908. In 1936 Griffin believed the Lord had called him to be a preacher, and over the next decade, he preached as a deacon and elder in Arkansas, Oklahoma, Missouri, and Oregon. His work in the military kept him moving. But after he married Daisy Green in 1945, Griffin took a job with the Southern Pacific Railroad in Salt Lake City. They initially joined Jack and Alberta Jennings at the Mount Zion congregation before relocating and beginning a church of their own in a community building in Washington Terrace, Ogden. The first few years saw many moves, from homes to trailers to boxcars. In 1949, Griffin mortgaged his car to get a loan to purchase a lot in West Ogden on 26th Street. Finally, in May 1952, they finished construction on their own building and dedicated it for worship. Affectionately known as the "church by the tracks," the West Ogden Church of God in Christ (later renamed the Griffin Temple Church of God in Christ) would eventually become the jurisdictional headquarters for the state of Utah.[49]

Several other congregations laid their foundations in the 1940s. Elder Ralph R. Girley and his wife Seretha left Elder Mike's congregation in Ogden to establish the Lincoln Avenue Church of God in Christ. In 1964, the congregation purchased a former Latter-day Saint ward house on the corner of 30th Street and Wall Avenue; in gratitude of Bishop Isaac Finley's leadership and work to purchase the building, they renamed the congregation the Finley Temple Church of God in Christ. Members continued meeting there until 2013 when Pastor Henry McAllister and his wife Daisy sold the old building and purchased a new property in Clearfield. Renaming the church the Journey of New Beginnings Church of God in Christ, Pastor McAllister continued to lead the congregation as of 2021.[50]

Around the same time that Elder Girley began his congregation, Elder Millard C. Thomas and his wife Janie transferred with the military to Camp Kearns in 1945. They worshipped at Mount Zion under R. E. Hurrington until starting a new Salt Lake City congregation called Ebenezer Church of God in Christ in 1952.[51] When the Mount Zion congregation closed its doors, Ebenezer remained as the oldest congregation in the capital city. In 2020, there were two Salt Lake City area congregations: Kingdom Church of God in Christ pastored by Bishop Bobby Allen and Full Gospel Deliverance Center Church of God in Christ, located in West Valley City and pastored by Apostle Jervis Lee. While others have come and gone, four congregations continue to hold weekly services in Utah.[52]

Most African Americans lived in Salt Lake City and Ogden, but a few lived or worked on farms in central Utah or in mining towns, which sometimes boasted sizable Black populations.[53] In the multicultural Carbon County, the white population predominating in Price was informally segregated from many of the racial minorities primarily living in Helper. Many immigrants made their way to Utah as strike breakers, and some continued living in Utah through the mid-twentieth century. African Americans in these communities became part of a mixed workforce that included recent immigrants and US citizens.[54]

The limitations of rural life in a mining community may have provided moments of toleration and interfaith activity not often seen in Utah's urban areas. With fewer congregations to attend and fewer physical structures in which to attend, churchgoers sometimes relied on denominational cooperation to create worship services despite theological differences. The Church of God in Christ opened a church among the coal camps sometime around 1946.[55] Billed as a church "for all races and denominations," the local church held services in Helper, Spring Glen, and Sunnyside under the direction of J. R. Green.[56] Green hoped to develop a church that interacted with the entire mining community, and he often reached out to others for support. As they constructed a chapel in Helper on the foundation of the old Catholic Church, they held a "chair rally" for donations of "any extra chairs or benches that would give his congregation something to sit on while attending services."[57] The COGIC congregation hosted barbecues to fundraise for the construction of the chapel and permitted an African American Baptist church to use the building as well after its completion.[58] Green must have reached out to the Church of Jesus Christ of Latter-day Saints; in 1948, Pastor Green received a one hundred dollar check from Latter-day Saint president George Albert Smith as a donation. Green and others expressed their appreciation for the "generous gesture of tolerance and goodwill from the dominant church in Utah."[59]

Yet the remote living arrangements of the coal camps and towns also revealed racial tensions. A Black man named Howard Browne remembered an incident at a pool hall in Price, one of the few places in Price where Black people could go. During a card game, an altercation occurred among Browne, a Mexican American man, and a white man:

> Something came up in the card game that this Mexican had said something to him and [the white man] said, "do you know who you're talking to?" He says, "You're talking to an American White Man." And so this Mexican fellow just said real low, he says, "I'm just as much of an American as you are." And so this guy says, "You can't be as much American as me as Black as you are." . . . Well, he done made me hot then. I said, "Hell, you can't be as much American as he nor me." I said, "I come from the Cherokee tribe. And your people came over here and took this country away from us. So how in the hell are you going to be as much American as me or him!"[60]

This incident illustrates the feelings of Utah Latinos and African Americans as they wrestled with racial discrimination and bias. Whites discriminated against Latinos and complicated their place in American society. Howard Browne, who reportedly had African American and Native American ancestry, found more accepting allies in non-whites who experienced similar discrimination. But African Americans endured the lion's share of racism in Utah, despite being the smallest minoritized group. Even work culture in the mines, where European immigrants worked alongside African Americans, reinforced racial hierarchies.[61]

"GOD HAS BROUGHT US A MIGHTY LONG WAY"[62]

To unify the fledgling congregations and create more support for a statewide community, Bishop Isaac Finley and bishops who succeeded him strongly supported the annual holy convocations in Utah. These meetings brought together the various small congregations. There they celebrated the achievements of the COGIC community and participated in charismatic worship, which included speaking in tongues, prayer circles, holy dance, and ecstatic worship.[63] These meetings also brought in speakers from other locations and encouraged past leaders to return and support the community. Bishop Isaac Finley and Mother Jennings, no longer residents of Utah by the early 1950s, maintained their roles from a distance as state bishop and state mother, respectively. Bishop Finley found the convocations to be important enough that he donated funds to purchase an old Latter-day Saint church building large enough to comfortably accommodate all of the congregations during the annual convocation. When Bishop Finley returned to take over the pastorate of Lincoln Avenue in 1955 upon Elder Girley's death, the building also served as the home location for what became known as the Finley Temple Church of God in Christ.[64]

The holy convocations of the Church of God in Christ constituted the majority of times that these congregations found their way into local newspapers.[65] The convocations allowed them the opportunity not only to come together as a religion but also to remind the cities around them about their existence and importance within the state. Bishop C. H. Mason, the founder and Senior Bishop of COGIC, and other national bishops for the denomination made appearances. New local leaders received assignments. Over time, these convocations even received recognition from local officials for their services to the community. When the Utah jurisdiction held its seventy-fifth anniversary in 2013, Utah governor Gary Herbert and the mayors of Salt Lake City and Ogden all expressed their appreciation for "your congregations' efforts to succor and uplift people from all walks of life, both spiritually and temporally, throughout the past seventy-five years."[66]

Members of COGIC also shared strong interfaith relationships with other churches in Utah. Tommy Vigil, pastor for the Apostolic Assembly of the Faith in Christ Jesus, remembered as a child how his father's church (Harold Vigil pastored the Apostolic Assembly), Griffin Memorial Church of God in Christ, and the United Pentecostal Church occupied three of the four corner lots around his home on Lake Street. Vigil recalled how these Pentecostal churches supported each other, despite differences in race and ethnicity.[67] France Davis, who pastored the Calvary Baptist Church in Salt Lake City from 1974 to 2019, recalled the "marvelous interdenominational organizations in Utah" and the associations between them that he considered to be unique to the state.[68] Close friends with Elder David Griffin and Bishop Bobby Allen, Davis has worked together for years with COGIC in ways that are almost unheard of in other parts of the country. These relationships prevented feelings of isolation and provided support for these small congregations. Summarizing his thoughts about the interfaith relationships over the years, Bishop Bobby Allen cited a scripture: "How pleasant it is for brethren to dwell together in unity."[69]

At times, the Church of God in Christ and the Church of Jesus Christ of Latter-day Saints sought to improve relationships between their two communities in Utah. Much of the time the two churches did not have much interaction, but on occasion, interfaith activities did occur. In July 1968, Melvin A. Givens Jr. and his family moved from Idaho Falls, Idaho, to Salt Lake City, where he felt called to start a new church. They managed to purchase land at 300 North 862 West but did not have the funds to build a church. Nevertheless, they began construction and held services for the small congregation in the tool shed on the property.[70]

Bishop Givens pursued the help of the wider Salt Lake City community to finish the building. In early 1970, he met with Ernest L. Wilkinson, president of Brigham Young University. They organized a benefit concert headlining Mahalia Jackson, the "Queen of Gospel," and a BYU choir and philharmonic orchestra.[71] John H. Vandenbeg, Presiding Bishop of the Church of Jesus Christ of Latter-day Saints, attended the concert and met with Bishop Givens. They discussed the possibility of working together to complete the Deliverance Temple church. Naming the fundraising project "Operation Good Samaritan," they enlisted the help of young men and women from both churches. "Youth from 566 Mormon wards washed cars, raked lawns, sawed fireplace wood, sold baked goods, cleaned garages, and did yard work to boost the building fund of the Negro church," reported the *Daily Herald* in June 1970.[72] They raised over $30,000 to complete the construction. At a banquet celebrating the event, Latter-day Saint leaders sat down with Bishop Givens and other leaders in the Utah Church of God in Christ and expressed appreciation for the spirit of camaraderie displayed in the previous months. "I may disagree with some of your teachings," Givens explained, "but that doesn't mean we have to pick up bricks and throw them at each other or that we have to start talking Black power."[73] They completed construction and dedicated the Deliverance Temple building on August 23–30, 1970.

Despite the goodwill and interfaith focus, "Operation Good Samaritan" felt insincere to some observers since it came at a time when the Church of Jesus Christ of Latter-day Saints denied full membership rights to Black members. Russell Stevenson argues, "Over the generations, racism had metastasized into a major aspect of Mormon society and culture."[74] The fundraising event in 1970 followed closely on the footsteps of several complicated public controversies for the Church of Jesus Christ of Latter-day Saints. Stanford University and the University of Wyoming staged boycotts and protests against BYU, and Civil Rights activists continued to attack the priesthood prohibition against African Americans. In 1969, the Latter-day Saints First Presidency released an official statement that both promoted civil rights and upheld the priesthood ban. Stevenson wrote that "the success of the Civil Rights protests had seeped into the Mormon consciousness, compelling Church leaders to walk the awkward border between support for Civil Rights and the continuing embrace of the priesthood restriction."[75]

Because of its timing almost immediately following the 1969 statement, "Operation Good Samaritan" appeared to be reparative work on the public image of the Church of Jesus Christ of Latter-day Saints. Bishop Givens viewed the interfaith project as a way to "join hands and be brothers and sisters in our community," but the moment was rife with implications.[76] Some members of the Church of God in Christ had no desire to be used as a "public relations ploy."[77] The politics of the national image of the Church of Jesus Christ of Latter-day Saints cast suspicions on the motivations of interfaith engagements with African Americans, despite the goodwill of many Latter-day Saints in Salt Lake City.

"I NEVER HAD A JAIL RECORD UNTIL I STARTED PREACHING."[78]

The 1970s provided new opportunities for the Church of God in Christ to emerge as an important part of the Utah landscape, thanks in large part to the work of Robert Harris. By the time the forty-second Utah state legislature began on January 10, 1977, the city of Ogden already knew well the personality of its recently elected representative, Robert Lee Harris. A pastor for the Church of God in Christ Congregational, owner of the Faith Market grocery store by day, and employee for the Union Pacific Railroad by night, the Reverend Harris became the first African American to win an elected office in Utah.[79] His passion for politics and religion carried him from a life of poverty in the South to the Utah state legislature. But his personality and savvy evangelization of his faith made him a household name among voters in Weber County.

Robert Harris pursued a life of faith and hard work. Born in Ft. Worth, Texas, in 1925, his father died when Harris was two years old, and his mother struggled to raise her eight children alone. She remarried, bore three more children, and became a widow for the second time. Remembering his childhood, Harris recalled that "when I was eight I threw a rock as a ball, because I was too poor to buy one."[80] He learned the value of hard work during the Great Depression and felt called to ministry within the Church of God in Christ Congregational.[81] In 1944, he relocated to Phoenix, Arizona, where he started his family.

In 1956, Harris moved to Ogden in pursuit of employment and found work with the Union Pacific Railroad. There, in Ogden, he met his second wife, Evelyn, and opened Faith Market, becoming the first African American grocery store owner in Utah.[82] He also established a congregation of the Church of God in Christ Congregational. Although small, Harris pastored the congregation over several decades. Robert and Evelyn became fixtures of the African American community in Ogden.

Pastor Harris used his pulpit as a platform to express his political concerns throughout the late 1960s and 1970s. He sought to represent the forgotten communities of Utah, including members of minority groups, people living in poverty, and the elderly. Mixing Christian social gospel with Civil Rights, Harris protested often in the Salt Lake City and Ogden areas. He demonstrated over sixty times and received jail time on at least a dozen occasions.[83] Harris blocked traffic with his vehicle to protest increased gasoline prices, laid down at the doors of the Utah State Capitol Building to protest mistreatment of the poor and elderly, and sang "White Man and Black Man Get Together Today,"—a song he wrote—at the steps of the Salt Lake City courthouse to protest the race riots of the late 1960s.[84] He ran for Ogden City Council three times but never managed to win a seat. "The Black man has never had anyone in office to speak for his rights," argued Harris, "and the poor people have never had anyone to speak for their rights."[85]

Yet when the Reverend Harris won the election for the Utah legislature's House of Representatives in 1976, he explained, "I'm not taking a racial approach. You walk through my district and you'll see there are far more white people in need than there are colored."[86] As the first African American in Utah to hold an elected office, Robert Harris vowed to fight for the beleaguered. And his Pentecostal faith, still unfamiliar to most Utahns, informed every action he made in office; "I will be on my knees in prayer for two minutes every morning immediately after the day's session begins."[87]

Unfortunately racial difficulties persisted throughout the twentieth century. "The fact that they were spread so thinly through the population," believed Utah historian James B. Allen, "contributed to a lack of familiarity that tended to slow down the process of acceptance."[88] "In the South, it [racism] was there," said Joan Nabors, thinking about her experiences in Utah in the 1960s and 1970s, versus other places. "I mean it was out in the open. Here . . . it was like, oh yeah, I mean, you know, on the surface things looked pretty good, but then you just go down just one layer, and you hit it, you know."[89] Henry McAllister moved from Arkansas to Utah in 1973 and worked at Hill Air Force Base. Reflecting on racism in Utah, he said, "It was more subtle. It was more covert rather than just straight out. Down south you knew where you stand. You knew where you couldn't go, shouldn't go. But some of the same issues that we had down south are present here in Utah."[90]

Terry Williams became the first African American state senator in Utah in 1983. As he traveled the state of Utah, he realized that for many rural Utahns, he was the first African American they met in real life. Addressing the racism he encountered in Utah through derogatory language and terminology, he developed his own approach to the subtle discrimination:

> As I have traveled around this state and I've heard that kind of terminology, if I were a militant person like in the late 60s with the Black Panthers, you know, you just jump off on that person and you rip them up and down verbally and you call them a racist and a bigot. These people have no bigotry in their heart. They don't have any hostility in using the terminology. It's something they grew up with since they were kids and it's just part of their vocabulary. . . . And recognizing that they've lived in a cocoon society with and using vocabulary that's offensive to me but they don't know it and they don't mean it hostilely, then my reaction should be to receive that and know that rather than jumping all over them.[91]

Despite the approaches to politics taken by Terry Williams and Robert Harris before him, race continued to plague the culture of Utah.

Harris failed to win reelection, but he remained a vocal, active member of his community, attending city council meetings and other events in the Ogden area. Working nights for the Union Pacific Railroad and days at his grocery store, Harris still made time for church and community. He volunteered to provide funeral escorts in town and donated free meals from his store. Even after he was no longer able to walk, Harris could regularly be seen around town in his motorized wheelchair, looking to help those in need. Loved by his community for his activism (not to mention his "Best Soul Barbecue Sauce" that he sold from his grocery store), many grieved for his family when he died on February 22, 2005.[92]

GROWTH AND CHALLENGES IN THE LATE TWENTIETH CENTURY

The Utah Church of God in Christ underwent a variety of changes during the late twentieth century. Many of the original members died or retired during these years, turning the congregations over to new leaders with new directions. These decades also marked important anniversaries for the history of the church in Utah. During the 1990s and early 2000s, a new group of leaders celebrated their history and made preparations for growth in the twenty-first century.

The churches in Ogden had grown the most during the early twentieth century and continued to grow in the 1980s and 1990s. Elder Sylvester V. Miller became the third pastor of Brealey B. Mike's Wall Avenue church in 1970. Under his direction, he believed the church could modernize, both spiritually and temporally. Because national church leader Bishop C. H. Mason had visited the church and the first convocations had been held there, the church guarded some important historical moments. But Elder Miller decided it was time for a change. He renamed the church the Emmanuel Church of God in Christ and began buying additional land around the building.

Elder Sylvester Miller, along with his son Elder John Miller, spent decades raising funds for additional land and a new building. Elder John Miller became pastor after his father and could often be heard preaching, "This corner is changing by the power of the Holy Ghost!" After many years of hard work, they broke ground for a new building in 2002 and dedicated it on August 22, 2004. Much more spacious and modern than the previous building, the new building could be utilized for decades to come.

At the fiftieth annual district meeting of the Ogden district in 1998, the church decided to take stock in its history. Henry McAllister, the pastor of Finley Temple Church of God in Christ since 1996, started collecting histories for COGIC in Utah. He compiled photos and memories, spoke with long-time members, and wrote short biographies and church histories. At the annual district meeting on March 2, 1998, leaders presented a brief history of the Utah Church of God in Christ for their members to keep.

Not only had Emmanuel Church of God in Christ changed over the years, but all of the other churches had too. The old Mount Zion building was sold and torn down. Elder Griffin and his congregation purchased a new building in April 1989, just before his death that September. Bishop Nathaniel Jones changed the church name to Griffin Memorial Church of God in Christ, in honor of the more than four decades that Elder Griffin had led the church. Bishop Jones then appointed Elder Bobby R. Allen as pastor.

Bishop Bobby Allen is a long-time fixture in the Utah COGIC community. Bishop Allen was born in 1938 and raised in Texas. He and his wife, Martha, moved to Ogden in 1960. Finding work was difficult, but Bishop Allen found various jobs as a car washer and a mechanic's assistant. While working at the Cream O'Weber dairy, Bishop Allen was the only Black employee there. Often his children were among the only African Americans in their schools, and his family were among only one or two in their neighborhoods. Despite adversity and racism, Bishop Allen eventually trained as a certified diesel mechanic and worked in that profession for more than fifteen years.

Already a believer in Pentecostalism, in 1961 Bishop Allen and Martha began attending the Griffin Temple Church of God in Christ. He became an elder in 1975 and was appointed pastor of the Idaho Falls Church of God in Christ in 1980.[93] For seven years, he commuted to Idaho Falls every week. On occasion, he pastored at more than one congregation in Idaho and Utah at the same time. About eighteen months after Elder Griffin's death, Bishop Nathaniel Jones appointed Bishop Allen to become pastor at Griffin Memorial Church of God in Christ. Shortly thereafter, Bishop Nathaniel Jones was appointed to a new jurisdiction in southern California, and Bobby Allen was appointed bishop of the Utah Jurisdiction in 1993. Having served in that position for over twenty-five years, Bishop Bobby Allen is one of the longest-serving bishops in the history of the jurisdiction, second only to Bishop Isaac Finley.[94]

The Church of God in Christ has not grown larger in Utah through the late twentieth and early twenty-first centuries. It remains one of the smallest Pentecostal denominations in Utah, probably in large part because African Americans remain the smallest minority group in the state. Yet stalwart members including Bishop Bobby Allen continue striving to strengthen and care for the community. In 2013 during the Holy Convocation celebrating the seventy-fifth anniversary of COGIC in Utah, Bishop Allen wrote, "As I reflect upon the past fifty-two years, I see God has brought us a mighty long way." Some steps along the way may have been more painful than others, but Bishop Allen believes that God "is yet taking us higher."[95] COGIC's continued presence in the state of Utah is a monument to their endurance and faith.

The history of the Church of God in Christ illustrates the complexities of race, ethnicity, and religion in Utah.[96] Rarely acknowledged by other Pentecostals and often uninvited by other religious communities in the state, they have struggled to find places of worship and maintain active congregations. The COGIC congregations never rivaled the size of other African American or white churches. And even as the Black population in Utah increased over the twentieth and twenty-first centuries, their congregations remained small. Without the finances for growth and enmeshed within a majority religious community unsure of how to structure its relationship with a growing racial and ethnic community, they soldiered on, developing their own unique subculture within Utah.

Despite cultural and financial hardships, the Church of God in Christ reveals how Pentecostal churches of all types have managed to establish themselves in even the most unlikely of places. For over eighty years, members of COGIC dedicated much of their lives to creating a community in Utah where they could comfortably worship according to their unique beliefs. Many studies of Utah religion focus on the Church of Jesus Christ of Latter-day Saints, sometimes to the exclusion of other religious groups. Viewing the struggles of minority churches in

Utah illuminates the religious diversity of the American West, even within areas saturated by strong religious majorities. The Church of God in Christ community is small, but they show no indication of going away. On the contrary, they are looking ahead to the next eighty years.

FIGURE 1. Photograph of the signs in Bountiful, Utah, before they were all removed, circa 1995. Public domain.

FIGURE 2. The American Fork Assembly of God congregation in American Fork, Utah. Pastor Warren J. Campbell and his wife, Dorothy, are on the far right, circa 1951. From the collection of Pat Christensen. Used by permission.

FIGURE 3. La Veda Francis and Robert Smith, circa 1950. From the collection of Robert Smith. Used by permission.

FIGURE 4. The Assembly of God church located at 469 29th Street, Ogden, Utah, sometime in the mid-1940s. Nathan Padgett is right of the door on the uppermost level. His brother, Alpha, is one step lower and to his right. From the collection of Loretta McIntosh. Used by permission.

FIGURE 5. Leo Waggoner is on the left, Pastor Overstreet is next to him, and Elsie Waggoner is singing at the podium. In Ogden, Utah, probably late 1950s. From the collection of Robert Smith. Used by permission.

FIGURE 6. The Gallegos family, circa 1943. Narciso and Romana are seated. Vidal Enriquez is standing on the far left. From the collection of Debra Rivera. Used by permission.

FIGURE 7. The Spanish Assembly of God church in Salt Lake City, circa 1957. Romana Gallegos is seated on the second row from the front, second to the far right. From the collection of Inez Perea. Used by permission.

FIGURE 8. Photo of the Spanish Assembly of God at 116 S 900 West, Salt Lake City, Utah. Romana Gallegos is in the back row, far left side, circa 1960. From the collection of Inez Perea. Used by permission.

FIGURE 9. Interfaith revival held at Griffin Temple Church of God in Christ. Bishop Isaac Finley preaching. Beginning second from the left, Elders David F. Griffin, R. E. Hurrington, Sylvester V. Miller, and Ralph R. Girley. Pastor Leo Waggoner is to the right of Finley, circa 1952. From the history collection of the Utah Church of God in Christ. Used by permission.

FIGURE 10. Church of God in Christ church leaders outside the old Griffin Temple building. From left to right: Elder R. E. Hurrington, Elder Bobby Allen, Deacon J. W. Sanders, Elder Justice Griffin, Elder William Golding, Elder David F. Griffin, Bishop Nathaniel Jones, unidentified. From the history collection of the Utah Church of God in Christ. Used by permission.

FIGURE 11. Pastor Robert L. Harris. From the history collection of the Utah Church of God in Christ. Used by permission.

FIGURE 12. The Assembly of God congregation in American Fork, Utah. They are standing outside the American Legion Hall. Pastor Warren J. Campbell is on the far left. Lilly May Strayer is on the back row, third from the right, circa 1950. From the collection of Barbara Burrows. Used by permission.

FIGURE 13. Layton Assembly of God Church at 100 South Main Street, Layton, Utah, circa 1953. From the collection of Barbara Burrows. Used by permission.

FIGURE 14. Lilly May Strayer, September 1961. Outside the Layton Assembly of God Church at 202 W. Golden Avenue, Layton, Utah. From the collection of Barbara Burrows. Used by permission.

5

"LABORERS ARE NEEDED IN THESE WESTERN STATES"

Pentecostal Woman Evangelists in Utah

In 2004, when the organization Standing Together successfully lobbied to have Ravi Zacharias speak in the Tabernacle in Salt Lake City, a newspaper touted the event as the first non-Latter-day Saint speaker in the Tabernacle since Dwight L. Moody in the late nineteenth century.[1] In 1926, however, an unlikely Pentecostal evangelist named Mae Eleanor Frey received the opportunity to preach from the pulpit of the famed dome building. Frey already had many years' experience preaching in the Northern Baptist Convention, and she received an evangelist's credential from the Assemblies of God in 1921 when she became Pentecostal.[2] As she traveled through the western United States as a newly credentialed evangelist for the Assemblies of God, she reported to the *Pentecostal Evangel* her concern that "laborers are needed in these western states, strong men and women who are willing to endure hardships for Jesus Christ, who are willing to blaze a trail across these western plains to the many needy souls for whom Christ died." In Salt Lake City, she and her secretary Miss Harrington received the opportunity from a "Mormon Bishop" to visit the Salt Lake Tabernacle. Upon discovering their profession, he invited them to hold a service there.[3]

Frey hesitated at the invitation but eventually agreed to preach. "I will have to preach the Gospel, not the Book of Mormon or Joseph Smith," she replied to the Bishop. The Bishop understood and promised a crowd all the same. Frey justified the occasion as she "remembered Brother Welch [referring to John W. Welch, General Chairman of the Assemblies of God from 1915 to 1919] say once that he would preach the Gospel from a Catholic altar if he got a chance." She and Miss Harrington proceeded to preach the next evening, thanking God for the opportunity to "give to them in their beautiful Tabernacle the full Gospel message of

Salvation, Baptism of the Holy Spirit, Healing, and the Coming of Christ according to the blessed Word of God."[4]

WHERE HAVE ALL THE WOMEN GONE?

Frey's experience preaching in the Tabernacle highlights the importance of female evangelists in Utah's Pentecostal history, as well as Pentecostal history generally. From the beginning of the Pentecostal movement in the United States, leaders debated the question of female preachers. Various denominations established alternatives to ordination that still allowed women to fulfill the scriptural reference in Joel 2 about women prophesying.[5] Prior to the revival of the early twentieth century, Phoebe Palmer developed the early Holiness Movement within Methodism and Maria Woodworth-Etter became nationally famous for her unique style of evangelism. They evangelized instead of pastoring. Once the revival started and denominations began aligning themselves with the Pentecostal message, leaders almost immediately took up concerns about the place of women. The Church of God in Christ developed the Women's Department, which created space for Church Mothers who wielded significant influence without the need for ordination. In the Assemblies of God, the question of women's authority was debated at the very first general council in 1914. According to Joy Qualls, "The authority to speak carried with it the right to exposit Scripture, which in turn meant teaching men."[6] Concerned that women might usurp the authority of men, it was resolved "that we recognize their [women] God-given rights to be ordained, not as elders, but as Evangelists and Missionaries, after being duly approved according to the Scriptures."[7] Other denominations created similar evangelistic roles for women.

Because of Utah's status in the United States as a Home Mission (similar to foreign missions within some Pentecostal denominations), women could participate in evangelization and played an important role in the early history of Pentecostalism throughout the state. Olive H. Walker opened the first Pentecostal mission in Salt Lake for the Assemblies of God.[8] Her mission would grow into a church following the visit of Woodworth-Etter a few years later.[9] A group of four women pioneered the earliest Church of God mission in Monticello. Grace Hall, Loretta Boyd, Ethel Perry, and Elizabeth Prickett worked for several years in southern Utah spreading the Pentecostal message in the late 1920s.[10] Romana Gallegos guided her family into the Assemblies of God in the early 1930s and then helped her children and others to organize the earliest Spanish-speaking Pentecostal churches in Utah. Her faith in healing and her ability to interpret tongues made her a central figure among the Monticello and later Salt Lake Assemblies.[11] Woman evangelists often traveled through Utah and preached at these early missions and churches. Women played a crucial role in evangelistic campaigns and early institution building around the state.

The importance of women in Pentecostal ministry continued through the 1940s and 1950s. Alberta Harris Jennings came to Utah in the late 1930s and organized the first Church of God in Christ in the state. She continued as state Mother until her death in February 1970.[12] Agnes DeVore pioneered the first Pentecostal church in the Provo area in the 1940s, Lilly Strayer pioneered the first Pentecostal church in Layton in the 1950s, and Addie Croasmun pioneered churches in Monticello, Blanding, and Mexican Hat through the 1960s.[13] Croasmun's mission churches were also the first Pentecostal churches among the Native Americans in Utah. Rosemary Cosby opened the doors of the independent Faith Temple Pentecostal Church in 1967.[14] Many of these churches planted by women continue to operate in Utah today.

From the late 1960s forward, however, fewer women could be found in leadership positions at Pentecostal churches in Utah. Permanent pastors replaced missionaries and evangelists. Despite many Pentecostal denominations permitting the ordination of women as pastors since the 1930s, the number of women currently pastoring in the state of Utah is almost zero. This trend in Utah supports the argument that most Pentecostal churches in the United States sought to limit the participation of women as the movement gained acceptability. Estrelda Alexander argued, "Pentecostals sought to distance themselves from any association with modernity and 'worldliness,' including ideas of the 'new woman' that were coming into fashion by the middle of the century."[15] In 1994, women accounted for only 8 percent of ordained pastors in the Assemblies of God worldwide.[16] In 2017, only 6 percent of women served as lead pastors in the Pentecostal Assemblies of Canada.[17] Fewer women held positions of authority over men across almost all classical Pentecostal denominations.

Trends suggest that the numbers of Pentecostal female pastors are growing in the twenty-first century, but the mid-twentieth century underwent a decline in overall numbers.[18] At present, a few Utah pastors are female (and a few more assistant pastors as well), but the vast majority of Pentecostal pastors in twenty-first-century Utah are male. Women continue facing complications in Pentecostal ministry in the United States. Charles Barfoot and Gerald Sheppard argued in 1980 that "the early equality of women in Pentecostalism was limited to the first stage of the movement."[19] Their data revealed that many more women than men joined the Pentecostal movement in its first two decades, which allowed more women to be involved in leadership roles than could be seen in other Protestant churches of the time. While it is true that women participated in ministry, more and more scholars disagree with the idea of a "Golden Age" for women.[20] The lack of men made opportunities available to women, but according to Qualls, "contradictions in message still existed regarding their role, abilities, and freedom to function within the organization."[21]

PLANTING AND NURTURING NEW CHURCHES

Women were a crucial part of the foundations of Pentecostalism in Utah because Utah was long considered a mission field and a difficult one at that. As described in other chapters, new church plants in Utah sometimes lasted no longer than the missionary or pastor had the energy to keep preaching. As soon as he or she left, the church scattered and members sought other congregations or worshipped alone at home. This meant there was almost always an opening to fill for a willing female missionary or evangelist in the spiritually bleak mountains and valleys of Utah.

In this sense, Utah serves as additional evidence of the complicated role of women within Pentecostal institutions. Qualls wrote, "While women had significantly developed and pioneered the work of the Pentecostal movement and the Assemblies of God, at every turn, their right to serve was challenged."[22] Leaders alternately praised and limited the work of woman evangelists in Pentecostal denominations. Alexander noted how Pentecostal "leaders willingly allowed them [women] to 'dig out' or plant new congregations and nurture them to the point of viability," only then to be asked to stand down from those works they spent years nurturing to let men take their places in the pastorate.[23] At other times, it meant accepting some of the hardest locations to preach because men were unwilling to go there. It also meant struggling to understand their place in their own Pentecostal institutions.

Lilly May Strayer's example of ministry in Utah serves as a vehicle for analyzing the ups and the downs of a woman navigating ministry within a Pentecostal organization. Arriving in Utah in 1948 and dying in 1991, her life of ministry covers most of the latter half of the twentieth century. And Strayer's experiences in Utah represent the missionary spirit of Pentecostal women in Utah, while also revealing the institutional tug of war that women participated in as they interacted with their leaders and their culture.

The profile of Strayer that follows, demonstrates how Pentecostal woman evangelists played a pivotal role in the creation of Pentecostal churches in Utah despite gender discrimination from their own organizations and congregations. They laid the groundwork for many congregations, and they modeled how women could be involved leaders within the Pentecostal movement. Alongside Kathleen Cummings's research about Catholic nuns in the United States, Pentecostal women's history in Utah reinforces Cummings's conclusion that it is not always true that "women who were faithful members of a patriarchal church were largely incapable of genuine work on behalf of women."[24] Women like Strayer showed how to be engaged with leadership throughout her life.

Strayer lived her early adult life in southern California. Born in 1913, she married Henry Al Strayer on September 3, 1930. Henry worked at North American Aviation in Inglewood, and they lived not too far away in Los Angeles. Strayer had been raised in the Church of Jesus Christ of Latter-day Saints, but Henry was Methodist and wanted nothing to do with the Latter-day Saints. Strayer sent her children to Sunday worship with Latter-day Saints in Inglewood for a while, but they eventually began attending a local community Christian church pastored by a man named Joe Bentley. During the late 1930s, she considered the Bible-centered teachings Pastor Bentley offered but loosely retained her membership and beliefs in the Church of Jesus Christ of Latter-day Saints.[25]

During a stressful stay in 1942 at the Centinela Hospital in Inglewood, California, Strayer felt what she described as a "born-again" experience. "I was frightened," she recalled, "terribly for I knew I was facing eternity and being taught salvation came through 'work' I knew I had nothing to offer God." Strayer's understanding of Latter-day Saint doctrine left her concerned that she had not done enough good to merit salvation. As she lay in the hospital, she "cried out again 'O God, help me, take away this pain and I'll do anything for you.'" The visionary experience that followed her plea left her certain that she must abandon her beliefs as a Latter-day Saint and dedicate herself to God in a new way.[26]

Over the next couple of years, Strayer became spiritually active and began worshiping with the Assemblies of God. She told her sister, Lola, about the changes, and Lola "sent missionaries out, wrote, called, and finally came herself" to try and convince Strayer to return to her former beliefs. This worried Strayer because Lola "always had dominated me and I knew I couldn't combat her." As her sister's visit drew near, Strayer pursued baptism in the Holy Spirit.

> I told Brother Walker and . . . we kneeled at the altar in the small basement chapel. Jane Handlos was on one side of me, Brother Walker on the other and the rest close by. I was truly in earnest and my need was great. Suddenly all around me faded out, light dimmed and the silence was heavy. . . . Then I was lifted up out of the power and was glorifying God in a strange language. The presence and the shaft of light went upward and out. I saw no face to be able to describe, just a presence of beauty, Jesus Christ, My Lord came and baptized me in the Holy Spirit.[27]

Having experienced a second witness of her new faith, Strayer gained the confidence she needed to speak with her sister and defend the choice she made.

By the late 1940s, Strayer felt called to be a missionary among the Latter-day Saints. Similar to foreign missions where churches often sent missionaries already familiar with native cultures or languages, having a prior connection to the Church of Jesus Christ of Latter-day Saints drew various Christians to Utah in the hopes of working among the Latter-day Saints. Later pastors like Alex Lucero would feel a similar call and responsibility to perform evangelistic work among adherents of their former faith. When pastors entered Utah without knowledge of the Latter-day Saints, many times they did not remain very long. Yet others, like Strayer, felt called to Utah because of their relationship and understanding of the Latter-day Saint religious community. In some ways, they knew what they were getting into, and it created a personal investment in their success. The added impetus to stay strengthened their commitment to the difficult nature of missionary work in the state.

Unfamiliar with Utah, the Strayers moved in 1949 from southern California to American Fork, Utah. Strayer offered her services to Warren J. Campbell, the pastor of a small congregation started a few years earlier in 1946. Strayer's husband Henry Al Strayer, although supportive of her call as a missionary, had no desires of entering the ministry himself. He worked to support the family while Strayer worked with the church. Life in American Fork, a town located in central Utah about an hour south of Salt Lake City, differed considerably from life in the Los Angeles area. The Strayer's children joined the very few non-Latter-day Saints at school, and it took a little time to transition to a more rural lifestyle.

Many Pentecostal women worked in similar family and financial circumstances as the Strayers. Romana Gallegos held Pentecostal worship meetings in her home, while her husband, Narciso, worked to support the family in Monticello. Grant Croasmun sold a successful trucking company he operated in New Mexico to support his wife Addie's desire to plant churches in southern Utah. In the mid-twentieth century especially, middle-aged, married women played active roles in small congregations in Utah, as they also did elsewhere. Lay service in congregations afforded Pentecostal women opportunities to assist ordained pastors in the work of evangelism. A newspaper article in 1950 noted how Strayer represented the Assembly of God church as she held a prayer service with a family prior to a funeral.[28] It also opened the door for women to lead evangelistic projects in the absence of ordained pastors. From 1922 forward, the Assemblies of God permitted women to perform "baptism, marriage, burial of the dead and the Lord's Supper when a man [is] not available for the purpose."[29] Often men were not available in rural Utah settings, and married women took the lead at church as their husbands cared for family finances.

When she began holding church meetings in a home in 1952, Strayer began her first solo church plant in Utah. Al found work at Hill Air Force Base, and the Strayer family moved north to Layton. No Pentecostal churches existed in the area, so she took the initiative to create one. They held meetings in the home of their friends the Pfaenders until they managed to sign a lease on an old building at 100 South Main Street in Layton. They added living space for the family in back and held their first meetings on New Year's Day of 1953.[30]

"I'VE TAKEN THE CHURCH AS FAR AS I AM ABLE"[31]

The struggles of participating in Pentecostal ministry as a woman manifested themselves within the first year of Strayer planting a church on her own. Despite being in active ministry for four years, in 1952 she petitioned the Rocky Mountain District to become a licensed minister. On the form, she explained to District Superintendent Russel G. Fulford that she came to Utah "because of God's call to my heart for this field." She recorded preaching 124 sermons in the previous year and hoped to receive the support of the District as she pioneered a new work.[32] She received a license, but without becoming an ordained pastor, it relegated her to a lower position than other pastors in Utah. In a letter to Fulford, she asked for assistance for the Layton church. "Bro. Roll seemed to think that I was going to press the district for money," wrote Strayer, "and he let me know very [definitely] that the ordained men come first. I don't want any help for myself," she explained. In all the years she would eventually spend pastoring churches, she never received pay for her service, and her letters suggest she did not expect it. "I too feel the ministers should have help. And I'm doing my best to see they get help. There isn't any one who is in the mission field that doesn't need help to establish a strong and healthy work. And I am not after any help for myself. If I ask for it, it is for the church and goes into the church."[33]

Strayer knew ordained men came before licensed ministers like herself, but she worried more about the health of new congregations. "The thing I do believe in," she declared,

> is that there is no use of going out in Personal evangelism and getting souls saved unless we have healthy churches to send them into so my call is to see that healthy Assemblies of God are established all over so that when God sends a renewal we will have a place for the people to be fed. And a healthy church is one that is self-supporting financially as well as spiritually.

The Layton Assembly of God was the seventh English-speaking Assembly planted in the state of Utah. Including her work in American Fork, already she had assisted with almost a third of the denomination's churches in the state, and she hoped to plant other churches still.[34]

Her 1953 letter discussed the matter of turning over the Layton church to a male pastor, and the conversation demonstrated the type of gender dynamics at play within the Pentecostal community in the mid-twentieth century. She worried that male pastors in the area thought she hoped only to siphon off funds from the district for her own gain. She worried that remaining in charge of a church might limit its potential growth. And she understood the cultural significance of male leadership over female leadership. In her letter, Strayer even presented her missionary role in gendered terms. "I'd like to turn over Layton Assembly to you as a healthy Growing Baby," she explained, "and see it grow. Then I'd be free to start another one where ever God bids me." The simile of the church as a healthy baby marked Strayer as its mother. As a mother, she birthed and nurtured churches in their infancy, until they were ready for a man's leadership. "I feel I've taken the church as far as I am able. It needs some man now to develop it into a full grown church." Strayer employed the societal roles of mothers and fathers to explain the importance of her evangelistic role in the state of Utah. She acknowledged the need for men to guide churches into strong congregations, but she also defended women's participation in creating new churches.[35]

The letter also revealed the almost adversarial position women in the ministry found themselves in. A little defensively, Strayer affirmed her faith in her denomination while simultaneously sharing reservations about it: "I believe in the Assemblies of God with all my heart. I believe we need assemblies all over Utah. But I don't believe we will see much of anything here in Utah until some things are cleaned up." Subtly, she hinted that some of the difficulties to be cleaned up had to do with the relationship between her and some of the men in the ministry in Utah. "Please believe me," she implored. "Regardless of the things that have been said—and I know of them—All I'm here for is to see Utah won for God." Her words suggested that, at times, women contended with not only the culture around them but also the culture of the church. The questioning of her intentions and the talk around her ministry all suggested the culture of suspicion that female ministers worked within.

Strayer vacillated between reaffirming her faith in the Assemblies of God as a denomination and confronting the denomination for inhibiting her work. Qualls, in analyzing the relationship of Pentecostal women to the institutional framework of the Assemblies of God, argued that women "faced challenges and constraints dictated not by those outside their faith communities but from within their own ranks, their fellow ministers."[36] In studying the role of women in the Church of God, David G. Roebuck argued that the denomination systematically relegated women to an inferior status in ministry because of their concerns about women leading.[37] This was certainly the case for Strayer as she negotiated the growth of the Layton Assembly of God.

Her ministry stretched over decades, demonstrating her conviction to evangelism. Despite trying to find men to replace her in Layton, she pastored the church from 1952 until about 1958. She stayed on as an assistant pastor and helped with the initiative to build a new building.[38] At the same time, she returned to American Fork as an interim pastor and guided their building program to completion.[39] She worked with Youth Camps in the Rocky Mountain District and participated in state camp meetings. She often assisted with funerals and printed Christmas greetings in local newspapers.[40] She continued to fill in as interim pastor at Layton and American Fork at various times throughout the 1960s, and she also served briefly as an assistant pastor for Pastor Peter Pilot at the Salt Lake Assembly.

Again writing to the Rocky Mountain district superintendent, Strayer made clear her acceptance and understanding of gender dynamics in congregational leadership. In 1961, she explained to Superintendent Fulford about finding another new pastor in Layton: "I love this church and feel that it is a very special place and that God has a very special man for the work." Strayer supported the effort to have a man pastor the church. "I see the need of a good man and the right one," she argued, because she admitted that she was "not able to do a lot of things that [were] needed to complete the work here." As in decades past, she agreed that male pastors increased the likelihood of growing successful churches, and she fully supported the policies of her denomination.

In the mission field of Utah, women commonly filled the role of interim pastor. During the early 1940s, Agnes DeVore placed dozens of ads in the paper for the Provo Assemblies of God church. At times, she listed herself as an exhorter, an acting pastor, as well as just pastor.[41] Ethel Perry remained committed to guiding the Church of God in Moab after other leaders moved on to other mission fields. "When many of the Church of God members left the church," reported the *Church of God Evangel*, "Sister Perry, her sister and son, of Summit Point, Utah, stayed true to the church."[42] Strayer too continued pastoring and supporting congregations on and off into the 1970s.

Strayer integrated her evangelism with politics in the community. As the state considered legislation against cigarettes in the 1950s, she reminded readers of the *Salt Lake Tribune* that "no one has given any testimony from the highest authority on the subject."[43] She engaged others in their use of the Bible in argumentation, wryly criticizing the way "people will use the Bible to prove anything and everything they wish proved even when they don't read it themselves."[44] Concerning Utah party politics or the now-famous exchange between Anita Bryant and Tom Higgins (who publicly pied Anita in the face because of her campaign against homosexuality), Strayer took to the editorials sharing her Pentecostal point of view.[45] Like Robert Lee Harris of the Church of God in Christ Congregational or Dean Jackson of the Rock Canyon Assembly of God, she believed society needed vocal religious advocates to participate in politics. Unlike Harris and Jackson, she did not pursue public office but instead worked to influence politics from a distance. The decision not to run for an office may have resulted from another cultural element of gender dynamics.

At times, Strayer's interactions with her denomination seemed defensive, and with good reason. In the mid-twentieth century, men accounted for nearly 80 percent of ordained pastors while women accounted for nearly 67 percent of the church membership.[46] The *Pentecostal Evangel* ran various articles petitioning for more men to engage in ministry.[47] Strayer herself, after over twenty-five years of ministry for the Assemblies of God in the state of Utah, was dismissed as a Licensed Minister by the Rocky Mountain District Presbytery. Referencing her "general attitude" as a "failure or inability to represent our Pentecostal testimony correctly," the district chose not to renew her license as an Assembly of

God preacher. Strayer's work with the Inter-Faith Christian Center in Farmington, Utah, along with difficulties between her and her male colleagues, resulted in her dismissal.[48] She had accepted additional opportunities to minister among congregations not directly associated with the Assemblies of God, which violated the general bylaws of the denomination.[49]

Years prior to her dismissal, Strayer had indicated that her loyalty to the call to ministry superseded denominational boundaries in importance: "My Call is of God and it is to see Utah Evangelized for God," she testified to Superintendent Fulford in 1953. She outlined her plan for accomplishing it: "My desire is to see it [Utah] won through the Assemblies of God. But if they haven't the vision, I'll still go on and do as God has put in my heart, and that is a Pentecostal church in this town."[50] Nevertheless, she felt devastated by the later loss of her credentials in the denomination she spent decades supporting.

Other Pentecostal women also explored ministry opportunities outside their denominations because of the limitations and strains placed on them by denominational regulations. Joy Langford argued, "It was within the confines brought about by the apparent institutionalization of the [Pentecostal] movement that women were less likely to be ordained."[51] Reviewing differences between classical Pentecostal denominations and charismatic or neo-charismatic nondenominational congregations, Langford found that women received greater opportunities for ministry in many nondenominational congregations because "within New Charismatic churches formal ordination is not a necessity for leadership. Leadership is rather conferred on an individual when their anointing has been discerned."[52] Like Strayer, some women who felt called to ministry and limited by their organizations sought out additional opportunities outside the bounds of their denominational structures. This led Alexander to observe how there is "a pronounced increase in the number of women leaving Pentecostal churches to pursue ministry within mainline or nondenominational bodies."[53]

Despite a lifetime of ministry, female ministers remained vulnerable to gender dynamics in Pentecostal institutions if they did not take care to adequately and appropriately groom their relationships with their superiors. The dismissal caused significant emotional pain for Strayer. She did not stop ministering among Pentecostals, but she no longer formally ministered within the Assemblies of God. Strayer's strong will and clear description of her spiritual loyalties over denominational loyalties may have worked against her place within a fixed denomination. In the debate between the spiritual call to preach and the institutional authority to preach, women remained far more vulnerable to the loss of their credentials than men.[54]

Dismissal from the Assemblies of God freed up time for Strayer to commit to her community. Prior to 1976, she worked and volunteered at the Davis County Recreation Center and Hill Air Force Base as an arts and crafts supervisor. She continued to do so through the later years of her life, volunteering at Bountiful's Golden Years Center, serving on the Senior Citizen's Nutrition Advisory Committee, and participating widely in community services. Until her death in 1991, she continued working to improve the community that she lived in.[55]

CONCLUSION

The roles women filled in Utah mirrored the roles Pentecostal women filled elsewhere in the United States, as they worked to spread the Pentecostal message in the twentieth century. Because of its designation as a Home mission by many denominations, Utah became an open door for women to work as missionaries, exhorters, and evangelists. As the Pentecostal community grew, however, opportunities for women shrank. Just as demonstrated through the life of Strayer, the Pentecostal community in Utah needed passionate women to help establish new churches and congregations. These women struggled as much to find converts to fill the pews as they did to maintain their positions of leadership in their organizations. They watched and even supported men take over the churches they planted. Sometimes, they received censorship or dismissal despite their years of service. And at the end of it all, many women continued supporting these institutions because of their spiritual convictions. In the announcement for Strayer's funeral, it stated how "it was her [Strayer's] desire that in lieu of flowers, donations be made to Abundant Life Assembly of God, North Salt Lake, to finish their kitchen."[56] After being dismissed from ministry and nearing the end of her life, she continued asking others to support the denomination she herself wrestled with on and off over the decades of her ministry.

Female Pentecostal ministers continue to straddle the complicated relationship in which they are forced to operate. They cherish and chastise their organizations, as both the means for spreading the Pentecostal message to the world and the means by which women are at times underappreciated for the services they render. Throughout the twentieth century, the institutional pull toward male pastors limited opportunities for women in Utah. Through the 1960s, women filled numerous pastorates in various denominations across the state. By the late twentieth and early twenty-first centuries, however, very few women led churches.[57]

Rosemary Cosby continued to pastor the independent church she founded until her death in 1997, and women such as Janie B. Thomas continued holding offices in the Women's Department of the Church of God in Christ.[58] The Rocky Mountain Ministry Network (formerly known as the Rocky Mountain District) of the Assemblies of God reported in 2017 a total of 581 ministers, with only 119 women. Men lead almost all of the approximately forty-five Assemblies in Utah, and other Pentecostal denominations in the state are statistically similar. Women continue to participate in the leadership of youth and children's ministries but not in congregational leadership.[59]

Pentecostal women in Utah are not the only religious women in the state struggling with gender dynamics in conservative institutions. Women in the Church of Jesus Christ of Latter-day Saints also grapple with their purpose and position in their church structure. The twenty-first century witnessed the creation of a movement within the Latter-day Saint community to ordain women to the priesthood. The movement "aspires to create a space for Mormon women to articulate issues of gender inequality they may be hesitant to raise alone."[60] While Pentecostal women in most denominations are already able to receive ordination, both Pentecostal and Latter-day Saint women continue seeking ways to engage the inequalities they perceive to exist within their own institutions. Certainly, other conservative religious institutions share some similar gender dynamics as well.

It is not surprising then that Pentecostal women continue to struggle for representation in ministry in the state of Utah. The examples of Lilly Strayer, Rosemary Cosby, Addie Croasmun, Alberta Harris Jennings, and Romana Gallegos all witness to the desires women felt to be a part of spiritual work and institution building. Even when those institutions limited women's ability to assist in the work, for the most part, these women remained involved. Discussing the anti-feminist personalities of Catholic women in the United States, Kathleen Cummings argued, "The bonds of Catholicism remained stronger than the bonds of womanhood, and as long as this remained true, feminism would hold little appeal."[61] Pentecostal women in Utah committed to "do as God has put in my heart," to heed their inward convictions to spread the Pentecostal message of salvation in Jesus Christ.[62] Like Cummings's example of Catholic nuns in twentieth-century America, Pentecostal women felt the theology of Pentecostalism empowered them to participate in and often convinced them to submit to the inequalities placed on them by their religious organizations. In the process, they laid the foundation for many of the early Pentecostal churches in the state of Utah, and they continue supporting and improving the role of women as leaders and members in the institutions of which they are a part.

6

GROWING PAINS

The Struggles of Pentecostal Church Growth in Utah

Growth in Utah did not come easy for Pentecostals. Religions in general struggled to plant churches and gain members in the state against the backdrop of the Church of Jesus Christ of Latter-day Saints. Catholics succeeded to some degree as newcomers migrated to Utah in the mid-twentieth century. Yet because Pentecostals and Latter-day Saints both understood themselves as religious outsiders, they clashed in their messaging and in their behavior toward one another. Pentecostals existed in Utah as a tiny minority for much of the twentieth century, and they labored to acquire and maintain resources in the religious culture of Utah. They struggled to find meetinghouses they could rent or buy, often requiring them to build their own structures. They struggled with being viewed as undesirable by local communities, both culturally and systemically, as children received ridicule in schools and pastors fought with city administrators for the rights to build churches. In some ways, these difficulties arose out of Latter-day Saint culture in Utah, which dominated day-to-day life in the state. In other ways, it resulted as a product of their own self-representation as exclusivist religious outsiders.

This chapter argues that the difficulties Pentecostals encountered in Utah differed from struggles elsewhere because of the similarities in perspective shared by Pentecostals and Latter-day Saints. On one hand, because Pentecostals understood themselves as religious outsiders, they rarely got along with Catholics or mainline Protestants. Pentecostals across the United States suffered difficulties at the hands of large Christian communities. On the other hand, because Pentecostals and Latter-day Saints both understood themselves as religious outsiders, Pentecostals encountered additional difficulties in Utah. They sometimes clashed in their messaging and in their behavior toward one another. Latter-day Saints did not particularly seem to view Pentecostals as a serious threat to their community but instead as a nuisance to be ignored or excised. This impassive view of Pentecostals by Latter-day Saints differed from other parts of the United States.

The exclusivist behavior and worldview of Pentecostals resembled the behavior and beliefs of Latter-day Saints in Utah and may have spurred the impassive response to their presence. When Pentecostals came to Utah, they attempted to promulgate an exclusive path for salvation to a community that literally tried to abandon the United States to pursue its own exclusive path for salvation. Pentecostal Evangelism often fell on uninterested ears among Latter-day Saints who already felt like they were on the right, exclusive theological path to salvation. Published theological discussions between the two groups were rare, and both Pentecostals and Latter-day Saints commonly rejected each other's messages outright.[1] So the friction between these two religious outsider communities more often manifested itself in their comportment as neighbors. Pentecostals in Utah ordinarily worked alone to build their congregations. When they did receive support from the Latter-day Saints in their community, the support seemed intended to demonstrate the virtues of the Latter-day Saint theology over their neighbors. As outsiders dedicated to their own exclusive paths, Pentecostals and Latter-day Saints commonly floundered in their local interactions with each other throughout the twentieth century.[2]

The difficulties of growing the Pentecostal community can be understood through three distinct periods over the twentieth century. As a new religious movement, early Pentecostals arrived in Utah and found themselves entirely alone. Due to prejudices against the new movement nationally and preexisting evangelistic agreements between Protestants locally, Pentecostals encountered opposition from all sides. These circumstances continued from the early 1900s until the late 1930s. During the second period, from about 1940 to 1980, Utah Pentecostals encountered resistance from individuals, and on more rare occasions from local communities, across the state as they attempted to plant churches. Although institutionally Protestant churches and the Church of Jesus Christ of Latter-day Saints became more amenable to some interfaith activities, local communities employed vandalism and exclusion in attempts to convince Pentecostals to give up their aspirations. Finally from about the 1990s forward, fewer incidents of direct conflict occurred, but Pentecostals continued to feel ostracized from Utah communal life in a variety of ways. These three periods of Pentecostal growth help describe the ways religions interacted with Pentecostals and viewed their growing presence in Utah over the twentieth century.[3]

AGREEING TO DISAGREE: PENTECOSTALS AND PROTESTANTS

Pentecostals did not receive a very friendly reception generally in the United States during the early twentieth century. At first, few people knew of the Pentecostal revival. "Till the 1950s," argued Grant Wacker, "most Americans had never heard of [Pentecostals.]"[4] Those most familiar with Pentecostals in the earliest decades of the movement, however, fought bitterly against them. Radical evangelicals like the Holiness churches and the Fundamentalist Christians combatted the growth of the Pentecostal movement fiercely. Many Pentecostals left these movements to become Pentecostals, and radical evangelicals felt the sting of the loss keenly. Wacker notes that the "most conspicuous divisions took place within the Church of God in Christ, the Fire-Baptized Holiness Church, the Holiness Church of North Carolina, and the Christian and Missionary Alliance."[5] As individuals left to join the Pentecostal movement, radical evangelicals attacked the movement as poor, unintelligent, American fanatics, whose ecstatic practices purportedly encouraged sexual immorality, social decay, and self-righteous arrogance.[6]

The criticisms were not one-sided, and Pentecostals feverishly shot back at radical evangelicals. To justify leaving their old beliefs, Pentecostals claimed the embrace of the "full gospel." It was full, meaning their previous beliefs came up short. "The genius as well as the heartbreak of the new message," lamented Wacker, "was that it compelled converts to acknowledge, upfront and without qualification, that their previous commitments had been not just incomplete but bogus."[7] To justify leaving their old beliefs, they condemned them. Pentecostals embraced an exclusivist view of doctrine and practice that distanced them from their old friends and institutions.

As the movement grew, other Christians would join in the criticisms against the Pentecostal movement. Many caricatured Pentecostals as the "rubbish of society" because of their poverty.[8] Others ridiculed the movement because of the many women who held authoritative positions in the early years, like Maria Woodworth-Etter and Aimee Semple McPherson. Even though most Pentecostals resembled any other American as far as their socioeconomic status, their penchant for vibrant worship and constant evangelism fed the stereotype of holy rollers and drifters.[9]

Pentecostal interactions with Protestants in Utah suffered because of the state's religious history. Nineteenth-century Protestant missionary efforts revealed little success in converting the Latter-day Saints, regardless of the variety of methods attempted. Charles Randall Paul argued that Protestant missionaries fought to achieve evangelistic success during the late nineteenth and early twentieth centuries using three methods: first, to convert individual Latter-day Saints away from their beliefs; second, to curtail the success of Latter-day Saint missionaries in converting Protestants; and third, to encourage the Church of Jesus Christ of Latter-day Saints to abandon its peculiar doctrines and practices.[10] None of these methods proved very successful for missionaries like John Danforth Nutting, William Mitchell Paden, and Franklin Spencer Spalding. Serving as Congregationalists, Presbyterians, and Episcopalians respectively, they all made efforts in the early twentieth century that failed to gain many converts for their causes.[11]

The previous attempts by mainline Protestants to convert the Latter-day Saints directly affected the early attempts of Pentecostals to develop churches in Utah. Because of the difficulties of evangelization in Utah, many of the mainline Protestant denominations developed associations and agreements to work together in their evangelistic efforts. The Salt Lake Ministerial Association supported John Nutting's Utah Gospel Mission, which began operations in 1900. The mission functioned as an "interdenominational missionary approach," which Nutting would later rebrand as nondenominational.[12] Nutting drew financial support for the mission from various Protestant denominations in the Eastern United States, and its operation continued until Nutting's death in 1949. They traveled around the more rural areas of Utah seeking to convert Latter-day Saints to a generalized Protestant Christianity. In 1916 William Paden organized the Utah Home Missions Comity Council, which worked to "assure that there were no overlapping denominational efforts to serve local Protestants and to proselytize the Mormons."[13] According to James B. Allen, "comity agreements sought to build one church in a community with enough members to support it adequately rather than to establish several smaller competing congregations."[14] Indeed, one comity agreement expressly stated that "a feeble Church should be revived, if possible, rather than a new one established to become its rival."[15] Almost all of the mainline Protestant denominations in Utah participated in these arrangements, which allowed them to work together ecumenically to finance congregations around the state.

As Pentecostals began opening missions and planting congregations, they did not participate in, nor were they invited to join, either the Salt Lake Ministerial Association or the comity agreements established by the Utah Home Missions Council. This caused friction between the mainline Protestant denominations and the Pentecostal missionaries and evangelists. The Utah Home Missions Council's Statement of Principles declared that "those denominations having churches nearest at hand, should … be recognized as in the most advantageous position" to maintain a Christian presence in the rural communities of Utah. As such, "A community being served by one or more evangelical denominations should not be entered by any denomination" beyond what was already established.[16] Because of the Protestant biases against Pentecostals (and vice versa) noted earlier in the chapter, neither Pentecostals nor Protestants desired to work together in evangelism. The ecumenical agreements among the major Protestant Christian denominations in Utah helped to support the growth and sustainability of their member congregations against not only the Church of Jesus Christ of Latter-day Saints but also the fledgling Pentecostal congregations.

By the mid-twentieth century, many of the mainline Protestant missionary programs slowed as the Pentecostal efforts increased. The Utah Gospel Mission reported very few converts over the years of its operations, and funding declined into the twentieth century. The Presbyterian school system, a strong force for evangelism in Utah in the late nineteenth century, dwindled from twenty-five schools in 1900 to four schools by 1915. Following the national debates associated with senator Reed Smoot concerned with continuing polygamy in Utah, funding for Protestant missions in the state diminished generally as the Latter-day Saints appeared to comply with marriage laws. Adventists, Presbyterians, Methodists, and Baptists all seemed to lose their evangelistic momentum and zeal for missionary work in the state. As their missionary endeavors wound down, the comity agreements of the early twentieth century began to fade away also.[17]

"WE WANT YOU OUT OF TOWN"[18]

Pentecostals, however, continued increasing missionary works and now began spreading out beyond the urban centers. And as pastors and their families embarked on new fields of labor in the state, they encountered resistance. Confrontations most commonly occurred in the process of purchasing land or constructing buildings for new congregations. Often local authorities complicated pastors' attempts to create a permanent presence and members of local communities discriminated against the new religious groups. Sometimes discrimination also came in the form of withholding assistance. Latter-day Saints assisted Pentecostals during the mid-twentieth century at the direction of their leaders and when it improved their image as good Americans. Overall, however, Pentecostals felt the sting of what it meant to be a small band of outsiders during the 1940s through the 1980s.

Utah Pentecostals did not suffer greater difficulties than Pentecostals in other places. Fundamentalists and Holiness adherents in the eastern and southern United States railed against the "mental instability" and "demon power" of the early Pentecostals.[19] Newspapers across the country printed sarcastic stories and reports about Pentecostal tent meetings. In some places, Pentecostals suffered far greater persecutions. In the southwestern United States Latino Pentecostals met rhetorical and violent persecution from the Catholic community most Pentecostal converts abandoned. [20] Pentecostals in Mexico received death threats and at times had to flee their homes.[21] During the 1932 Salvadoran massacre known as "La Matanza," and later on during the Salvadoran Civil War, many Pentecostal converts lost their lives.[22] Only in very rare cases did Utah Pentecostals fear for their lives.

Utah Pentecostals did not suffer greater difficulties, but they did in some ways suffer them silently. Rather than Utah newspapers printing disparaging articles about Pentecostal fanaticism, they printed nothing at all about Pentecostals. Instead of attacking Pentecostal theology, Latter-day Saints ignored their teachings. Or perhaps worse, they pitied Pentecostals because of their teachings. Nephi Jensen, a mission president for the Church of Jesus Christ of Latter-day Saints, reported to Latter-day Saints in a general conference about a visit he made to a Pentecostal church. Describing the Pentecostals he observed as "honestly but vainly striving . . . to get close to the Father of All," he felt bad for their purported failure to find God.[23] Outside of Utah, Pentecostals met oppositions head on. Inside of Utah, Latter-day Saints just ignored them most of the time. For a religious movement deeply invested in evangelism, this presented a curious dilemma: How does one evangelize among a people who view your message with unenthusiastic indifference?

Some of the disputes and encounters that did occur in the mid-twentieth century may have been a byproduct of the clash of religious outsiders in close quarters. R. Laurence Moore argued that outsider status helped the members of some churches to "find themselves" in the complex web of American society.[24] Pentecostals found affirmation of their unique beliefs through adversity. According to Grant Wacker, "Religious boundaries needed to be rigorously enforced, and social boundaries needed to be smashed."[25] If Pentecostals endured difficulties from their neighbors, it served to strengthen their resolve. Latter-day Saints also found theological security in adversity, but in Utah, they far outnumbered their competitors. And their history of developing closed religious and economic communities (the United Order communities developed under the direction of

Brigham Young) may have encouraged some individual members of society to view Pentecostals as undesirable additions to their neighborhoods. Although Latter-day Saint leaders abandoned efforts at communal living long before Pentecostals arrived, some of the principles of communal living remained as they continued urging converts to gather to Utah through the early twentieth century.[26]

Despite generally avoiding interactions with Pentecostals, resistance to Pentecostal growth did still materialize in the form of taunting, bullying, and vandalizing. "Religious opposition has been unrelenting," reported the *Pentecostal Evangel* in 1954.[27] Vandals damaged the doors of Guy Heath's Assembly of God Church half a dozen times in the early 1950s. During the construction of the building, they broke windows and stole tools from the site.[28] After Willard Coleman purchased an old Latter-day Saint building in Richfield to use for the Assembly of God, teenagers broke into the building and spray-painted "Go Away" on the walls and blackboards. Another break in in Richfield shortly after the first resulted in the damage of additional property.[29] When the Abundant Life Assembly of God church purchased a building in North Salt Lake in the early 1980s, someone painted on the exterior wall of the building "We don't want you here." The constructing or purchasing of physical property for a new church signaled a desire for permanency, and often anonymous representatives from the community took it upon themselves to let the newcomers know what they thought of such desires.[30]

Children and adolescents faced hardships at school. Max Croasmun, the son of pastor Addie Croasmun, recalled vividly the feel of an egg or tomato (depending on the occasion) smashing into his back, thrown at him by students driving by in their vehicles as Max walked home from high school. They attended school in the southeastern town of Monticello in the early 1950s. He and his brothers often fought with students at school, and Max believed it was due to their outsider religious status:

> That year that I spent there, I whipped all but two boys in that school. Them two were the bullies in the school. I fought one of them, and we come in kind of a draw. He didn't whip me, I didn't whip him. And after that they showed me respect and that part of it stopped. But my brother just younger than me. There was at least two times I remember, they pulled his pants down in the hall. You know, this kind of stuff. There was a family that started coming to the church. They came in and were there a while, and this boy, there was a boy and two girls in the family, and he helped me one day. Well they beat that poor boy to a pulp. That was the

> kind of persecution. I'm not telling you, I'm not stretching anything. I'm telling you exactly what was happening to us.[31]

In some ways, children struggled more than their parents as they tried to fit in at school and elsewhere. During the early 1970s, the children of pastor Murray Kemper in Santaquin recalled how they ran home from school every day in a hail of rocks from their classmates.[32] The children of Willard Coleman in Richfield suffered similar experiences.[33]

The blending of social and religious structures in many Utah towns shut Pentecostals out of community activities. Weddings, social events, and youth events revolved around the Latter-day Saint worship practices and youth programs. Because of the strong relationship in Utah between the Boy Scouts of America and the Church of Jesus Christ of Latter-day Saints, Pentecostal youth joined predominantly Latter-day Saint Scout troops. Attempts at conversion blended imprudently into the Boy Scout experience for many youth. Informed by local Scout leaders that they would need to attend church meetings to complete the requirements for religious badges, Pentecostal parents occasionally had to step in and fight for their sons' rights to attend their own churches.[34]

Disruptions accompanied new Pentecostal services. Guy Heath reported how "a group of fifteen to thirty people would visit the church, and then walk out in the middle of the sermon to disturb the spirit of the service."[35] This scene repeated itself over the years, in Assembly of God churches, Pentecostal Church of God churches, and independent churches like the First Apostolic Church pastored by William Fitzgerel.[36] Around April 1978, a gentleman interrupted Pastor Willard Coleman's services in Richfield by feigning to have a gun, pointing at the pastor, and declaring that "if they did not leave town, then next time it would be the real thing."[37]

Rarely did the troublemakers identify themselves by name or religious affiliation. Hiding behind anonymity, individuals and groups namelessly expressed their dislike for the Pentecostals. Therefore, it could be the case that anti-Pentecostal sentiment in Utah came from Catholics, Protestants, and Latter-day Saints alike. Certainly, in the early twentieth century Protestants objected to Pentecostal presence in Utah. Yet given the considerable majority Latter-day Saints maintained over other religious groups, especially in rural areas, it was probable that most agitators came from the Latter-day Saint community.[38]

At least on one occasion, the only non-Latter-day Saint church in Santaquin (a small town in central Utah about twenty miles south of Provo) during the 1970s received the disruption from their neighbors with smiles on their faces. During one of their services, children outside threw rocks at the windows of the building where the Santaquin Assembly of God met on Sunday. They did not intend to damage the building—just disrupt the meeting. Their taunts about "holy rollers" could be heard inside the service. So the pastor, pacing at the pulpit in the front, declared, "Well if I'm gonna be called that, I might as well be it." And away he went, rolling across the floor, the congregation breaking up in laughter at the pastor's jest.[39]

In rare instances, individuals aggressively mistreated Pentecostals and pressured them to leave. Returning from a Pentecostal fellowship meeting in Moab to their humble home in Monticello, the Croasmun family discovered that while they were gone, someone broke into their home and scattered all of their belongings outside. They worked late into the evening finding their things and bringing them home, including their beds, stove, and refrigerator. On another occasion, when Grant Croasmun answered the phone in their home, an unidentified man informed them that "we want you out of town." Despite several years of poverty and difficulties, the Croasmuns continued their work planting churches in southern Utah.[40] On the first evening that Willard Coleman arrived in Richfield in 1976, he brought some youth members from the West Valley Assembly of God Church to assist in surveying and evangelizing the city. A few young gentlemen stopped them in the street, pulled out a gun, and threatened them with violence if they did not leave the city.[41] Although no physical harm occurred, the tension continued in Richfield for several years.

More commonly, local city governments signaled their dislike of Pentecostals by complicating the process of constructing physical church buildings. It took Reverend B. B. Mike of the Church of God in Christ seven years to complete a small church in Ogden because neighbors continuously complained about the construction of the new church and dramatically slowed the building's progress.[42] In Monticello, the Croasmuns spent over a year getting permission to run electricity and water to the property where they hoped to build a church because of city council interference.[43] The Assembly of God Church in Santaquin chased out bats each Sunday morning from the only building in town they could find to rent.[44] The Abundant Life Assembly of God church in North Salt Lake received various permit rejections for routine renovations on their building that smacked of intolerance.[45] City governments at times dramatically slowed the process of planting churches, with no clear explanation for the impediments.

A city struggle concerning a proposed building plan in Tropic, Utah, exemplified the opposition Pentecostals occasionally encountered from rural communities. On May 3, 1979, the Garfield School district placed an ad in the newspaper for "anyone interested in removing or moving the old house on the Marshall property adjacent to Bryce Valley High School." They offered the building up at "no charge."[46] A man named George Wilson responded to the ad and received a verbal claim to the building, as long as he removed it by June 1 and cleaned the land. Mrs. Kristy Shakespear, a member of the fledgling Assembly of God community in Tropic, offered to purchase the building from Wilson so that they could move it, refurbish it, and use it as a church building in town. Wilson agreed, they prepared a notarized contract of sale, and the small Pentecostal congregation began making preparations to move the building.

Controversy over the transaction erupted. The Garfield County School District Board, led by Superintendent Henry Jolley, rescinded their offer to give the building away and opened a bidding process for the building to be demolished. Mrs. Shakespear and Willard Coleman, the pastor of the Richfield Assembly of God Church, attended School District Board meetings and city council meetings, arguing their right to the building and threatening legal action against the city. Once while attempting to inspect the building, the city sheriff insisted Pastor Coleman was trespassing and warned that if he returned to the site, he would be shot.[47]

The small Pentecostal community protested the unfair treatment, arguing, "There had been no complication until it was learned that Mrs. Shakespear and others had intended for the building to be used as a meeting house."[48] Editorials and articles graced the pages of the local newspaper as the school district tried to resell the building and the Assembly of God church tried to move the building. Later, the newspaper summarized the entanglement: "A battle over an old building which the Garfield School District planned to destroy and which the Tropic Assembly of God church sought to use for its meeting after rehabilitation dominated the news for three weeks with the church apparently losing the battle."[49]

By the conclusion of the conflict, the Assembly of God congregation could find no other explanation beyond religious discrimination. The District relented over the purchase of the building by Mrs. Shakespear but maintained the requirement to move it before June 1. Otherwise, they would lose their claim to the building. Yet a new problem arose from the resolution of the old one; no one in Tropic would sell the Assembly any land. The newspaper reported, "In seeking to acquire property on which to locate the building, Shakespear stated that they 'had been turned down repeatedly, with some residents refusing sale simply because an Assembly of God church was to have been placed on the site.'" A few people considered offers to sell but ultimately backed out of the offers "due to outside pressure against use of the property by the Assembly of God Church." "We hope the attitude evidenced in the difficulties in Tropic," lamented Mrs. Shakespear, "were not truly representative of the feelings of the community at large." The evidence, however, seemed to strongly support Mrs. Shakespear's suspicions. [50]

Many small cities like Tropic, Monticello, and Richfield remained resistant to new religious influences through much of the twentieth century. Local officials who often also held positions in the Latter-day Saint community carried enough sway with their neighbors and constituents that events like those in Tropic could still occur. Founded in 1891, the population of Tropic has never exceeded more than about 500 people. When the Croasmuns experienced discrimination in Monticello in the early 1950s, around 1,200 people lived there. The discrimination in Richfield occurred in the late 1970s, when Richfield had a population of around 5,000. North Salt Lake in the 1980s was roughly the same size as Richfield when the Abundant Life Assembly of God opened its doors. It required fortitude and persistence to break through local religious intolerance as Pentecostals experienced the growing pains of planting congregations and defending their own religious path in different Utah communities.

Sometimes engaging the community for support worked, but other times it fell flat. When Pentecostals could not find buildings to purchase, they constructed new ones. But finding adequate funding for construction always plagued new churches. The success of community fundraisers during the 1960s and 1970s hinged on the institutional involvement of the Church of Jesus Christ of Latter-day Saints. Leaders could mobilize members to offer their support, but more often than not, neither Pentecostal leaders nor Latter-day Saint leaders desired to engage each other. When they did, the reasons for their actions occasionally felt less than sincere by outside observers. Two specific examples that follow demonstrate the complications of seeking community support in the 1960s and 1970s.

Paul Harvey drew quite the crowd when he spoke at BYU in 1967. Born in 1918 as Paul Harvey Aurandt, he worked diligently as a young man to become one of the most famous radio broadcasters in American history. Better known by his middle name, Paul Harvey reported on stories of all types, but he had a gift for feeling the pulse of the nation, identifying American concerns, and encapsulating them into five minute musings to be published in papers or sent out to the American public on the radio waves across the country. On President Ernest L. Wilkinson's invitation, Harvey accepted the opportunity to be the featured speaker for BYU's "American Week," a weeklong series of counsel, music, and pageantry honoring and supporting the foundational principles of the United States of America.[51]

The audience at BYU exuded their excitement at being with Harvey and supporting his work. In a climactic evening event, "200 musicians, 1,000 voices, and pageantry" operated as a prelude to the message Harvey left with the crowd he obviously respected. Reporting on the event the following day, Harvey admitted "I don't know what I had expected. . . . These days many young eyes are prematurely old from countless compromises with conscience. But young lads and ladies of BYU have that enviable head start which derives from discipline, dedication, and consecration." Paul Harvey marveled at the attention he received from the audience of 15,000, filling the Smith Fieldhouse to overflowing. "The spontaneity," Harvey fervently reported, "the instant response of students and Faculty to the words of a prayer, or a pledge, or a song. It was an evening like re-dedication celebrations used to be!"[52] Despite their religious differences, Latter-day Saints connected with Paul Harvey because, as Mike Huckabee put it, Harvey "was not just the VOICE of America—he embodied the VIRTUES of America."[53]

Through the late 1960s and early 1970s, Paul Harvey's radio show reached millions of Americans multiple times a week, including multiple newspapers and radio stations in Utah. "By the beginning of 1971," wrote Harvey's biographer Paul J. Batura, "Paul Harvey held the world in the palm of his hand." Over 120 television outlets and 250 newspapers aired or printed his radio broadcasts, including Provo's own *Daily Herald*.[54] He spoke at events like BYU's "American Week" nearly a dozen times a month, receiving a speaker's fee of $5,000 per event. Like newspaper readers across the country, the *Daily Herald's* predominantly Latter-day Saint readership engrossed themselves in Harvey's interpretation of the American way.

Yet, in spite of such popular sentiment and support for his work, when Paul Harvey visited Utah again just a few years following his BYU visit, five times fewer people came to hear him speak. Planned for the evening of March 24, 1972, the visit included a dinner at the Prudential Banquet Plaza in Salt Lake City, followed by a public rally at the recently constructed University of Utah Special Events Center. Mayors Verl G. Dixon of Provo and E. J. Garn of Salt Lake City, as well as Utah governor Calvin L. Rampton, also attended the dinner as special guests. Tickets to the event cost $4 for reserved seating, $3 for general admission, and $2.50 for students, with the expectation that the 15,000 seating capacity of the Special Events Center might not be enough based on the attendance at Harvey's previous visit five years earlier.[55]

Raymond Ansel, pastor of the newly renamed Rock Canyon Assembly of God Church, organized Paul Harvey's 1972 public rally as a fundraising event to assist his church with the completion of their new building in Provo. Pastor Ansel was a licensed contractor in the state of Utah at that time, and he assisted with the construction of various church buildings in the state, from Logan and Brigham City in the north, to Cedar City in the south. For the project in Provo, they previously raised over $50,000, and Pastor Ansel hoped to raise another $40,000 from Harvey's visit to complete the building. So they rented facilities in Salt Lake, invited local and state officials as additional honored guests, and advertised the event in the newspaper. But they failed to raise the funds for the building. "It was a flop," Pastor Ansel reported. "I thought thousands of people would come, but only about 2,500 people had come and just barely covered the costs of what we had done."[56]

Only two years earlier, Pentecostal Bishop M. A. Givens Jr. of the Church of God in Christ worked closely with the Church of Jesus Christ of Latter-day Saints to complete a very similar fundraising campaign. Under the direction of Givens and leaders of the Church of Jesus Christ, Latter-day Saint youth raised over $30,000 to complete a church in Salt Lake City. BYU choirs joined acclaimed gospel singer Mahalia Jackson on stage for a benefit concert.[57] The Deliverance Temple building was completed and dedicated in August 1970.[58]

The outcomes of these two events illustrated the subtle difficulties Utah Pentecostals struggled with as they sought to grow into a permanent establishment in the state of Utah. On one hand, when prominent Latter-day Saint leaders promoted community works or service projects alongside Pentecostal leaders, church members supported those initiatives. The Church of God in Christ, a predominantly African American Pentecostal church, may have benefitted from the timing of Bishop Givens's request for aide. Over the late 1960s, Latter-day Saints received a significant amount of bad press nationally over their policies concerning African Americans and their access to the priesthood within the church institution. The newspaper headlines following the fundraising event, headlines like "Mormon Teens Raise $33,000 to Aid Salt Lake Negro Church" and "Negro Faith, LDS End Fund Campaign," appeared to intentionally highlight the great relationship between Latter-day Saints and the Utah African American community.[59] The Latter-day Saint community contributed very charitably, but some reports suggested self-interest motivated the participation.[60]

On the other hand, when Pentecostals attempted to engage the Utah community without representation from prominent Latter-day Saint leaders, they seldom received any community support. From Pastor Ansel's perspective, "The Mormons really listened to Paul Harvey."[61] And based on Harvey's previous visit and the syndication of his column in the local newspapers, he was right. Yet when the newspaper identified in bold that a Pentecostal church sponsored the event, it may have deterred the Latter-day Saint public from attending. Latter-day Saints did love Paul Harvey; they did not, however, often participate in local interreligious activities through much of the twentieth century. "There are not many roads that lead to heaven," stated J. Reuben Clark Jr., a member of the First Presidency of the Church of Jesus Christ of Latter-day Saints, in 1960 during the general conference of the church. "There is one and one only, and that is the road that we profess to travel and should be traveled."[62] Instead of filling the Special Events Center to its capacity of 15,000 (as happened at the Smith Fieldhouse in 1967), Harvey spoke to an almost empty house.

Teachings from leaders of the Church of Jesus Christ did not strictly prevent members from working with other religious groups, but they may have conflated motivations between neighborly kindness and missionary proselytization. Speaking to a convention of ministers in Salt Lake City, LeGrand Richards explained the importance of "Mormonism." "It is true that you can find some of the things that are in the Bible in the church, that is why we have hundreds of them, but you cannot find any other church in all the world that has all of the things that the Lord has promised."[63] His explanation, like Pentecostal explanations of the "full gospel," unabashedly declared that other Christian faiths did not contain the entirety of Christian belief. J. Reuben Clark Jr. worried similarly when he lamented:

> [As I] talked and heard others talk, that there may be a feeling, in fact, I know there is among some, that it does not make very much difference to what church we belong, what creed we may have, and not too much difference, within very broad limitations, what we do.... For we will all go to heaven anyhow, do what we will, think what we will, believe what we will, have faith as we may.

Without equivocation, he concluded, "I find great fault with that." Teachings like these, while never explicitly permitting the mistreatment of others, may have inadvertently led Latter-day Saints in Utah to oppose neighbors who followed different creeds or belonged to different churches. In defense of the faith, they kept their distance from those "pretenders of being the offspring of our Heavenly Father's gospel and principles."[64]

Pentecostals endured more difficulties from the 1940s to the 1980s than any other period. Even though some of the difficulties, like not receiving fundraising support, would likely not be considered harmful, the taunts, threats, and property damage affected the lives of Pentecostals significantly. And in some ways, it continued to reinforce their identities as religious outsiders. Pastors and missionaries achieved considerable growth from the 1970s into the early twenty-first century. Spurred by the missionary emphasis of Pentecostal theology and perhaps refined by the difficulties encountered in Utah, the Assemblies of God especially began reaching out to new cities across the state. Spreading out from Salt Lake churches, evangelists and pastors like Willard Coleman secured locations for congregations and then received ministerial assistance and financial aid from their home congregations. Many Assembly of God churches in southern Utah developed from coordinated efforts between congregation members and young pastors willing to travel extra hours and volunteer labor on new buildings. By the early twenty-first century, Pentecostal churches could be found in most cities across the state.

"I DON'T THINK THE MORMONS LOOKED AT US AS A THREAT"[65]

From the 1990s to the present, increasing diversity in Utah positively affected the treatment of Pentecostals in the state. Pastors rarely fought with local officials about construction regulations or reported threats of violence or vandalism. Instead, they almost got lost in the evolving religious culture within the state. Whatever concerns that previously filled neighbors with anxiety became muted. This was an improvement, but Pentecostals still felt like unwanted neighbors. The cultural atmosphere changed from intolerant to tolerant. Yet toleration is not necessarily the ideal condition for interactions with neighbors. Feelings of isolation replaced concerns about safety. Even though by the end of the twentieth century some Pentecostals and Latter-day Saints would vote together and occasionally work together on national issues, living together proved more complicated and less genial.[66]

Due to their continued minority status, Pentecostals in Utah remained community outsiders within their neighborhoods. Pastor Ray Ansel, who spent two decades pastoring in Vernal and Provo, concluded, "I don't think the Mormons looked at us as a threat."[67] The harassment Pentecostals received from time to time felt more like attempts at isolating newcomers and encouraging them to leave. Pentecostals did not suffer from systematic or defensive aggression provoked by the institutional Church of Jesus Christ of Latter-day Saints, nor did church leaders often mention the Pentecostal movement by name. In fact, in some ways the institution hardly seemed to notice they were even there. Of course, there were a few signs that they noticed. Beginning in 1975, the Church of Jesus Christ of Latter-day Saints began assigning missionaries to proselytize around the state of Utah. Previously they did not recognize a need for it beyond the missionaries that welcomed tourists to Temple Square in Salt Lake City.[68] Overall, however, the church seemed to be focusing more and more outwardly and internationally, diverting its attention from Utah.

With less visibility, Pentecostals missed out on opportunities to integrate into the community. Many social functions and activities intertwined with church functions because of the Latter-day Saint configuration of geographical boundaries for congregations. As a result, Pentecostals found themselves ostracized within their own neighborhoods. Holiday activities vividly highlighted the effects of religious boundaries. "We didn't even have to buy candy" on Halloween, remembered Judy Williams, because "people would come to this fence, walk across the street, go to that house, and then walk back across the street, and go to the next house. This happened for years," laughed Judy.[69] When Pentecostals did receive invitations, they often became the focus of proselytizing efforts. Pentecostal youth in Orem received invitations to sleepovers with classmates at school, only to discover that they were not being invited as friends, but as potential converts. Pentecostal youth felt like missionary work was often masked by false friendships. When religion came up in public school settings and Pentecostal youth became outed as non-Latter-day Saints, it affected their ability to make friendships or even simple relationships. Like in many communities with a large religious majority, religious minorities felt ostracized and removed from even their neighbors.

This was not unique to Pentecostals. Non-Latter-day Saints felt trapped in similar circumstances. Catholic students at BYU reported comparable experiences, from feeling left out to having trouble establishing relationships after revealing their religious affiliations.[70] The Church of Jesus Christ of Latter-day Saints now makes up only around 55 percent of adults in Utah in the present, but it remains more than twice as large as the number of unaffiliated people, and more than ten times the size of the Catholic population (the next largest religious denomination at 5 percent).

Over the last one hundred years, non-Latter-day Saints fought an uphill battle to grow churches in Utah, and Pentecostals found themselves pitted against most other religious groups in the state at one time or another. They competed with other Protestants who had no interest in including them in their evangelistic associations. They competed against Latter-day Saints, who pressured them to leave and then isolated them when they chose to stay. They brought their families and watched their children get drawn into religious disputes. On a school trip in the early 1990s, Dean Jackson's son pointed out his church (Rock Canyon Assembly of God in Provo) to another student on the bus. To which his seatmate replied, "My daddy says that those places that have a cross on them—they lie."[71] They created some of the problems themselves by claiming to be the keepers of the "full gospel." As a minority of exclusivist outsiders among the largest concentration of religious outsiders in the American West, Pentecostals butted heads at times with their neighbors. Latter-day Saints were as much to blame and on many occasions more to blame than the Pentecostal newcomers.

A majority of the time, Pentecostals dealt with being ignored and isolated from the community. Elsewhere in the country, Pentecostals managed to grow against the odds by combatting with other Christians verbally. Their boisterous meetings often drew curious people in. Utahns did not seem to respond in kind. Left in silence to themselves, Pentecostals struggled to collect the resources they needed to grow their community within Utah. Regardless of their difficulties, and despite the hardships sustained during the twentieth century, by the early twenty-first century Pentecostals managed to grow and mature into one of the largest Protestant communities in Utah.

7
MEET THE MORMONS

George O. Wood, former General Superintendent of the Assemblies of God, spoke to a large audience of students and faculty of Brigham Young University on September 16, 2013. He met with members of the Quorum of the Twelve Apostles from the Church of Jesus Christ of Latter-day Saints, including Elder Jeffrey R. Holland, prior to his speech. Some identified this occasion as the first time a Pentecostal leader spoke to a body of BYU students. Yet nearly sixty-four years earlier, in March 1949, Warren J. Campbell presented on the history of the Assemblies of God church before a class of about eighty students. He presented the information to multiple classes as they studied contemporary Christianity and Latter-day Saint Church history and doctrine. In both cases, the meetings with members of the different faith groups exemplified an interfaith approach to the conversation over differences between Pentecostals and Latter-day Saints.[1]

Over the twentieth and early twenty-first centuries, Pentecostals and Latter-day Saints engaged each other in a variety of ways, evolving from antagonism to indifference and eventually settling into a tentative and aloof relationship. Set in

Note: Although members of the Church of Jesus Christ of Latter-day Saints prefer to be called Latter-day Saints, the term Mormon has been used as well by both insiders and outsiders of the faith to describe them. On August 16, 2018, Russell M. Nelson, president of the church, stressed the importance of using the formal name of the church over any of its nicknames or acronyms and updated their publication style guide accordingly. With respect to these requests, I will most often use the term Latter-day Saint. In some cases within this chapter, however, I will also use the term Mormon as it was used by the institutional Church of Jesus Christ of Latter-day Saints in its public media campaigns of the early twenty-first century. I will also occasionally use the shortened "Church of Jesus Christ" to reference the Church of Jesus Christ of Latter-day Saints in this chapter.

exclusivist understandings about truth claims within Christian theology, neither Pentecostals nor Latter-day Saints pursued ecumenical or interfaith conversations during the early twentieth century. Conversion to the truth, both churches supposed, provided unity and purity more amply than nondenominational alliances. Pentecostals and Latter-day Saints attacked what they perceived as the false doctrines taught by each other. Hoping to convert souls by exposing errors, many early Pentecostals in Utah aggressively antagonized distinctive aspects of the Church of Jesus Christ of Latter-day Saints. Failing to convert Latter-day Saints en masse to Pentecostal Christianity, pastors in Utah developed a kind of social indifference toward the majority faith in the state, which enabled them to focus more fully on strengthening small congregations and developing methods of attracting non-Latter-day Saints to their organizations. Yet by the early twenty-first century, political and social developments in the United States at large paved the way toward first attempts at institutional engagement.

This evolution of engagement helps make sense of the evolution of Pentecostals and Latter-day Saints within the American religious mainstream. Building on the work of Robert Wuthnow's *The Restructuring of American Religion*, Neil J. Young argued that Catholics and Latter-day Saints also played an important role in the realignment of American Protestants into liberal mainline Protestants and conservative evangelicals.[2] As Catholics, Latter-day Saints, and evangelicals modified their interfaith approaches toward one another, it "produced some closer inter-Christian relationships but also hardened religious lines."[3] Missing from this analysis of the new American religious mainstream is the expanding role of Pentecostal churches. Young's analysis lumps Pentecostals into the community of evangelicals in the United States, but he provides very little analysis of Pentecostals apart from the larger evangelical community.[4]

This chapter helps reframe the importance of Pentecostalism within the American evangelical movement by focusing on Utah as a case study of the ways Pentecostals interacted with other conservative religions. Theological differences encouraged Pentecostals to strive for conversion over coexistence during the first half of the twentieth century. Pentecostals succeeded at converting members from various evangelical Protestant groups during the early twentieth century and had quite a bit of success among Catholics in the Southwest as well. Very few Latter-day Saints converted to Pentecostalism, however. Settling for coexistence, Pentecostals developed their own networks and institutions among themselves during the latter half of the twentieth century. By the early twenty-first century, however, both conversion and coexistence took a back seat to cooperation within a nation perceived by conservative Christians as becoming increasingly secular and liberal. Pentecostals reoriented themselves from labeling the "Mormons" as "a Satanic cult like all the rest of the demon movements of the last days," to compatriots of a religious "experience that others didn't understand."[5]

"THE LOVE OF THE TRUTH AND WHAT IT WILL SAVE US FROM"[6]

Similarities in charismatic worship practices within Pentecostal and Latter-day Saint churches likely created negative perceptions of each other in the early years of the Pentecostal revival. Pentecostals embraced spiritual gifts such as healing, tongues, and prophecy, as indications of a spirit-filled believer. Seventy years earlier, Latter-day Saints embraced the same gifts as they sought to restore all parts of Christ's original teachings. Since the church's inception, Latter-day Saints observed and recorded spiritual occurrences as evidence of the validity of their new religion. In 1835, Joseph Smith wrote, "When faith comes, it brings its train of attendants with it—apostles, prophets, evangelists, pastors, teachers, gifts, wisdom, knowledge, miracles, healings, tongues, interpretation of tongues, etc."[7] Throughout the nineteenth and early twentieth centuries, Latter-day Saints embraced various forms of charismatic worship. Many of the practices began fading away in the first decades of the twentieth century, but recollection of such things remained in the communal memory of Latter-day Saints. The similarities in spiritual expression would lead to charges of counterfeiting and deception hurled back and forth at each other as Pentecostal and Latter-day Saint adherents encountered one another in the flesh.

Utahns occasionally found opportunities prior to the Pentecostal Revival of 1906 to examine and discuss charismatic outsiders. Some examples came from within the family of Latter Day Saint churches themselves.[8] In a series of editorials between John Powell, a Latter-day Saint in Utah, and Joseph Smith III, president of the Reorganized Latter Day Saints in Missouri, Powell contested the validity of "revelation in tongues, interpretation, prophecy, visions, dreams, etc.," among members of the Reorganized Church of Jesus Christ of Latter-day Saints (RLDS) church. "A man need not be much of an observer to know what sort of a spirit they were of," retorted Powell.[9] A few years later, J. W. Wright, an apostle in the RLDS church, spoke in an unknown tongue during the April 1908 conference.[10] These examples made the news not only because of the shared historical and religious origins but also because Latter-day Saints found charismatic worship interesting.

Other examples came from new religious movements making their way to Utah. Alma White's "Pentecostal Jumpers," as the media popularized them, established a congregation of the Pillar of Fire Church in Ogden, Utah, in 1905. Because of their unique worship style, crowds of Utahns gathered to their street meetings, to watch as the street preachers, "both male and female, participated in a dance, which to the unregenerate was of a most amusing nature. . . . The majority of those who attended the meeting," reported the *Ogden Standard*, "regarded it as a rather 'serious' joke," because "they display religious enthusiasm amounting to mania."[11] The controversial ministry of Alexander Dowie also often found its way into newspapers in Utah, as it did across the country. Newspapers and church periodicals in the early twentieth century sensationalized the religiosity of these individuals and congregations.[12]

Long considered charismatic outsiders themselves, Latter-day Saints understood spiritual gifts to be a theological evidence of the restoration of true Christianity. Although charismatic practice diminished in the early twentieth century, its theological importance to the defense of the restoration often appeared in sermons by church leadership through the 1930s. Dozens of examples from general conference discourses in the late nineteenth to early twentieth centuries argued similarly to Andrew Jenson's defense in 1905:

> Now, my brethren and sisters, if the true church of Christ in this age had been rejected of God, the first thing we would have had to find an excuse for would be why the blessing and gifts of the Gospel had ceased, why there was no demonstration of the power of God as there was in the beginning. The fact that these things have continued in the Church, the fact that they have increased in the Church, the fact that there have been abundant witnesses raised up in this land as well as in every land where the Gospel has been sent, has been and ought to be in and of itself one of the grandest proofs we can have in regard to the divinity of this church and the perpetuity of it.[13]

Spiritual gifts reinforced the divine origins of the Latter-day Saint movement. Furthermore, leaders understood such manifestations to offer "temporary comfort" in difficult times.[14] Since the earliest days of the church, members embraced charismatic manifestations and through the years leaders developed and refined their place within Latter-day Saint theology and practice.[15]

Charismatic expression informed and established Pentecostalism as separate and unique from mainline and Holiness Protestants. Encompassing a fourfold emphasis on Jesus Christ as Savior, Baptizer in the Holy Spirit, Healer, and Coming King, Pentecostal theology positioned charismatic manifestations of spiritual gifts within the core concepts of their theological framework.[16] "It must be immediately admitted," explained Donald W. Dayton, "that all the elements of this fourfold pattern occur separately or in various combinations in other Christian traditions," but that the Pentecostal proclivity toward outward charismatic expression defined the Pentecostal experience in contrast to the experience of other Protestants.[17]

As the Pentecostal Revival exploded out of the works of Charles F. Parham and William J. Seymour, Latter-day Saints' initial perceptions of Pentecostals arrived in print just prior to any mentions by Pentecostals about Latter-day Saints. In March 1907, the *American Fork Citizen* reported on the Christian Assembly Church of Denver, Colorado, pastored by Gilbert E. Farr. "They assert," the editorial skeptically announced, "that a great majority of the 600 languages in existence today have been used by their members in their little church on Welton street." Explaining where the belief in the gift of tongues originated, Pastor Farr told of how the previous August, two women from Los Angeles spoke at their camp meeting in Colorado. Having received the gift of tongues, manifesting itself in Arabic, they were on their way to serve a mission in Jerusalem. "Many of our members began to seek it for themselves," Pastor Farr concluded.[18] The women, likely Louise Condit and Lucy M. Leatherman, received their faith in the gift of tongues at William J. Seymour's Azusa Street mission in Los Angeles. In early August 1906, they had announced their intention to go to Jerusalem and headed out from Los Angeles.[19]

Utah newspapers published reports from Spokane, Washington, about missionaries of the "Apostolic Light mission" who planned to leave for "China, India, Africa, and other lands." They planned to leave without any provisions, "neither are they to study the languages of the countries to which they go," because they believed to "have received the miraculous gift of tongues and will be enabled to speak without study."[20] Through the winter and spring of 1907, Florence Crawford traveled from the Apostolic Faith Mission in Los Angeles to plant Pentecostal missions across northern California, Oregon, and Washington. A second time Utahns heard accounts of the expansion of Pentecostal Christianity as it spread out from the Los Angeles Azusa Street mission.

Claude T. Barnes introduced Charles F. Parham and the "Apostolic Faith movement" to Latter-day Saint readers in August 1907 with an article titled "The Unconscious Illapse." One of many Latter-day Saints who pursued education in the eastern United States during the early 1900s, Barnes attended the University of Michigan from 1906 to 1907.[21] His education led him to believe that "the religious thought of the world is a confusion."[22] In answer to the confusion, Barnes argued that religions began unwittingly turning toward the "truth of Mormonism." "As a loosened buoy floats slowly inland, by the soft propulsion of an evening breeze," Barnes described, "so are the unsettled minds of the world, unconsciously, drifting towards one little island—The Isle of Truth, 'Mormonism.'" Barnes believed that seekers found bits and pieces of truth, but remained stubbornly unwilling to "make their way up the river, up the mountain to its summit, there to look with gladness upon the delectable island of truth about them."[23]

And the nascent Pentecostal movement served as an example for Barnes's argument:

> On January first 1900, people were somewhat startled to hear that a Miss Agnes Ozman, of Topeka, Kansas, had spoken with other tongues, as did the disciples of Jesus on the day of Pentecost. Since that time many more have spoken with tongues; and now an "Apostolic Faith movement" claims that the gift is restored. Mr. Parham, one of the leaders, says: "We truly are in the days of the restitution of all things which God has spoken by the mouth of all his holy prophets since the world began." A writer in *The Wesleyan Methodist* says that the sincerity of these people is undoubted; but, however, that it is a matter of history that in the early days of the "Mormon" Church whole days of speaking meetings were devoted to it. The Latter-day Saints have always taught that the gift of tongues is one of those "signs which shall follow them that believe;" hence, this late manifestation of the gift can therefore be regarded only as another evidence of the unconscious illapse into "Mormonism."[24]

Barnes perceived of the Apostolic faith movement's adoption of speaking in tongues as an inadvertent foray into the true doctrines of Jesus Christ already restored by the Church of Jesus Christ of Latter-day Saints. All Pentecostals needed was a little explanation about the theological gem they had discovered. "The world is in a quandary," explained Barnes, "because it knows not towards what it is tending." And his solution to their confusion? "It behooves us to open its eyes."[25]

Because the gift of tongues stood out as a unique identifier for Pentecostal Christians, the earliest Latter-day Saint responses to Pentecostalism focused directly on the concept of counterfeit spirituality. In the fall and winter of 1907 and 1908, a handful of editorial articles in the *Liahona* appeared to respond to the growing interest in Pentecostalism due to its outward charismatic manifestations. Spiritual gifts identified the "true faith," and "those creeds of so-called Christianity which do not possess this power, do not possess a fullness of the gospel of Christ."[26] According to an article in October 1907, because spiritual gifts could be imitated, they served a minor role in identifying true Christianity. Their presence was paramount but under scrutiny at the same time: "If there were no genuine spiritual gifts being made manifest the devil would not need to counterfeit them."[27] Another article published in January 1908 explained how "supernatural manifestations may have their source in a good or an evil power."[28] It addressed questions of authenticity concerning prophecy, healings, and tongues: "When we hear speaking in tongues, how can we determine whether the gift comes by the Holy ghost, or an evil spirit? These are important questions, and they are rapidly becoming more so, because miracle workers, or alleged miracle workers, who have no part nor lot with Christ or His people, are becoming more and more numerous and are displaying more and more power."[29]

Concerning tongues specifically, an article followed the previous two in February 1908, which directly refuted reports of Pentecostal missionary activities abroad. Discussing missionaries like T. J. McIntosh and Pastor A. G. Garr, both connected to the Azusa Street Revival, the editorial excoriated their belief in the gift of missionary tongues, labeling their attempts to speak foreign languages a "fiasco" and their belief in spiritual gifts as "deluded."[30] The editorial pointed to the linguistic failings of Pentecostal missionaries, as compared with the "hundreds of elders of the Church of Jesus Christ of Latterday [sic] Saints" who successfully received the gift of tongues and spoke foreign languages fluently as missionaries. The article specifically critiqued the belief in xenolalia, or missionary tongues. Both Pentecostals and Latter-day Saints believed that the Holy Spirit could empower a person to speak in a foreign language previously unknown to the individual, expressly for the purpose of missionary work. In answer to the question of why Latter-day Saint missionaries received the gift of tongues and Pentecostal missionaries did not, the article declared, "because that Church [the Church of Jesus Christ of Latter-day Saints] is the only one in the world which possesses divine authority to confer upon converts the Holy Ghost, of which the genuine gift of tongues is at once a fruit and a proof."[31]

In the early twentieth century, Latter-day Saints perceived Pentecostal charismatic worship as mimicry of a practice long expressed among members of the Church of Jesus Christ of Latter-day Saints. Articles explained how to tell the differences between "bogus" gifts and real ones, and they pointed members to explanations given by leaders. In May 1909, the *Liahona* even reprinted Joseph Smith's April 1842 sermon "Try the Spirits," in its entirety, as a rebuke against increasing charismatic manifestations among other Christian churches. In that sermon, Joseph Smith gave his most comprehensive explanation against charismatic manifestations outside of the Church of Jesus Christ of Latter-day Saints, including methods of identifying counterfeit spiritual gifts. Latter-day Saints in the 1900s sought to employ the same arguments against the Pentecostals that Smith used against the Irvingites in the 1840s.[32]

A few sources divulged a modern perception of charismatic manifestations among Latter-day Saints. An article reported on journalist William T. Ellis's recounting of the revival at Pandita Ramabai's Mukti mission in India. The article in *Goodwin's Weekly* seemed to satirize the entire subject of tongues, demonstrating a changing perception about tongues within the church itself. "We do not question Mr. Ellis," opined the editor, but rather "refer to the matter merely to tell him that he went a long way around to find the marvel. Could he have come to Utah, it would but have required a journey of three and a half days and here he could have found more gifts of tongues than all India can supply." It then spoke of Englishmen speaking in Swedish and Americans speaking in Welsh. It also suggested that "it has never been possible to make an Irishman pray in modern Egyptian," explaining that "there is a lack of coordination" necessary for such a gift to manifest. "India has no monopoly on miracles," the editor quipped, concluding that "we often hear what Mr. Ellis heard in India—people praying in a tongue that no man can interpret."[33] Many practices of the Church of Jesus Christ of Latter-day Saints underwent changes during the Progressive Era, including using spiritual gifts. While most members still believed only the Church of Jesus Christ enjoyed the authority to practice authentic charismatic manifestations, fewer and fewer Latter-day Saints appeared to believe such manifestations should happen very often, if at all.[34]

WHAT IS MORMONISM?

Pentecostals certainly had their own perceptions about the Latter-day Saints as well. Three themes emerged from early Pentecostal publications about Latter-day

Saints: Latter-day Saints were not Christians, the Church of Jesus Christ of Latter-day Saints was growing, and Pentecostals needed more home missions to defend against Latter-day Saint expansion. During the early twentieth century, these themes appeared consistently across Pentecostal publications. Often mentioned alongside Christian Science, Hinduism, New Thought, and Mohammedanism, early Pentecostal perceptions of the Latter-day Saints viewed the religion as a stumbling block for the righteous at best, and "paganism veneered with Christian terminology" at worst.[35] And for many, conversion from the Church of Jesus Christ of Latter-day Saints to Pentecostalism seemed to be the only way to combat the growth of the movement.

Through question and answer columns and editorials, various Pentecostal publications sought to distinguish the Latter-day Saints from the Pentecostal movement. In a series of "questions concerning tongues," one reader of the *Bridegroom's Messenger* asked, "why don't you write about the Mormons talking in tongues?" The editor replied, "I know of no well authenticated facts concerning the 'tongues' movement of that people. I am not willing to receive the statements of their leaders upon that or any other subject."[36] Few Pentecostals knew very much about the Mormons, as they were called, and fewer still associated directly with members of the Church of Jesus Christ of Latter-day Saints in the West, or its counterpart the Reorganized Church of Jesus Christ of Latter Day Saints in the Midwest. And the political battles over polygamy in the late nineteenth century still cast suspicion on the morals of the Latter-day Saint community. As Pentecostals began responding to the questions of their adherents, many views remained influenced by the past. The editorialist in 1908 defended his statements with a story of his visit to Utah in the 1870s, which for him, "was not approving—so far as their conduct or their word was concerned."[37]

Others gave far less mild responses to questions and concerns about the Latter-day Saints. When E. N. Bell, the first chairman (later known as general superintendent) of the Assemblies of God, responded to the question "what is Mormonism," he resolutely decried, "It is a false system of religion invented by Joseph Smith." Calling its doctrines "rank heathenism," he warned, "none of our people should listen to a Mormon preacher two minutes," because "it would take volumes to expose all the false things in the history of Mormonism."[38] When the next year, a reader of the *Pentecostal Evangel* asked "who are the Latter-day Saints," Bell again reinforced, "They are entirely different from the Assemblies of God in the Pentecostal Movement."[39] G. F. Taylor pointedly explained, "The Pentecostal Holiness Church is utterly opposed to Mormons," and Andrew Fraser remarked,

"We cannot countenance anything that savors of Mormon theory or of Mormon practice in the Pentecostal movement."[40] Leaders from across the emerging Pentecostal denominations spurred their followers to "stay away from Mormonism."[41]

Some of the anxiety over Latter-day Saints appeared to grow from the fear of conversion. Basing evidence on stereotypes about Latter-day Saint missionaries, concerned critics claimed, "Elders are making a house to house canvass throughout the country, with the sole purpose of making converts to 'celestial marriages.'" Referring to polygamy, they worried that Latter-day Saints believed "in the future God will re-establish polygamy as the rule over all the earth," and women especially remained vulnerable to these "smooth-tongued" missionaries.[42] The *Latter Rain Evangel* warned:

> They trap the unwary by laying stress on the growing apostasy, and emphasizing some of the great truths of Scripture, such as the resurrection of the body, miracles, revelations, millennial rule of Christ, tithing and the gifts of the Spirit, and keep in the background the dangerous and blasphemous claims in their book until they have the confidence of those who are not well-informed, and then the soul who is really seeking for God is caught in the meshes of this false net that is spread for his feet.[43]

In 1911, a silent film entitled *A Victim of the Mormons*, vividly depicted the almost hypnotic power Mormon missionaries held over those foolish enough to listen to their teachings.[44] This kind of sensational media, along with news articles and federal government distrust, supported a real concern among the American public generally over the possibility of conversion to the Church of Jesus Christ of Latter-day Saints.

Pentecostals worried about the religious and cultural dominance the Latter-day Saints maintained over the western United States. "Do you know," inquired a concerned editorialist, "that a man on horseback can travel from Alberta, Canada, to the interior of Old Mexico and sleep every night under a Mormon roof?"[45] The breadth of settlements established by Latter-day Saints throughout North America threatened the potential growth of the Pentecostal message. Latter-day Saint organization and care for their youth represented this same concern. Pentecostals noticed the "religion classes" developed by the church and taught around the state of Utah. Known as the seminary program, the church established religion courses for their youth, taken in conjunction with high school education at public schools. "The equipment of these Mormon church schools is usually the most modern," observed a home missions editorial in 1911. And Pentecostals needed to provide alternative options to prevent further indoctrination: "In mission schools only can the Mormon child get the Bible without the accompanying Mormon interpretation, which is as different from the conception of the evangelical churches as day is from night."[46] In various ways, the success of the Church of Jesus Christ of Latter-day Saints vexed Pentecostals trying to expand their own movement across the country.

The basis for their concerns grew out of the common perception of Latter-day Saints at the time of the Pentecostal revival, mixed with emerging theological concerns among conservative Christians. As Spencer Fluhman argued, "By 1900, then, Mormonism hovered between Christianity and a non-Christian religion."[47] Without polygamy and theocracy, the church preached a theology very Christian-like, with some eccentricities of its own design. Theosis or deification, as well as the Book of Mormon as additional scripture, compelled many Pentecostals to associate Latter-day Saints with cultism. Theosis presented the possibility of more than one God, a heretical concept for Pentecostals. "It teaches that there are many gods, who were formerly men and women, have flesh and bones, are sinners, and often live in polygamy," scoffed the *Bridegroom's Messenger* in 1914.[48] Oneness Pentecostals would receive similar accusations of heresy for their views of the singular nature of Jesus as God.[49] The Book of Mormon presented a problem for the fundamental emphasis on the Bible. "We believe that the Christian Scriptures are the final revelation of God," defended A. A. Boddy, "and need not to be explained either by a Book of Mormon or by Mrs. Eddy's 'Science and Health.'"[50] Elsewhere, in declaring extra-biblical works as anti-Christian, the *Latter Rain Evangel* declared, "The Koran and the Book of Mormon have been most pernicious in their working."[51] The pivot from polygamy to extra-biblical literature occurred smoothly and easily among Pentecostals who believed in the Bible as the literal and sole source of the word of God. The other eccentricities merely reinforced the perception of Latter-day Saints as heretics or worse, anti-Christ. "We have given these few facts about Mormonism," explained a Pentecostal editor, "to acquaint our readers with this anti-Christian system of religion which is so rapidly spreading over our country."[52]

The perceptions that Latter-day Saints and Pentecostals developed about each other in the early twentieth century differed from the perceptions of others concerning these minority faiths. When the Latter-day Saints first appeared in the American landscape, most other Christians expected the church to manage only a brief stint within the American religious milieu. Philip Schaff, who earlier in his career almost entirely disregarded the Latter-day Saints as insignificant, by the late nineteenth century still viewed its presence in American society only as a case study in determining the limits of religious freedom in American democracy.[53] When the Pentecostal movement ignited in 1906, most other Protestants worried little about its potential. As put by Robert Mapes Anderson, "Denominational ministers tended to regard the Pentecostal movement as a convenient means for draining off the undesirable members of their congregations."[54] The major Christian denominations did not immediately worry about Latter-day Saints or Pentecostals because few predicted these religious outsiders would have lasting impacts on American society. [55] Many would change their minds later on.

The perceptions that Pentecostals and Latter-day Saints held about the other resulted from their close competition with each other for converts. Latter-day Saints perceived of Pentecostal charismatic worship as a counterfeit in order to strengthen and defend their own historical claim of restoring spiritual gifts first, and Pentecostals labeled Latter-day Saints as members of an unchristian cult in order to keep their curious new adherents from considering Latter-day Saint teachings. Other radical evangelicals, such as the Holiness movement, similarly perceived of the Pentecostals and Latter-day Saints as significant threats to their struggling communities. Their focus on missionary work not just abroad but also among the established denominations in the United States, made them direct competitors and increased the anxiety associated with their perceptions of each other.

"THE TRUTH ABOUT THE 'MORMONS'"[56]

As both Pentecostals and Latter-day Saints grew into significant American religious institutions by the end of the twenty-first century, past perceptions played a role in insulating the movements from interacting with other religious groups. Instead, they developed methods of interacting with American religion exclusively. The evolution of the interactions between Pentecostals and Latter-day Saints demonstrates the way that both groups pursued religious interactions generally. Evolving from the pursuit of converts to a forced coexistence and finally to a tenuous cooperation, Pentecostals and Latter-day Saints employed comparable methods for increasing their presence and prominence in the emerging American religious mainstream of the twenty-first century.

As minority religious institutions in the United States, both Pentecostals and Latter-day Saints pursued new converts rigorously. The Latter-day Saints sent missionaries and Pentecostals sent preachers, each hoping to save humanity from a growing secularity that they felt existed in the Christian institutions all around them. Nephi Jensen, president of the Latter-day Saint Canadian mission during the early 1920s, remarked in general conference:

> Everywhere I find pathetic proof of the lack of this inspiring belief in God. I detect it in the insipid singing in the sectarian churches. I notice it in their hollow prayers. I discover it in their old sermons that speak of a distant God in high sounding theological phrases. Last Sunday afternoon I was more than usually impressed with the sectarian lack of the power to get in contact with God. I attended a Pentecostal meeting in Winnipeg, Canada. At this meeting I saw an audience of several hundred people, who have discovered the hollowness and coldness of modern religion. These people were honestly but vainly striving, in song and prayer and sermon, to get close to the Father of All.[57]

Many mainline Protestants avoided or belittled confrontations with Pentecostals and Latter-day Saints in the pursuit of converts. Often, however, Pentecostals and Latter-day Saints engaged each other, as they worked to build up their separate understandings of the kingdom of God.

During the early twentieth century, most contact between Pentecostals and Latter-day Saints took place outside of Utah. A few Pentecostal congregations existed in Utah prior to 1940, but they struggled to maintain their presence and suffered from changing leadership and organizational infighting.[58] Outside Utah, missionaries and preachers occasionally reported on crossing paths. As with the example of Nephi Jensen, Latter-day Saints left more published accounts of their interactions with Pentecostals, leaving the historical record skewed in their favor. Pentecostals welcomed visitors to their meetings and allowed them to share their thoughts, and Latter-day Saint missionaries took advantage of the opportunity. Many times elders (as Latter-day Saint missionaries are commonly called) preached in Pentecostal churches or camp meetings. At times they debated pastors at outdoor services. These elders related their successes in being able to "put a great many of the principles of the gospel before the people."[59] At times, audience members agreed with the things taught until finding out the affiliation of the preachers. After a bystander found out that the speaker was a Latter-day Saint, "There was a noticeable flinch, yet he admitted it was gospel truth nevertheless."[60] One minister explained how "he did not know they were Mormons or he never would have given them the opportunity he did," to speak before his congregation.[61] Others allowed the elders to speak that they might engage them in debate. Elders Scheselaar and Driggs reported of a debate in Waynesboro, Pennsylvania, that continued every Saturday for six weeks. "The debate arose," explained the elders, "because of statements made by the minister about the Latter-day Saints and their belief, and the elders, whose meeting followed that of the Pentecostal organization, felt the statements made should not go unchallenged."[62] Around the country, Pentecostals and elders sparred with each other's messages.

The reports coming from the elders tended to relate successful confrontations or faith promoting encounters. After all, missionary reports were meant to encourage the work, not hinder it. Elders in Rochester, New York ran into a Pentecostal minister who "was at one time a member of the Church and that try as he might, he cannot get away from the Gospel." The minister assisted the elders with two dollars before parting ways.[63] When elders preached by invitation in Pentecostal churches, they noted the audience size as a measure of the success of their preaching.

A few reports suggested that engaging Pentecostals did not always go the way the elders hoped. "The meetings held in Grand Junction and Fruita are well attended," an elder in Colorado reported, "and although there has been considerable opposition of late from the Pentecostal Church, who seem to delight in running down other churches, the 'Mormons' in particular, still it has caused investigation to be more pointed and the Elders are getting more chances to explain the Gospel truths to the people."[64] The elder's perception of "running down the Church" may just as well have been evidence of the Pentecostal pastor's effectiveness in countering the elders' efforts at conversion.

As the century rolled on, religious tracts played a significant role in the ways that Pentecostals and Latter-day Saints made sense of each other. Latter-day Saint tracts, while exploring the principles of Latter-day Saint theology, seemed unintentionally to reinforce cultural depictions of Latter-day Saints as Mormons and not Christians. And Pentecostal tracts published in Utah intentionally aimed at doing the same thing.

Latter-day Saints employed tracts and pamphlets since the formation of the church in the early 1800s, but they tried to systematize missionary use of tracts in the early 1900s. B. H. Roberts's *On Tracting* and John A. Widtsoe's *Tracts and Tracting* educated elders on how to employ tracts more effectively. They encouraged tracts be given out in a particular order to build an enticing and cohesive conversation about the restored gospel. They motivated elders to persevere. A poem by Frank Kooyman depicted the difficulties of missionary work and the power of tracting. The poem told of "tight-shut doors," longing for home, and the anguish of evangelistic failure. Against the many hardships of evangelism, the elder shared in prayer his concerns to the "Sweet Whisp'rer," hoping for relief. And at the end of each verse, he received the same response: "Tract on! Tract on and on!"[65] Like the Sweet Whisp'rer in the poem, Latter-day Saint missionaries placed great emphasis on using tracts in the early 1900s.

Interestingly, many of the tracts used in the early twentieth century adopted cultural language about "Mormons," instead of vehemently endorsing the use of the formal title of the church. Tracts like "The Origin and History of 'Mormonism,'" "Why Mormonism?," "The Mormon People," "The Truth About the 'Mormons,'" "The Fruits of Mormonism," "The Philosophical Basis of Mormonism," and "What 'Mormons' Believe," all used the popular language associated with the Church of Jesus Christ of Latter-day Saints in introducing and explaining the beliefs of the Church of Jesus Christ of Latter-day Saints.[66] As missionaries explained the history of "Mormonism," from the vision of Joseph Smith in 1820 to the "five fundamental characteristics of a truly great people" outlined in "The Truth About the 'Mormons,'" they repeatedly pointed out differences between the Latter-day Saints and other Christians.

Antagonists labeled Latter-day Saints "Mormons" since the 1830s, but as the Church of Jesus Christ adopted the use of this language to explain itself, it may have inadvertently confused others. Especially in Utah, Pentecostals recalled how not until the late twentieth century did Utah Latter-day Saints begin calling themselves Christians instead of Mormons.[67] The training many missionaries received in the early twentieth century, training that incorporated tracts that emphasized the language of Mormonism, may have affected the ways in which Utah Latter-day Saints conversed about themselves. Some of the tracts, like "What 'Mormons' Believe," remained in use among Latter-day Saint missionaries as late as the early 1970s.

DWIGHT C. RITCHIE

When Pentecostals first began publishing tracts in Utah in the early 1940s, they also employed the language of Mormonism, but with the intent to discredit and expose. Dwight C. Ritchie, pastor of the First Assembly of God in Salt Lake City from 1941 to 1945, produced a variety of tracts and pamphlets while laboring in the state of Utah. In 1944, Ritchie explained how he had been "engaged in religious work in Utah and Idaho for eight years."[68] His missionary efforts focused on converting Latter-day Saints by convincing them of the errors in their doctrines and leaders. Formally ordained on February 12, 1943, Ritchie and his wife, Margaret, had almost a decade of experience preaching the Pentecostal message in Utah and Idaho at the time they left Utah.[69]

Ritchie's experiences in Utah convinced him of the need to uncover and expose what he perceived as the falsehoods of the Church of Jesus Christ of Latter-day Saints. His tracts written in Utah from 1943 to 1944 focused on polygamy and false leadership. His later tracts from the 1950s focused on the Book of Mormon and Joseph Smith. They attempted to demonstrate how the tenets and beliefs of the Latter-day Saints contradicted the doctrine of the Bible and Christianity. In each category, Ritchie's tracts form an example of the ways Pentecostals sought to engage Utahns and convert them to the Pentecostal message.

Ritchie viewed polygamy as a problem with a practical solution for the Church of Jesus Christ of Latter-day Saints: remove references to it from the books that the Latter-day Saints considered sacred. In a poem called "Signs!," referencing the signs of the times, Ritchie mentioned false prophets and places where "men are taking many wives."[70] Clearly, the continued practice of polygamy concerned Ritchie. Like the Presbyterian evangelist William Paden, Ritchie worried that Latter-day Saints intended to restore the practice of polygamy at some future date.[71] A resident of Idaho and Utah for many years, his concern over the topic increased during one of the first large-scale attempts of the twentieth century to convict individuals of polygamy. A particular case involving seventy-year-old William Chatwin and fifteen-year-old Dorothy Wyler proved very disconcerting.[72] Ritchie wrote:

> After the polygamy exposures of a few months ago, in which it was revealed that Section 132 of the Doctrine and Covenants had been used to convert a fifteen-year old girl to belief in polygamy and to lead her into an illegal marriage, I presented to the leaders of the Mormon church complete scriptural proof that this document was not inspired of God, suggesting that they consider removing it from the official literature of their church, as it was being used as an excuse for illegal and immoral acts, and causing the ruin and disgrace of young girls.[73]

From his perspective, Latter-day Saint leaders should repudiate not only the practice of, but also the belief in, polygamy.

Through letters, public lectures, and a series of tracts, Ritchie attempted to engage leaders of the Church of Jesus Christ and the Salt Lake community. He produced a series of tracts, with titles like "Origin of Polygamy in America," "Polygamy Disproved," "The Case Against Polygamy," and "Revival of Polygamy Presents a Challenge to the Mormon Church."[74] The course of action seemed reasonable enough to Ritchie: "Few Americans would be foolish enough to become followers of Mohammet if he came to America with his doctrine of polygamy, attempting to further his religion with the sword."[75] So he reasoned, "leaders of the L.D.S. church today are educated and intelligent men, unlike many of the early followers of Joseph Smith. . . . They should have no reason therefore for wishing to keep in their literature a revelation which shames their organization when exposures of polygamy are made and excommunications result."[76] To strengthen his case, Ritchie railed against the doctrine of polygamy through biblical exegesis and historical examination of the Latter-day Saint practice of polygamy.

In early 1944, Ritchie reached out directly to the First Presidency of the Church of Jesus Christ of Latter-day Saints, and to former Salt Lake City mayor John F. Bowman.[77] He hoped either to meet in private to discuss the problem of polygamy, or to meet in public debate on the topic. The secretary of the First Presidency responded to Ritchie with a letter informing him that "Mr. Grant refuses to enter into a discussion with me 'regarding the inspiration behind any of the principles of the Gospel as taught by the Church of Jesus Christ of Latter-day Saints,' and goes on to charge me with 'clearly seeking to destroy Truth and not to search after it.'" John F. Bowman responded indirectly, reading parts of Ritchie's letter during his public lecture about the polygamists in the news and the beliefs of the Church of Jesus Christ. Bowman's discourse, according to Ritchie, "did not advocate" for the practice of polygamy, "but made it plain that his church believed it to be a divinely inspired doctrine and had no intention of removing it from its official literature."[78] Despite reaching out to them, no face-to-face dialogue would be established.

Instead, Ritchie initiated a preaching campaign in Salt Lake City. "Since the leaders of the Mormon church cannot be dealt with in a courteous and friendly manner," he impugned, "it is necessary to adopt the harder method of exposing them as false teachers."[79] Following Bowman's public address on January 23, 1944, Dwight C. Ritchie gave a public address of his own in the evening titled "Mormonism Disproved." Beginning Sunday evening, Ritchie gave "six friendly messages to Latter-day Saints," one each night through Friday, January 28, 1944.[80] He also unleashed a series of tracts and pamphlets outlining his concerns about

Mormonism. Ritchie had previously published a popular bulletin for the First Assembly of God in Salt Lake, which he mailed to subscribers around the country. It predominantly included sermon subjects and Christian poetry.[81] These later tracts and pamphlets included attacks on plural marriage and the history of the Church of Jesus Christ of Latter-day Saints. "Many of the doctrines agree perfectly with the Bible," admitted Ritchie, but "we all recognize the danger of a mixture of truth and error."[82] The hope for dialogue dissolved into open religious warfare on Latter-day Saint doctrine, Latter-day Saint leaders, and the Latter-day Saint past.

Even after leaving Salt Lake to pastor in Idaho and Montana, Ritchie continued to publish missionary pamphlets denouncing Latter-day Saint beliefs. Like many Pentecostals of the time, he worried that Latter-day Saints focused too much on works and not enough on grace. "The most serious error of this false faith," posited Ritchie, "is the belief that salvation must be gained by working for it.... Hundreds of Joseph Smith's followers perished in trying to work out their salvation by marching across the plains to Utah. You will perish also if you try to work your way to heaven."[83] This argument would continue to follow Latter-day Saints throughout the twentieth century.

The Book of Mormon and Joseph Smith's claim to have translated it also created concerns for Pentecostals. In 1954 and 1956, Ritchie wrote pamphlets titled "The Mind of Joseph Smith" and "The Book of Mormon Hoax." "A study of the words of the founder of Mormonism revealing twenty-four symptoms of mental derangement," the pamphlet on Joseph Smith discredited Joseph's visions and translations, it depicted his participation in plural marriage as immoral, and it viewed his belief in being called of God as deceitful.[84] The pamphlet on the Book of Mormon included copies of the characters from the Anthon transcript purported to be from the Book of Mormon, as well as examples of Egyptian hieroglyphs translated by the famed Champollion by means of the Rosetta Stone.[85] Ritchie mailed a copy of it to J. Reuben Clark in 1956, with a request: "As an honored leader of the Church of Jesus Christ of Latter-day Saints, I trust that you will inform them of the facts concerning the origin of the Book of Mormon. I hope that you will then lead them into full faith in the Scriptures of the Bible, for they offer to men the only certain way to eternal life and happiness."[86] There is no record of a reply, but Ritchie would likely be happy to know that at the very least, President Clark kept the letter.

Ritchie's missionary tracts demonstrated an offensive approach to missionary work, as compared to the defensive tracts produced by the Church of Jesus Christ of Latter-day Saints. The content of the Latter-day Saint tracts sought to defend their beliefs and practices against the claims made by outsiders, while the Pentecostal tracts sought to highlight Latter-day Saint beliefs and practices they believed to be dangerous and anti-Christian. Both styles toyed with the popular language of "Mormonism" to influence the popular image of "Mormonism." In the state of Utah, the approach may have been too forceful a method of interacting with Latter-day Saints; there did not seem to be much growth under Ritchie's ministry in Salt Lake. His campaign hoped to save souls and not necessarily make friends. "Perhaps you are beginning to think by this time that my letters are anything but friendly," Ritchie wryly observed. "However, I assure you that the hard things that are being written about Joseph Smith and the Book of Mormon are being presented in the interests of truth. If your house were on fire you would not think a neighbor unfriendly if he told you the truth about it and warned you to get out before you lost your life."[87] Despite still desiring the mass conversion of Latter-day Saints to the gospel truth, most Pentecostal denominations operating in the state began adjusting their approach from a focus on conversion to a focus on coexistence.

THE FAITH ONCE DELIVERED TO THE SAINTS[88]

Pentecostals in Utah during the mid-twentieth century pursued a style of missionary campaigning less focused on conversion and more focused on permanently coexisting inside the Latter-day Saint majority state. Canvassing campaigns worked to plant sustainable congregations and spread the word that Pentecost was here to stay among the cities of Utah. As Pentecostal denominations became more organized and capable of funding home missions in the state of Utah, they developed methods of expanding deeper into the state and building permanent homes for their parishioners.

Within their own denominations, Pentecostals quite frequently interacted and cooperated with each other. The annual state camp meetings of the Assemblies of God began in 1945 with the few congregations meeting together for worship in a revival setting. Prior to that, congregations traveled once a month to meet together. From month to month, they headed to different locations. Among the Pentecostal Church of God around Ogden and the Church of God around Monticello, similar fellowship meetings occurred in the mid-twentieth century. These meetings strengthened the small communities and gave them opportunities to come together for worship in large groups. Occasionally these meetings transgressed denominational boundaries but not very often. In 1951, prior to the Greek Full Gospel Assembly affiliating with the Assemblies of God, they held joint New Year's services with the Assemblies of God, also including the Salt Lake Spanish Assembly of God.[89] Harold Laster, a district superintendent of the Pentecostal Church of God, asked "ministers of other churches in the city to attend a series of Saturday services . . . in the interests of greater church unity in the work of God."[90] Chaplains at Hill Air Force Base, in some ways ahead of the interfaith curve because of their military affiliation, hosted Easter Sunrise services for all Protestants including Pentecostals, through the late 1950s.[91] Otherwise, Pentecostals mostly interacted only with churches of their own denominations.

Neither Pentecostals nor Latter-day Saints, however, desired any kind of ecumenism or cooperation with each other. Books like *Who Are the False Prophets?* and *Mormonism Under the Searchlight* offered treatises on the Church of Jesus Christ of Latter-day Saints as a cult dangerous to Christianity.[92] These materials available to most Pentecostals portrayed Latter-day Saint beliefs as misguided or demonic. It turned dialogue with Latter-day Saints into a spiritual danger. And the Latter-day Saint hierarchy did not exactly pursue interfaith opportunities either. According to Neil J. Young, "The frequent emphasis on the LDS Church's status as the 'one true church' during the McKay era provided an implicit rebuke to ecumenism."[93] Young argued that the Latter-day Saint institution attempted to be neighborly with other churches in the state of Utah, but really "the LDS Church signaled its toleration of other churches in its midst while it reasserted its standing as Utah's de facto church."[94] On the ground, Pentecostals living in the state often invented creative ways of acknowledging the Latter-day Saint majority while poking fun at its so-called exclusive distinctiveness. Ads in the newspapers, for churches such as Rosemary Cosby's Faith Temple, appropriated Latter-day Saint language to their own ends.[95] These acknowledgments of each other suggested that cooperation of any kind might yet be a long way off.

By the 1960s, the Assemblies of God was ready to embark on considerable expansion in the state of Utah. Congregations in Salt Lake and Ogden became launch pads to more rural areas in the state. Pastors like Guy M. Heath, Peter Pilot, and Robert Smith weathered the initial difficulties of planting churches and prepared themselves to push out into new terrain. Converts helped to strengthen congregations, of course, but in Utah building churches and handing out tracts mattered just as much. Reporting on home missions in Utah, Rocky Mountain District Superintendent R. G. Fulford said, "progress has been quite slow, as is the usual experience in Utah, but every time we start a new church it helps to break the strength of the forces against us which are so keenly felt."[96] The missions program for the 1960s and 1970s took this concept to heart as it planted churches as far across the state as it could manage.

The Home Missions of the Assemblies of God enlisted their youth to orchestrate major canvassing events in conjunction with new church plants. Milton Newman began work in Tooele, Utah in October 1962. The town of Tooele sat about thirty miles west of Salt Lake City in central Utah. Evangelizing on his own, he laid the groundwork for a congregation in the area. They dedicated the First Assembly of God in Tooele in March 1964 as a Breakthrough project for the Rocky Mountain district.[97] Prior to this dedication, however, in August 1963 they enlisted a group of Christ's Ambassadors from Colorado and Utah to "leave a personal witness at every home in Tooele (a town of approximately 5,700) and to conduct special services in the evening."[98] Christ's Ambassadors, the youth organization of the Assemblies of God, believed youth could grow spiritually by engaging in the work of evangelization. The door-to-door evangelizing helped make nearby non-Latter-day Saints aware of a Pentecostal congregation in their city. "Although the city is overshadowed by the Mormon religion, the teams discovered over one hundred prospects with over a hundred more potential prospects."[99] In little over a week, they made 3,000 solicitations and distributed 2,500 *Pentecostal Evangel* magazines.

Promoted as an opportunity to "engage in front-line soul winning with many other teen-agers," the Rocky Mountain District Christ's Ambassadors descended again on Utah in 1964.[100] Approximately one hundred youth from Utah, Colorado, Arizona, California, Idaho, and Texas spent a week in August canvassing in Salt Lake City, Ogden, Roy, Layton, American Fork, Moab, Monticello, Roosevelt, Kearns, Provo, and Midvale. Several of the areas already had small missions. They hoped to solidify these missions and turn them into permanent congregations. "Experiences ranged from total rejection at the door (including the 'slammed door' and anger) to complete acceptance with hour-long conversations, conversions and prayer," the *Evangel* reported. Twelve thousand home visits later, with 26,000 pieces of literature distributed, the youth returned to their homes. Additional "invasions" were scheduled for Cedar City and other locations. [101]

Large-scale canvassing effectively established and reinforced the fifteen Assemblies of God churches in Utah in the early 1960s. These youth crusades did not convert masses of Latter-day Saints to Pentecostalism; they strengthened the resolve and identity of local Pentecostals, publicized the presence of Pentecostal churches and reached out to individuals unaware of the opportunity to worship. Despite the overwhelming religious majority maintained by the Latter-day Saint community, the Assemblies of God created evangelizing opportunities for their youth and greater stability for their Utah members. They also introduced the full gospel message to many Latter-day Saints for the first time in a personal way by reaching out to them in their homes.

Through the 1970s, the Assemblies of God continued its focus on coexisting with other churches throughout the state. No other Pentecostal church managed to support and expand their congregations so effectively. The early part of the decade witnessed new works in northern Utah. "So far as can be determined," printed the *Pentecostal Evangel*, "the Assemblies of God churches established at Santaquin, Brigham City, Logan, and Bountiful are the first full-gospel churches in their areas."[102] Pastors and youth spent long hours traveling south to St. George, Richfield, and Tropic to plant churches and missions in the late 1970s as well.[103]

Other Pentecostal denominations also sought greater permanency and employed canvassing tactics to establish themselves in the state. The United Pentecostal Church (UPC) held its General Conference at the Salt Palace in October 1973. Over 8,000 members of the denomination traveled to Utah to plan and worship together.[104] "These people had a purpose in mind," revealed the *Outreach* periodical of the UPC, "to evangelize Salt Lake City."[105] With only two churches in Utah, they hoped to expand their presence. Adults and youth went door-to-door, placed posters in storefront windows, and advertised the church on the radio. They even paid for several large billboards in the Salt Lake area. Prior to canvassing, evangelists received a course from Brother Rutzen, who "taught over two hours on Wednesday on Mormonism and truth." At the close of the conference, they reported, "Because of the tireless efforts of dedicated individuals the two existing churches in Salt Lake City have been blessed and a new church formed to carry this spiritual revival forward."[106]

The efforts of the conference produced results in the same way as the canvassing events undertaken by the Assemblies of God. In January 1974, pastors Paul Russell and Keith Clark reported on the progress of the new church: "We have been evangelizing on a person-to-person basis from door to door, following up on the contacts made during the Pentecostal crusade held in October."[107] The success of the conference propelled the denomination to repeat the idea. The UPC held six General Conferences in Salt Lake and each time worked to strengthen the existing churches and plant new churches. Frank Bounds described to the *Salt Lake Tribune* in 2006 how the 2004 general conference drew people together from all walks of life and planted a diverse congregation in what he called "the last frontier for Pentecostals."[108] Even into the twenty-first century, Utah remains a vibrant center for missionary work among Pentecostals.

The shift from wholesale conversion to established coexistence allowed Pentecostalism to expand in Utah from one or two churches in 1940 to dozens of churches by 1980. These large-scale events attracted the attention of newspapers, and countless thousands of Utah citizens gained in-person opportunities to meet with Pentecostals and discuss their beliefs. In some areas of the state, these were first opportunities for Latter-day Saints to encounter the charismatic worship styles and contemporary worship music in their communities. A few communities, like Richfield and Tropic, attempted to prevent Pentecostal growth. Pastors received violent threats and buildings were vandalized. City officials in Tropic fought publicly with Pentecostals as they tried to secure a permanent location in town.[109] Yet, in most cases, these kinds of canvassing events laid a long-term foundation for the coexistence of Pentecostals among the other religious options of Utah, as well as the initial groundwork for cooperation between Pentecostals and other religious groups along the Wasatch Front.

"OH GOD, HELP US NEVER TO BE ROCK-THROWERS!"[110]

"Like the LDS we were a very marginalized minority, and even persecuted," George O. Wood, General Superintendent of the Assemblies of God, told BYU students on September 16, 2013. As he discussed Pentecostal history in Provo, Wood found parallels and points of similarity between Pentecostals and Latter-day Saints. He identified shared perspectives on politics. Discussing Elder Jeffrey R. Holland's (apostle in the Church of Jesus Christ of Latter-day Saints) concerns for strengthening youth perceptions about the teachings of Jesus Christ, he warmly agreed, "Any Assembly of God preacher could say the same thing. We just absolutely share that in common."[111] The leader of one of the largest Pentecostal denominations in the world stood in one of the most statistically Latter-day Saint cities in the world and expressed his appreciation for the things these two religious organizations shared in common.

Twenty-first century dialogue between Pentecostals and Latter-day Saints at first glance appears as different as night and day from the conversations held between them in the mid-twentieth century. Many things transpired in the intervening years. One of the most significant shifts in the interactions between

Pentecostals and Latter-day Saints included a transition from mere coexistence to nuanced cooperation between Pentecostals and Latter-day Saints at the local level. Pentecostals first began cooperating with each other and eventually reached out to Latter-day Saints as well as the twentieth century came to a close.

In fits and starts, Pentecostals engaged with Latter-day Saints throughout the latter half of the twentieth century. Most often, these friendly events occurred in smaller communities around deaths and holidays. When Narcizo Gallegos died in November 1944, Assemblies of God pastor Paul Reed conducted the funeral in a Latter-day Saint chapel in Monticello. Bishop L. Frank Redd of the Church of Jesus Christ spoke briefly of his "pleasant association with Mr. Gallegos and the respect he had for him as a neighbor and Christian gentleman," followed by a sermon from Reverend Reed.[112] In 1954, the Vernal religious community came together for an "all-faith" Thanksgiving service. For the first time in that small northeastern Utah town, Pentecostal Pastor E. F. Chopper participated in an event with other denominations including the Latter-day Saints. Reverend Richard E. Lundberg of the Episcopal church suggested to the 300 in attendance that "this yearly concentration of thanks should remind us that every day of our existence should be for us a day of returning thanks to Him for His great gift of our Lord Jesus Christ."[113] By pooling funds and coming together as a community, a few rural Utah cities managed to cooperate much earlier than in urban settings.

Cultural events worked at times to connect Pentecostals and Latter-day Saints in the community. Ray and Cathi Smith produced an Easter passion play called *The Master Mender* at Valley Assembly of God in the Salt Lake metropolitan area. Over the last three decades, the play became a method for Valley Assembly, and later the Salt Lake Christian Center, to engage and interact with the religious community in a nonthreatening way. Volunteer actors, musicians, and artisans assist in the construction of sets and the theatrical production itself. *The Master Mender* continues to be popular among Salt Lake Christians generally, even more than thirty years after its initial introduction.[114]

A pastor in Provo made initial inroads with his community through municipal and volunteer positions. In 1991, Dean Jackson became the pastor of the Rock Canyon Church (affiliated with the Assemblies of God) located in Provo, Utah. Admittedly, Jackson expressed early in his pastorate that "he did not really love LDS people; he saw them only as cultists to be converted."[115] Even so, Jackson reached out to the community through civic engagement and public dialogue. Over the years Jackson worked with the Provo Chamber of Commerce, the Rotary Club, and the chaplaincy at the Utah Regional Hospital.

Interfaith activities developed slowly, perhaps because the direct interactions were so rare. He recalled a time when a Latter-day Saint youth class visited Rock Canyon. "There they were," remembered Jackson. "Two whole pews of girls in nice dresses and boys in white shirts. My congregation took one look and got suddenly icy."[116] Provo remains one of the most statistically dominated areas on earth by its concentration of Latter-day Saints, and religious differences caused problems at times. Jackson's children underwent difficulties at school, and much of the Rock Canyon congregation wanted nothing to do with their Latter-day Saint neighbors.

Decisions over the late 1990s among Jackson's congregation led to an innovative approach at interfaith relations. The church board all agreed with Jackson that the congregation should reach out to the Latter-day Saint institution and ask forgiveness for past grievances. They prepared a formal statement of reconciliation:

> In an effort to allow God's ministry of reconciliation to us to be evident in our lives, we the undersigned do hereby declare that in times past our attitudes and actions toward members of The Church of Jesus Christ of Latter-day Saints have been completely unlike that which was demonstrated through the example of our Lord and Savior Jesus Christ. We therefore join in solidarity with the Pastoral Staff, Executive Board and Leaders of Rock Canyon Assembly Worship Center in humble and sincere repentance for this behavior. Having received forgiveness from God, we now ask for forgiveness from the members of The Church of Jesus Christ of Latter-day Saints. We declare 1998 The Year of Repentance. We pledge to live our lives as ambassadors for Christ, as though He were making His appeal through us.[117]

Dean Jackson and his congregation shared their request for forgiveness before a mixed audience of Pentecostals and Latter-day Saints on November 29, 1998.

Reactions varied dramatically concerning the decision not only to interact with Latter-day Saints, but also to ask their forgiveness. Stephen E. Robinson, a well-known Latter-day Saint scholar, reflected on the event, stating, "I am embarrassed that they had to make the first move."[118] Many Latter-day Saints expressed appreciation for the peaceful gesture from the small Pentecostal community in their midst. And the community got smaller because many of Jackson's congregation disagreed with the action and abandoned his church. Disappointed by the pushback, Jackson lamented, "I . . . have a file of negative responses that would choke a maggot—responses from around the world, believe it or not."[119] More than half the congregation left during the interfaith meetings, and the congregation remained at about fifty members through the early 2000s.[120]

The direct institutional engagement between Pentecostals and Latter-day Saints illuminated a transitioning religious landscape in Utah during the turn of the twenty-first century. Prior to this period, many evangelical churches in Utah offered anti-Mormon ministries, including some Pentecostal churches. Yet from the mid-1990s forward, a "growing sensitivity to anti-Mormon ministries" emerged in the urban centers of the state.[121] Greg Johnson, a Baptist minister from the state of Utah, developed a coalition called *Standing Together* in 2001. The coalition sought to unite evangelical churches in Utah, but also to develop and encourage dialogue between evangelicals and Latter-day Saints. Some of the largest affiliated churches are Pentecostal churches. Working closely with Robert Millett, a Latter-day Saint professor of religious education at BYU, Johnson and Millett organized events intended to bring the two faith groups into discussion. They engaged students, faculty, and the general public through dialogues orchestrated at various locations around the state, and even eventually developed national and international dialogue opportunities. Many Pentecostals supported the efforts, but as Ray Smith (pastor of Salt Lake Christian Center, an Assemblies of God church) acknowledged, some members chose to leave their home churches if they participated in or facilitated the dialogue events for *Standing Together*.[122]

The cooperation and engagement between Pentecostals and Latter-day Saints in the late twentieth and early twenty-first centuries remains predominantly isolated to Utah. "The regular things you could do anywhere else in the country, don't work here," explained Alex Lucero, pastor of the Abundant Life Assembly of God in North Salt Lake.[123] Few congregations outside of Utah have the same degree of familiarity with the Church of Jesus Christ of Latter-day Saints. Without that familiarity, Pentecostals in other parts of the country rarely interacted with Latter-day Saints and preferred it that way. Forced to interact with Latter-day Saints almost on a daily basis, Utah Pentecostals developed methods of engagement for which Pentecostals elsewhere had no desire. Political cooperation on a national level blossomed a few years earlier with the emergence of the Moral Majority, but cultural and social cooperation is rarer outside of the Beehive State.[124] Within the state, both institutions found value in improving social relations between their communities.

Within the Utah Latino community, Pastor Roy Cazares worked with Catholics, Latter-day Saints, Baptists, and other Protestants to worship together. From about 2001 to 2006, the Latino Assemblies of God Centro de Vida Christiana participated in a program where church members worshipped with members of different faiths. "It was amazing when they asked me to minister at an LDS ward," remembered Pastor Cazares. "I thought whoa! I had a Catholic priest come up here [to Centro de Vida Christiana] and speak. That was the whole idea of it. You give us your view, and we'll pray together. It was just an amazing thing."[125] The logistics of organizing the events made it complicated to continue the program beyond 2006.

This kind of cooperation was strictly cultural and social. *Standing Together* brought together evangelicals, Pentecostals, and Latter-day Saints, not to merge theological traditions but to open channels of communication among institutions. Theological boundaries between Pentecostals and Latter-day Saints remained impassable. Yet in other ways, the churches learned to cooperate socially. Pentecostal pastors credited Greg Johnson's access to Latter-day Saint leadership as instrumental in interfaith funerals, dinners, and public events that allowed religious groups to cooperate with each other at arm's length. Greg Johnson asked the question in the early 2000s: "What if the Mormon church were to let us have an event in the Tabernacle?"[126] The Tabernacle on Temple Square in Salt Lake City held the general conferences of the Church of Jesus Christ from October 1867 until the dedication of the Conference Center in 2000. An interfaith dialogue in the Tabernacle could work toward bridging the long history in Utah of attempting to convert each other or coexist without acknowledging each other. Significant concerns existed among evangelicals about asking to use the Tabernacle for a public event. On one hand, it might be compromising theological principles to request assistance from the Latter-day Saints. On the other hand, Greg Johnson argued, "It would be just as hard for them [the Latter-day Saints] to say yes as it would be for us to even ask.... What if we pulled it off? That would be the coup of the century because it would show that we don't have to hate each other."[127]

The event organized by *Standing Together* on November 14, 2004 represented the same kind of unprecedented transgression of denominational boundaries as the formal statement of reconciliation offered by the Rock Canyon Church just a few years earlier. Christian philosopher Ravi Zacharias, along with Fuller Theological Seminary President Richard Mouw became the first non-Latter-day Saint preachers in the Tabernacle since the early twentieth century.[128] Mouw, just like Jackson, sought to make public amends: "Let me state it clearly. We evangelicals have sinned against you."[129] The controversial apology rattled evangelicals in Utah, including some Pentecostals. These Utahns characterized *Standing Together* as Utah evangelicals who had "developed unhealthy, lopsided relationships with the Mormon apologists."[130]

Despite the controversy, the 2004 public event led to increasing cooperation through the new century. In March 2011, the National Association of Evangelicals (NAE) held an annual board meeting in Utah for the first time, where several board members attended a separate meeting with Latter-day Saint leaders.[131] And finally in September 2013, George O. Wood visited BYU and the Church of Jesus Christ of Latter-day Saints headquarters. Wood also acknowledged *Standing Together* and the NAE meeting as influences on his decision to accept a speaking invitation in Utah.[132] For many outside Utah, Wood's decision was rash and unacceptable. From inside the state, however, some Pentecostals viewed it differently. "I do not pretend to know what the Holy Spirit might be doing within the LDS leadership," wrote Ray Smith, pastor of Salt Lake Christian Center, "but I do believe the Spirit opened this door."[133] The majority of Utah Pentecostals seemed to agree that more cooperation between Pentecostals and Latter-day Saints could prove beneficial in the long run.

Many of the advances in cooperative interactions between Pentecostals and Latter-day Saints in the twenty-first century developed through the efforts and willingness of Pentecostals, but Latter-day Saints too altered their interfaith approach. They did not initiate interfaith engagements as often as Pentecostals, but they began accepting invitations to participate. Their willingness to participate in interfaith activities signaled a change in the institution's public presence. Since the Winter Olympics in 2002, the Church of Jesus Christ of Latter-day Saints appeared to begin reviewing its public image and revising its religious presence. At roughly the same time that Robert Putnam and David Campbell argued that the "coexistence of religious diversity and devotion" in the United States is created through "a web of interlocking personal relationships among people of many different faiths," the Church of Jesus Christ was exploring new advertising ideas to develop a campaign whose tagline would become "I'm a Mormon."[134] Elder Quentin L. Cook, an apostle and senior leader in the church, specifically cited Putnam and Campbell's book in a general conference talk given in April 2011.[135] This suggested that the findings in *American Grace* were being discussed among leaders of the Church of Jesus Christ at the time of the initiation of the "I'm a Mormon" campaign, and the campaign very likely revolved around the finding of Putnam and Campbell that "when Americans associate with people of religions other than their own—or people with no religion at all—they become more accepting of other religions."[136] The "I'm a Mormon" campaign and the subsequent film titled *Meet the Mormons,* appeared to fit the goal of introducing more people to the Latter-day Saint community to foster greater toleration for Latter-day Saints in the public eye. The kind of religious bridging advocated for by Putnam and Campbell almost exactly matched the types of cooperative social engagements organized by *Standing Together*. In this sense, the Latter-day Saint institution also saw value in accepting the invitations from Pentecostals for more dialogue.

The willingness of Pentecostals and Latter-day Saints to engage each other in dialogue represents significant changes in the ways both groups are engaging society at large. In Utah society, the divisive tracts and theological conflicts of the twentieth century are rarely seen any longer. Instead of constantly trying to convert one another, they developed a relationship that allowed more social and political cooperation. George O. Wood was invited to BYU as part of the growing interest in religious freedom manifested by the Church of Jesus Christ of Latter-day Saints. Wood shared that interest. After Donald Trump's election to the US presidency in 2016, Wood encouraged members of the Assemblies of God to pray for the newly elected administration: "Our most basic freedom—religious liberty—has faced the largest threat it has in our nation's history."[137] Wood also made clear that he was not bending on theological principles. "I did have private discussions with several in LDS leadership regarding the differences that separate us doctrinally," wrote Wood, "but also we discussed where we could work together within the public square on religious liberty and issues of morality."[138]

Yet the cooperation remains strained. Neil J. Young found that in the late twentieth century evangelicals, Catholics, and Latter-day Saints "defined and emphasized their differences from each other so as to clarify their unique religious messages against the perception of political unity."[139] For some, political cooperation felt too much like theological cooperation. Many pastors of smaller Pentecostal denominations have no interactions with the Church of Jesus Christ of Latter-day Saints. They participate in Utah society but find no value in reaching out to the Latter-day Saint institution.

Larger organizations like the Assemblies of God, however, have begun to pursue political unity so long as it does not require any theological concessions.[140] Conversion and coexistence as methods of social interaction bring with them a myriad of complications like those described in this chapter. Social cooperation, however, like the dialogues between Greg Johnson and Robert Millett, or the ones between Dean Jackson and the Latter-day Saint community in Provo, function to bring together people of differing faiths in a way that promotes political and cultural cooperation as well. As one of the larger members of the evangelical community in Utah, Pentecostals fit Neil J. Young's analysis of the problems of interfaith politics. Their transition from spiritual rivals focused on converting one another to uncomfortable political partners mirrors Pentecostal and Latter-day Saint behaviors elsewhere and reinforces our understanding of ongoing realignments among conservative faiths within the American mainstream.

Yet while Young's analysis focused on national political behaviors, this study focuses on local theological and social behaviors. Pentecostals continue to grow in influence among American evangelicals, and their history of local interactions in Utah may help understand their actions in other parts of the country in the future. For much of their history, Pentecostals have been able to remain apart from society to some degree. Their growth in the United States through the twentieth and twenty-first centuries no longer permits the same kind of behavior. As in Utah where Pentecostals eventually found it necessary to engage with their religious neighbors in new ways, congregations and individuals elsewhere may soon need to adapt similar methods as those employed among believers of the full gospel in Zion.

EPILOGUE

Pentecostals in Utah during the twentieth century exemplified the struggle to plant and sustain religious movements in the American West. From the earliest mission organized by Olive H. Walker in 1914, Pentecostals fought to convert the citizens of Utah to their brand of Christianity. For the most part, they failed, but they succeeded in gaining permanency and adding to the religious variety of the state.

Pentecostals managed to grow among the Latter-day Saints by shifting the focus of their missionary work from the Latter-day Saints to the non-Latter-day Saints of Utah. When other Protestant denominations began to slow down the work of evangelism, Pentecostals filled the void left behind and continued gathering members into their congregations throughout the twentieth century. Where other missionaries before them developed comity arrangements and promoted ecumenical alliances, Pentecostals worked alone to spread the full gospel in Zion. As a community in Utah, Pentecostals managed to grow in size throughout the twentieth and early twenty-first centuries.

The demographic changes that took place during the twentieth century fed the growth of Pentecostal churches. Ethnic churches developed in the African American, Greek, and Latino communities. Pentecostals and unaffiliated individuals moved to Utah for work as the federal government increased its presence in the state. As the non-Latter-day Saint population grew, Pentecostals benefited from the influx of new people to the community.

Although adversarial at first, Pentecostals transitioned from trying to convert Latter-day Saints to developing a peaceful disposition toward their neighbors, which allowed them to create comfortable places of worship for their congregations. Existing within a Latter-day Saint majority, they focused their resources and charitable work on affecting the non-Latter-day Saint population. Missions and food kitchens reached out to individuals and families not supported by the infrastructure of the Church of Jesus Christ of Latter-day Saints. Pentecostal churches developed networks of their own to support their small congregations and continue evangelizing among Utah residents. This less adversarial approach may have ultimately had a greater effect on the Utah religious community by improving Pentecostal growth in the state and increasing Pentecostal visibility in the community.

NEGOTIATING RELATIONSHIPS

In my research among Pentecostals in Utah, I have wondered about the effect of my personal beliefs on my interactions with the Pentecostal community. Robert Orsi observed, "To study a world of meaning and practice other than one's own, as many scholars do, whether this is in another country or in another time, means making one's arduous way from an initial experience of difference that may be deeply disorienting or even alienating toward understanding."[1] I hoped to make sense of the religious experience of Pentecostals living among my own people, the Latter-day Saints. Although not native to the state of Utah, I identified with the majority demographic. How would my past and present biases affect my engagement with the Pentecostal community?

There is a tendency in religious studies, expertly identified by Orsi, for religious studies scholars "to keep their lives out of their research."[2] Doing so creates the illusion of objectivity; the researcher is merely looking in from the outside and reporting their findings. Orsi argues that leaving out an analysis of the relationship between the scholar and the subject is an incomplete way of understanding religious communities. "Scholars of religion do not study churches, mosques, synagogues, and so on, they study in these religious environments, and what we learn is about life itself in these places, not about 'religion.'"[3] As I entered the churches and homes of Pentecostals in Utah, I felt constantly under pressure to negotiate and reconcile my personal beliefs with the beliefs of those around me. Being a member of the Church of Jesus Christ of Latter-day Saints, I represent one side of the historical conversation on display in this book. Often, I felt the unfamiliarity and strain of the relationship between Pentecostals and Latter-day Saints. In 2016 I presented at the annual conference for the Society for Pentecostal Studies. The presentation consisted of a comparison between the historical use of speaking in tongues among Latter-day Saints and among Pentecostals in the United States. I began my presentation by identifying my religious background. During the rest of the conference, many others came up to me and shared their appreciation for my interest in Pentecostal history and my scholarly participation at their conference. In these interactions, I recognized my place outside of the community, as did those members of the community with which I interacted.

When I presented on Utah Pentecostal history in 2017 at the Annual Utah History Conference, a few individuals expressed to me their surprise at the presence of Pentecostals in the state. Neither Pentecostals nor Latter-day Saints knew much about the other, which highlighted to me the historical deficit and limits of institutional interactions. In the conversations at the conference that followed, no one assumed that I was Pentecostal despite the content of my presentation. I wondered why and again fretted over the methods I was employing in my analyzing and retelling of Pentecostal history in Utah.

I wondered about how communities remembered these religious interactions for better or worse. Moments of progress would be followed by defeats or voids. Churches would open, gain converts, and then fade from the historical record. Steps toward communal harmony, hard-fought though they might have been, would fade from local memory. When in 1998 the Rock Canyon Church in Provo decided to act and created the Declaration of Reconciliation discussed in the last chapter, they took a considerable risk. And the risk resulted in a powerful interfaith moment between Pentecostals and Latter-day Saints. During the ceremony at Brigham Young University, the Rock Canyon Church presented to the Religious Education department a beautiful plaque including the Declaration that was then placed prominently on the walls of the building. When I visited Brigham Young University in 2018 to see it, almost no one knew about its existence or where to find it. Eventually we discovered it stored in an electrical closet. Twenty years later, and all but forgotten.

I wondered how my personal beliefs might influence the conversations I had with Pentecostals themselves. On some occasions, I shied away from promptly identifying my religious affiliation, worried that it might inhibit individuals from sharing their experiences with me. At other times the concern evaporated under the conversations of history and life experiences. When members of the Pentecostal community discovered I was not Pentecostal, some immediately and naturally began evangelizing. Conversations about history transformed into conversations about theology and salvation. My presence in worship meetings sometimes went unnoticed and other times became the focus for the sermon. My interest and presence affected the context of the experiences I witnessed.

As I formulated arguments and organized historical narratives, I continued to fret about the effect of my biases on the finished product. But I believe that my experience researching and writing about the Pentecostal community in Utah is demonstrative of the history itself. My concerns about and efforts in engaging the Pentecostal community mirror the concerns and efforts of Latter-day Saints and Pentecostals throughout the twentieth century. The relationship between these two groups was and is constantly being negotiated and renegotiated as historical circumstances evolve. It is what Orsi described as "religious messiness," and the necessity of seeing "religious spaces as always, inevitably, and profoundly intersected by things brought into them from outside, things that bear their own histories, complexities, [and] meanings different from those offered within the religious space."[4]

The story of Pentecostalism in Utah becomes a story of religious engagement and entanglement. Pentecostals were very aware of the religious makeup of the community they entered upon coming to Utah, and Latter-day Saints became aware of the Pentecostal community as it grew over the 1900s. At various points other religious organizations also found themselves caught up in the web of interactions. Over the course of their history, Pentecostals worked and reworked the terms of their engagement with Utah society. From the zealous pursuit of souls to institution building and church construction and finally hesitant acceptance, Pentecostals navigated their way along the valleys and mountains of Utah. And over the twenty-first century Pentecostals will continue evolving in Utah along with the religious community at large. Ultimately Utah Pentecostal history contributes additional voices and perspectives on the growth of Pentecostalism in the United States. The stories and struggles of men and women from various ethnicities and backgrounds coming together to create a religious community in Utah reveals additional depth to the reach of the full gospel in even the most unlikely of places.

NOTES

INTRODUCTION

1. A photograph of this very small news article is in the author's possession. I have not been able to identify the date of the article or the specific newspaper. I believe it is the *Davis County Clipper* or the *Ogden Standard-Examiner*. Notes on the event described come from an interview with various members of the Abundant Life Assembly of God church near the Bountiful area.
2. On August 16, 2018, Russell M. Nelson, president of the Church of Jesus Christ of Latter-day Saints, stressed the importance of using the formal name of the church over any of its nicknames or acronyms. Commonly called the "Mormon Church" or "LDS Church" in the past, the official style guide for the Church of Jesus Christ of Latter-day Saints requests that these names no longer be used in publications. With respect to these requests, I will attempt to follow the guidelines provided. For more information, see the announcement at https://www.mormonnewsroom.org/article/name-of-the-church, accessed November 26, 2018. See also the official style guide at https://www.mormonnewsroom.org/style-guide, accessed November 26, 2018.
3. Thomas Corwin Iliff, as cited by J. Alton Templin, Allen DuPont Breck, and Martin Rist, eds., *The Methodist, Evangelical, and United Brethren Churches in the Rockies, 1850–1976* (Rocky Mountain Conference of the United Methodist Church, 1977), 471.
4. First reference comes from Doctrine and Covenants Section 100:16. The second reference comes from Orson Hyde, "Discourse by President Orson Hyde," *Journal of Discourses* Vol. 16 (London: Latter-day Saints' Book Depot, 1874), 230. Orson Hyde liked the description: "I will make a few remarks upon the idea of our being a peculiar people. You know that we are regarded as such, and if we look upon ourselves from a proper point of view, we shall readily admit that in this respect outsiders have given us an appropriate name; for we are a peculiar people whom God has chosen to serve and honor him."
5. E. K. Fisher, as cited by Grant Wacker, *Heaven Below: Early Pentecostals and American Culture* (Cambridge, MA: Harvard University Press, 2001), 178.
6. R. Laurence Moore, *Religious Outsiders and the Making of Americans* (New York: Oxford University Press, 1986), 46.
7. Moore, 205–8.
8. Moore, 31.
9. Wacker, *Heaven Below*, 177.

10. Wacker, *Heaven Below*, 196.
11. Claude T. Barnes, "The Unconscious Illapse," *Improvement Era* 10, no. 10 (August 1907): 789.
12. Heber J. Grant, a senior apostle of the Church of Jesus Christ of Latter-day Saints and church president from 1918 to 1945, spoke often of the importance of charismatic expression in the history and theology of the Latter-day Saints. There are more than thirty published discourses from 1900 to 1941 spread evenly across the years in which President Grant recounted spiritual manifestations or witnessed to the power and necessity of spiritual gifts in the lives of church members. These discourses can be found in all the various publications of the Church of Jesus Christ of Latter-day Saints during the early twentieth century, from the conference reports of the annual and semi-annual general conferences, the *Liahona* missionary publication, the *Juvenile Instructor* and *Instructor*, as well as the *Woman's Exponent* and the *Relief Society Magazine*. Even though most Latter-day Saints no longer publicly participated in such a wide variety of charismatic expressions, church leaders continually supported their historical importance to the movement as signposts of their distinctive outsider theology.
13. From Richard D. Poll, general ed., *Utah's History* (Provo, UT: Brigham Young University Press, 1978), 692–93; Pew Research Center, "America's Changing Religious Landscape," May 12, 2015, 145; and Matt Canham, "Utah Sees Latter-day Saint Slowdown and Membership Numbers Drop in Salt Lake County," *Salt Lake Tribune*, January 5, 2020, available at https://www.sltrib.com/religion/2020/01/05/utah-sees-latter-day/?mc_cid=ef4ce4e988&mc_eid=fce4404805. The editors note that the data for the 1880s and 1890s on Latter-day Saint membership in the state of Utah may be inaccurately low "for reasons associated with the legislative and judicial campaign against the church in this period." As the federal government continued arresting polygamists for cohabiting with their spouses, many members of the Church of Jesus Christ of Latter-day Saints may have decided not to publicly identify as members of the church.
14. There is some media debate about whether people that live in Utah are known as "Utahns" or "Utahans." Although many media outlets continue to use the latter form, Utahns themselves do not. See Stephanie Grimes, "Is it Utahn or Utahan?," March 5, 2013, available at https://www.ksl.com/article/24207511.
15. Ferenc M. Szasz, *Religion in the Modern American West* (Tucson: University of Arizona Press, 2000), xii.
16. Patricia Nelson Limerick, *The Legacy of Conquest: The Unbroken Past of the American West* (New York: W. W. Norton & Company, 1987), 18–31.
17. Neil J. Young, *We Gather Together: The Religious Right and the Problem of Interfaith Politics* (New York: Oxford University Press, 2016), 1–5.
18. Stanford J. Layton, ed., *Being Different: Stories of Utah's Minorities* (Salt Lake City, UT: Signature Books, 2001); and Eileen Hallet Stone, ed., *A Homeland in the West: Utah Jews Remember* (Salt Lake City: University of Utah Press, 2001).
19. Edmund W. Hunke, *Southern Baptists in the Mountain West (1940–1989), A Fifty-Year History of Utah, Idaho, and Nevada Southern Baptists* (Franklin, TN: Providence House Publishers, 1998); and Carl Joseph Ballestero, *How High My Mountain* (Bloomington, CA: Carl Joseph Ballestero, 1991).

20. Martin Mitchell, "Gentile Impressions of Salt Lake City, Utah, 1849–1870," *Geographical Review* 87, no. 3 (July 1997): 334–52.
21. Utah State Historical Society, *Utah Centennial County History Series*. Each of the twenty-nine counties have a book in this series, as well as one book on Native Americans in Utah. This is a valuable source of local history for the state of Utah.
22. *Directory of Churches and Religious Organizations in Utah*, prepared by the Historical Records Survey Division of Women's and Professional Projects Works Progress Administration (Ogden, UT: Historical Records Survey, 1938); Robert J. Dwyer, *The Gentile Comes to Utah: A Study in Religious and Social Conflict, 1862–1890*, rev. 2nd ed. (Salt Lake City, UT: Western Epics, 1971); Thomas G. Alexander and James B. Allen, *Mormons and Gentiles: A History of Salt Lake City* (Boulder, CO: Pruett Publishing Co., 1984); and Jan Shipps and Mark Silk, *Religion and Public Life in the Mountain West: Sacred Landscapes in Transition* (Walnut Creek, CA: AltaMira Press, 2004).
23. The exception here is Jan Shipps and Mark Silk, whose data for the region is still quite helpful. For other examples, see Randall Rathjen, "The Distribution of Major Non-Mormon Denominations in Utah" (master's thesis, University of Utah, 1966); A. J. Simmonds, *The Gentile Comes to Cache Valley: A Study of the Logan Apostasies of 1874 and the Establishment of Non-Mormon Churches in Cache Valley, 1873–1913* (Logan: Utah State University Press, 1976); and Ferenc M. Szasz, *Religion in the Modern American West* (Tucson: University of Arizona Press, 2000).
24. Richard D. Poll, general editor, *Utah's History* (Logan: Utah State University, 1989). The only reference to Pentecostalism is found on pages 692–93 in a chart listing membership of various religious denominations in Utah. However, no Pentecostal denomination is listed despite their growing presence. Instead, it is assumed that Pentecostal congregations are lumped into the "other" category, which showed growth over the twentieth century. Beyond this, no Pentecostalism in any form is mentioned.
25. James B. Allen, *Still the Right Place: Utah's Second Half-Century of Statehood, 1945–1995* (Salt Lake City, UT: Charles Redd Center for Western Studies and the Utah State Historical Society, 2017). Jesse Bushman worked with James B. Allen to complete a series of interviews on which the religion appendix is based. Bushman then went on to complete additional interviews to finish his master's thesis. See Jesse Bushman, "A Quantitative Analysis of the Non-LDS Experience in Utah," (master's thesis, Brigham Young University, 1995).
26. Ronald G. Coleman, "A History of Blacks in Utah, 1825–1910" (PhD diss., University of Utah, 1980); Jorge Iber, *Hispanics in the Mormon Zion, 1912–1999* (College Station: Texas A&M University Press, 2000); and Juanita Brooks, *The History of the Jews in Utah and Idaho* (Salt Lake City, UT: Western Epics, 1973). For more research on ethnic or racial groups, see Robert E. Lewis, Mark W. Fraser, and Peter J. Pecora, "Religiosity Among Indochinese Refugees in Utah," *Journal for the Scientific Study of Religion* 27, no. 2 (June 1988): 272–83; Helen Z. Papanikolas, *The Peoples of Utah* (Salt Lake City: Utah State Historical Society, 1976).
27. T. Edgar Lyon, "Evangelical Protestant Missionary Activities in Mormon Dominated Areas, 1865–1900" (PhD diss., University of Utah, 1962); Stanley B. Kimball, "The Utah Gospel Mission, 1900–1950," *Utah Historical Quarterly* 44, no. 2 (Spring

1976): 149–55; and Peggy Pascoe, *Relations of Rescue: The Search for Female Moral Authority in the American West, 1874–1939* (New York: Oxford University Press, 1990).

28. Frederick G. Burton, *Presbyterians in Zion: History of the Presbyterian Church (USA) in Utah* (New York: Vantage Press, 2010); R. Douglas Brackenridge, "Hostile Mormons and Persecuted Presbyterians in Utah, 1870–1900: A Reappraisal," *Journal of Mormon History* 37, no. 3 (Summer 2011): 162–228; R. Douglas Brackenridge, "Presbyterians and Latter-day Saints in Utah: A Century of Conflict and Compromise, 1830–1930," *The Journal of Presbyterian History* 80, no. 4 (Winter 2002): 205–24; and Jana Kathryn Riess, "'Heathen in Our Fair Land': Presbyterian Women Missionaries in Utah, 1870–1890," *The Journal of Presbyterian History* 80, no. 4 (Winter 2002): 225–46.
29. For Methodism see Henry Martin Merkel, *History of Methodism in Utah* (Colorado Springs, CO: Dentan Printing Co., 1938); and *The First Century of the Methodist Church in Utah* (Salt Lake City: Utah Methodism Centennial Committee, 1970).
30. For Catholic history see Bernice Maher Mooney, *Salt of the Earth: The History of the Catholic Church in Utah, 1776–2007* 3rd ed. (Salt Lake City: University of Utah Press, 2008); Francis J. Weber, "Catholicism Among the Mormons, 1875–79," *Utah Historical Quarterly* 44, no. 2 (Spring 1976): 141–48; and Carol Ann Morrow, "Catholics Among the Mormons," *St. Anthony Magazine Online*, October 1997, available at www.americancatholic.org/messenger/oct1997/feature1.asp, accessed June 26, 2012. For Congregational history, see Dee Richard Darling, "Cultures in Conflict: Congregationalism, Mormonism and Schooling in Utah, 1880–1893," (PhD diss., University of Utah, 1991). For Baptist history, see France Davis, *Light in the Midst of Zion: A History of Black Baptists in Utah, 1892–1996* (Salt Lake City, UT: University Publishing, 1997); and R. Maud Ditmars, "A History of Baptist Missions in Utah, 1871–1931" (master's thesis, University of Colorado, 1931). For Episcopal history, see Frederick Quinn, *Building the "Goodly Fellowship of Faith": A History of the Episcopal Church in Utah, 1867–1996* (Logan: Utah State University Press, 2004). Quinn has several journal articles on Episcopal Church history in Utah, and Mary Donovan has written about female Episcopal missionaries, Mary S. Donovan, "Women Missionaries in Utah," *Anglican and Episcopal History* 66, no. 2 (June 1997): 154–74.
31. For Hare Krishna, see Sara Black Brown, "Krishna, Christians, and Colors: The Socially Binding Influence of Kirtan Singing at a Utah Hare Krishna Festival," *Ethnomusicology* 58, no. 3 (Fall 2014): 454–80; and www.utahkrishnas.org/category/about-us/history/. One journal article written by me briefly addresses early Pentecostal history in Utah. See Alan J. Clark, "'We Believe in the Gift of Tongues': The 1906 Pentecostal Revolution and Its Effects on the LDS Use of the Gift of Tongues in the Twentieth Century," *Mormon Historical Studies* 14, no. 1 (Spring 2013): 67–80. Buddhists, Muslims, Jehovah's Witnesses, and other smaller communities have virtually no research done concerning their history in Utah.
32. For more examples of early Christian missionaries in Utah, see Charles Randall Paul, *Converting the Saints: A Study of Religious Rivalry in America* (Draper, UT: Greg Kofford Books, Inc., 2018).

33. From Richard D. Poll, general ed., *Utah's History* (Provo, UT: Brigham Young University Press, 1978), 692–93; and Pew Research Center, "America's Changing Religious Landscape," May 12, 2015, 145.
34. For global and US statistics, see Allan Anderson, *An Introduction to Pentecostalism: Global Charismatic Christianity*, second edition (New York: Cambridge University Press, 2014), 3, 69. Pentecostals and Charismatic Christians differ predominantly in their denominational affiliations. Pentecostals are Christians specifically affiliated with denominations that identify themselves as Pentecostal. Pentecostals are similar to evangelical Christians in that they are Bible-centered and often identify as born-again Christians. They differ in their desire to experience a more charismatic or spirit-filled worship experience, which often includes the expression of spiritual gifts. Charismatic Christians are identified as non-Pentecostal Christians who accept charismatic spiritual experiences akin to those practiced by Pentecostals.
35. Harvey Cox in the foreword to Gastón Espinosa, *William J. Seymour and the Origins of Global Pentecostalism: A Biography and Documentary History* (Durham, NC: Duke University Press, 2014), xii.
36. There is a growing literature on the history and origins of Pentecostalism. See Robert Mapes Anderson, *Vision of the Disinherited: The Making of American Pentecostalism* (Peabody, MA: Hendrikson Publishers, 1992); Harvey Cox, *Fire From Heaven: The Rise of Pentecostal Spirituality and the Reshaping of Religion in the Twenty-First Century* (Cambridge, MA: Da Capo Press, 1995); Grant Wacker, *Heaven Below: Early Pentecostals and American Culture*, (Cambridge, MA: Harvard University Press, 2001); Cecil M. Robeck, *The Azusa Street Mission and Revival: The Birth of the Global Pentecostal Movement* (Nashville, TN: Thomas Nelson, Inc., 2006); Allan Anderson, *An Introduction to Pentecostalism: Global Charismatic Christianity*, second edition (New York: Cambridge University Press, 2014); and Gastón Espinosa, *William J. Seymour and the Origins of Global Pentecostalism: A Biography and Documentary History* (Durham, NC: Duke University Press, 2014).
37. While the basis for these three periods is explained more specifically in chapter one, generally the work of Pentecostal missionaries in Utah seems to fit into three waves of evangelization, with the final wave continuing to the present.
38. US Census quick facts, available at https://www.census.gov/quickfacts/UT. See also US Census Bureau, *Demographic Trends in the 20th Century: Census 2000 Special Reports*, prepared by Franklin Hobbs and Nicole Stoops (Washington, DC, November 2002) A1, https://www.census.gov/prod/2002pubs/censr-4.pdf.
39. Table titled "Membership of Religious Denominations in Utah—1870–1975," in Richard D. Poll, general ed., *Utah's History* (Logan, UT: Utah State University Press, 1989), 692–93. The 2016 statistics come from the Newsroom of the Church of Jesus Christ of Latter-day Saints, available at https://newsroom.churchofjesuschrist.org/facts-and-statistics/state/utah.
40. Camp Douglas, later renamed Fort Douglas, began operating as a military garrison in 1862. Zion National Park, the first national park in Utah opened in 1919. For a brief history of Utah public lands, see "BLM Utah History," available at https://www.blm.gov/about/history/history-by-region/utah, accessed November 26, 2018.

41. Charles S. Peterson and Brian Q. Cannon, *The Awkward State of Utah: Coming of Age in the Nation 1896–1945* (Salt Lake City: University of Utah Press, 2015).
42. See Helen Z. Papanikolas, "The New Immigrants," in *Utah's History*, Richard D. Poll general ed. (Logan: Utah State University Press, 1989), 447–62.
43. For a full account, see Kathleen Flake, *The Politics of American Religious Identity: The Seating of Senator Reed Smoot, Mormon Apostle* (Chapel Hill: University of North Carolina Press, 2004).
44. T. Edgar Lyon and Glen M. Leonard, "The Churches in the Territory," in *Utah's History*, Richard D. Poll general ed. (Logan: Utah State University Press, 1989), 317.
45. This is the Seventh Article of Faith, originally written by Joseph Smith in 1842. It would be canonized as a part of *The Pearl of Great Price* in 1880.
46. James E. Talmage, "The Gifts of the Spirit Contrasted with the Spurious Manifestations of the Evil Power," *Liahona The Elders' Journal* 29, no. 5 (August 1931): 98–9.
47. According to Robert P. Jones and Daniel Cox, *America's Changing Religious Identity*, Public Religion Research Institute, released on September 6, 2017, available at https://www.prri.org/research/american-religious-landscape-christian-religiously-unaffiliated/. It notes that the most religiously diverse states are in the northeastern United States, with much of the West coast following behind it.
48. Frederick Jackson Turner, "The Significance of the Frontier in American History," given at the American Historical Association in Chicago during the World Columbian Exposition, July 12, 1893.
49. Patricia Nelson Limerick, *The Legacy of Conquest: The Unbroken Past of The American West* (New York: W. W. Norton & Company, 1987), 26.
50. Richard White, *It's Your Misfortune and None of My Own: A History of the American West* (Norman: University of Oklahoma Press, 1991), 57.
51. Robert V. Hine and John Mack Faragher, *The American West: A New Interpretive History* (New Haven: Yale University Press, 2000), 11.
52. Hine and Faragher, *The American West*, 11.
53. Eldon Ernst, "American Religious History From a Pacific Coast Perspective," in *Religion and Society in the American West: Historical Essays*, ed. by Carl Guarneri and David Alvarez (Lanham, MD: University Press of America, 1987), 12.
54. Ferenc M. Szasz and Margaret Connell Szasz, "Religion and Spirituality" in *The Oxford History of the American West*, ed. by Clyde A. Milner II, Carol A. O'Connor, and Martha A. Sandweiss (New York: Oxford University Press, 1994), 389.
55. Szasz, *Religion in the Modern American West*, xvi.
56. Laurie Maffly-Kipp, "Eastward Ho! American Religion from the Perspective of the Pacific Rim," in *Retelling U. S. Religious History*, ed. by Thomas A. Tweed (Berkeley: University of California Press, 1997), 130.
57. Maffly-Kipp, 128.
58. Fay Botham and Sara M. Patterson, eds., *Race, Religion, Region: Landscapes of Encounter in the American West* (Tucson: University of Arizona Press, 2000), 3.
59. Botham and Patterson, *Race, Religion, Region*, 10.
60. Jan Shipps and Mark Silk, *Religion and Public Life in the Mountain West: Sacred Landscapes in Transition* (Walnut Creek, CA: AltaMira Press, 2004), 143–44.
61. Todd M. Kerstetter, *Inspiration and Innovation: Religion in the American West* (Malden, MA: John Wiley & Sons, Inc., 2015), 3.

62. See Lee Davidson, "Utah's Minority Populations Are Growing Rapidly—Adding 130K People in Seven Years," *Salt Lake Tribune*, June 20, 2018, available at https://www.sltrib.com/news/2018/06/20/utah-minorities-grew-by-139k-since-2010-equivalent-adding-a-city-the-size-of-of-west-valley-city/.
63. Estrelda Alexander in *Philip's Daughters: Women in Pentecostal-Charismatic Leadership*, Estrelda Alexander and Amos Yong, eds. (Eugene, OR: Pickwick Publications, 2009), 7.
64. Kathleen Sprows Cummings, *New Women of the Old Faith: Gender and American Catholicism in the Progressive Era* (Chapel Hill: University of North Carolina Press, 2009), 4.

CHAPTER 1: A BRIEF HISTORY OF THE ASSEMBLIES OF GOD IN UTAH

1. "Church News," *American Fork Citizen*, August 9, 1946, 1.
2. "From Humble Beginning to 3 Stakes, 20 Wards," *American Fork Citizen*, July 7, 1976, 14.
3. "Citizens Approve Recreation Program," *American Fork Citizen*, April 29, 1948, 3, and "Rev. Campbell Addresses BYU Religion Class," *American Fork Citizen*, March 17, 1949, 5.
4. Warren J. Campbell, "Assembly of God Church," *American Fork Citizen*, December 20, 1951, 10.
5. "Church to Be Host to State Fellowship Meet," *American Fork Citizen*, November 22, 1946, 1.
6. These figures come from Margaret M. Poloma and Brian F. Pendleton, "Religious Experiences, Evangelism, and Institutional Growth within the Assemblies of God," *Journal for the Scientific Study of Religion* 28, no. 4 (December 1989): 415. These figures can be compared with data from the Association of Religion Data Archives online. Statistics for the Assemblies of God can be found at http://www.thearda.com/Denoms/D_1021.asp. This data suggests that there were 50,000 members by 1925 and not 1914.
7. "Adherents 1975 through 2016," available at https://ag.org/About/Statistics. These numbers are provided by the statistics department of the Assemblies of God.
8. James B. Allen, "Religion in Twentieth-Century Utah," in *Utah's History*, eds. Richard D. Poll et al. (Logan: Utah State University Press, 1989), 609.
9. Nils Bloch-Hoell, *The Pentecostal Movement: Its Origin, Development, and Distinctive Character* (New York: Humanities Press, 1964), 57.
10. "Religion Plays Constant Part in State History," *Salt Lake Telegram*, July 8, 1942, 20. See also *Directory of Churches and Religious Organizations in Utah (Not Including the Church of Jesus Christ of Latter-day Saints)*, prepared by the Historical Records Survey Division of Women's and Professional Projects of the Works Progress Administration (Ogden, UT: Historical Records Survey, September 1938). In the survey, they listed three Pentecostal churches, which may be the same three referred to in the newspaper article: the Pentecostal Lighthouse in Ogden, the Full Gospel Assembly in Salt Lake, and a Foursquare Church in Salt Lake.
11. "Assemblies of God US Vital Statistics by County, 2000 Estimates," produced by the Flower Pentecostal Heritage Center. Copy in my possession.

12. "Assemblies of God US Vital Statistics by County, 2010 Estimates." This data varies to some degree from the data collected by the Association of Religion Data Archives (ARDA). For the year 2000, they estimated there were 8,176 members of the Assemblies of God in Utah, compared to the 12,391 estimated by the denominational records.
13. It may even be the case that the Assemblies of God outpaced the Southern Baptists by 2010, depending on which statistics are used. Regardless, according to the data from ARDA for membership reports in Utah from 1980 to 2010, the Assemblies of God accumulated gains in each report, while many others peaked around 1990 and began declining thereafter.
14. "Religious Landscape Study," Pew Research Center, Washington, DC (2014), http://www.pewforum.org/religious-landscape-study/state/utah/, accessed December 21, 2017. Comparative membership numbers are extrapolated from these statistics, as well as the previous ARDA growth statistics.
15. Bloch-Hoell, *The Pentecostal Movement,* 61.
16. Thomas O'Dea, *The Mormons* (Chicago: University of Chicago Press, 1957), 115. John Turner also cites O'Dea and others in his analysis of theocracy and nineteenth century Utah under the guidance of Brigham Young. See John G. Turner, *Brigham Young: Pioneer Prophet* (Cambridge, MA: Belknap Press of Harvard University Press, 2012), 200–206.
17. Ethan R. Yorgason, *Transformation of the Mormon Culture Region* (Urbana and Chicago: University of Illinois Press, 2003). The concept of the Mormon Culture Region includes the geographical area where Latter-day Saints colonized cities in the American West.
18. C. P. Lyford, *The Mormon Problem: An Appeal to the American People* (New York: Hunt & Eaton, 1886), 187.
19. C. P. Lyford, *The Mormon Problem,* 188.
20. R. G. Fulford, "Home Missions in Rocky Mountain District," *Pentecostal Evangel,* no. 2251 (June 30, 1957): 21.
21. Edith L. Blumhofer, *The Assemblies of God: A Chapter in the Story of American Pentecostalism,* two volumes (Springfield, MO: Gospel Publishing House, 1989), 110 & 134 respectively.
22. Blumhofer, 201.
23. Blumhofer, 269.
24. Blumhofer, 257.
25. Fred Eiting, "The Largest Untouched Field in the United States," *Weekly Evangel,* December 9, 1916, 15.
26. This story about Herbert Buffum comes from Eric Steinkamp, "History of the Rocky Mountain District of the Assemblies of God," Flower Pentecostal Heritage Center (Springfield, MO).
27. "Requests for Prayer," *The Weekly Evangel,* May 20, 1916, 15.
28. Letters from Utah to these newsletters demonstrated the reach of the newsletters. In one case, the *Salt Lake Tribune* reported on the religious diversity of Salt Lake City. See "Church Census is Almost Completed," *Salt Lake Tribune,* March 10, 1914, 14. In a survey of Salt Lake completed by the Association of Bible Schools of Salt Lake, they found two individuals who identified with the Apostolic Faith,

most likely out of Los Angeles or Portland. Sometimes the newsletters themselves listed the locations of their subscribers. For another example, see A. J. Tomlinson, editorial, *Church of God Evangel*, June 4, 1921, 2.

29. Dwight C. Ritchie, "Friendly Open Letters to a Latter-day Saint," published by Dwight C. Ritchie, Salt Lake City, 1944, Church History Library, The Church of Jesus Christ of Latter-day Saints, Salt Lake City, UT. Quote taken from Letter No. 4.
30. For the Assemblies of God, speaking in tongues is part of the doctrine of initial evidence. The Assemblies of God states, "The baptism of believers in the Holy Spirit is witnessed by the initial physical sign of speaking with other tongues as the Spirit of God gives them utterance. The speaking in tongues in this instance is the same in essence as the gift of tongues, but different in purpose and use." From *Minutes of the 53rd Session of the General Council of the Assemblies of God*, 93. This passage as well as much greater context concerning contemporary speaking in tongues can be found in Aaron T. Friesen, *Norming the Abnormal: The Development and Function of the Doctrine of Initial Evidence in Classical Pentecostalism* (Eugene, OR: Pickwick Publications, 2013).
31. This is the mission statement of The Genesis Project in Ogden and Provo, Utah. Mission statement available at https://www.genesisutah.com/ourstory, accessed October 5, 2018.
32. Gastón Espinosa, *William J. Seymour and the Origins of Global Pentecostalism: A Biography and Documentary History* (Durham, NC: Duke University Press, 2014), 72.
33. Gastón Espinosa, 70.
34. "Claim Strange Gift," *American Fork Citizen*, March 16, 1907, 4.
35. Grant Wacker, *Heaven Below: Early Pentecostals and American Culture* (Cambridge, MA: Harvard University Press, 2001), 155.
36. "Church Census Is Almost Completed," *Salt Lake Tribune*, March 10, 1914, 14.
37. Minutes of the General Council of the Assemblies of God in the United States of America, Canada, and Foreign Lands, April 1914, 12, Flower Pentecostal Heritage Center (Springfield, MO), available at ifphc.org.
38. "Salt Lake City," *The Christian Evangel*, October 24, 1914, 4.
39. For more about the founding of the Industrial Christian Home, see Peggy Pascoe, *Relations of Rescue: The Search for Female Moral Authority in the American West, 1874–1939* (New York: Oxford University Press, 1990), 20–31. Her analysis of the institution continues throughout the book.
40. In October 1915, the *Salt Lake Tribune* began announcing Pentecostal worship meetings at 523 South 400 East in Salt Lake City. Olive Walker is never mentioned, nor is any specific denomination. In the fall 1916, the announcements include mention of the Woodworth-Etter revival. This is probably the mission opened by Walker, but it is not entirely clear. Walker is listed as a Licentiate in Salt Lake City, Utah, in *The Weekly Evangel*, January 8, 1916, 16. So she was still in town in early 1916, but we next find her listed in Portland, Oregon, in the January 1918 ministerial directory. See Ministers Directory General Council, 1914–1917, Flower Pentecostal Heritage Center (Springfield, MO), 16. Following the revival, no more Pentecostal meetings are announced at this location.

41. Robert H. Lowe, "Woodworth-Etter Meeting at Salt Lake City, Utah," *The Weekly Evangel*, September 16, 1916, 15. Robert H. Lowe first appears in Salt Lake City on the AG national ministerial roll in 1916. See Minutes of the General Council of the Assemblies of God, October 1916, Flower Pentecostal Heritage Center (Springfield, MO), 20.
42. Lowe, "Woodworth-Etter Meeting at Salt Lake City, Utah," 15.
43. "The End of the Sidney, Iowa Meeting," *The Weekly Evangel*, October 28, 1916, 15.
44. For the schedule, see "In the Churches," *Salt Lake Herald*, October 15, 1916, 29.
45. August Feick, "The Etter Meeting at Salt Lake City," *The Weekly Evangel*, November 4, 1916, 15.
46. Eiting, "The Largest Untouched Field in the United States," 15.
47. Feick, "The Etter Meeting at Salt Lake City," 15.
48. "Interest Manifest in Work of Revival," *Salt Lake Tribune*, October 15, 1916, 13.
49. Lowe, "Woodworth-Etter Meeting at Salt Lake City, Utah," 15.
50. Eiting, "The Largest Untouched Field in the United States," 15.
51. "Interest Manifest in Work of Revival," *Salt Lake Tribune*, October 15, 1916, 13.
52. Eiting, "The Largest Untouched Field in the United States," 15.
53. Thomas Griffin, "Salt Lake City, Utah," *The Weekly Evangel*, May 5, 1917, 14. For the quote, see "Salt Lake Sunday Church Services," *Salt Lake Tribune*, May 27, 1917, 16.
54. Robert H. Lowe, "Fellowship in Christ," *The Weekly Evangel*, April 21, 1917, 14. In this article, Lowe is listed as R. S. Lowe. More often, however, he is listed as Robert H. Lowe. I have chosen to use the latter name.
55. Thomas Griffin, "A Word of Cheer from Salt Lake City, Utah," *The Weekly Evangel*, May 19, 1917, 11.
56. See the Combined Minutes of the General Council of the Assemblies of God in the United States of America, Canada, and Foreign Lands 1914–1917, Flower Pentecostal Heritage Center (Springfield, MO), 30, 31, 33. See also the 1918 and 1919 editions of *Polk's Salt Lake Directory* (Salt Lake City, UT: R. L. Polk & Co. of Utah), and the Church Directory in the *Salt Lake Telegram* during 1917.
57. P. D. McCabe, "Reports from the Field," *Pentecostal Evangel*, December 27, 1919, 14.
58. Combined Minutes of the General Council of the Assemblies of God in the United States of America, Canada, and Foreign Lands 1914–1917, Flower Pentecostal Heritage Center (Springfield, MO), 31.
59. Isaac Gordon and Martin Linden, Correspondence to N. R. Nichols, September 20, 1923, Flower Pentecostal Heritage Center (Springfield, MO).
60. All quotes from J. D. Wells, "Young Man, Go West!", *Pentecostal Evangel*, April 28, 1923, 11.
61. David Utter, "Mormonism Today," *Ogden Standard*, April 10, 1897, 5.
62. "King at the Tabernacle," *Salt Lake Tribune*, May 3, 1910, 6.
63. These percentages are estimates based on demographic data in the appendices of Richard D. Poll, general ed., *Utah's History* (Logan: Utah State University, 1989). Utah vital statistics come from page 688 and denominational statistics on page 692.
64. William H. Boyles, Correspondence to J. W. Welch, Flower Pentecostal Heritage Center (Springfield, MO), ID19-42, August 9, 1923, and Robert H. Lowe, Correspondence to J. W. Welch, Flower Pentecostal Heritage Center (Springfield, MO), ID19-42, August 21, 1923.

65. Isaac Gordon and Martin Linden, Correspondence to N. R. Nichols, Flower Pentecostal Heritage Center (Springfield, MO), ID19-42, September 20, 1923.
66. "This Week's Cover," *Pentecostal Evangel,* May 30, 1954, 10.
67. G. W. Wagner, "Reports from the Field," *Pentecostal Evangel,* June 21, 1924, 12.
68. "This Week's Cover," 10.
69. Orson F. Whitney, "Stay Where You Are!," *Latter-day Saints' Millennial Star* 83 (September 15, 1921): 585.
70. Charles L. Peterson and Brian Q. Cannon, *The Awkward State of Utah: Coming of Age in the Nation, 1896-1945* (Salt Lake City: University of Utah Press, 2015), 231.
71. Whitney, "Stay Where You Are!," 585.
72. Peterson and Cannon, *The Awkward State of Utah,* 266.
73. Much of the data in this paragraph and its preceding paragraph is found in Peterson and Cannon, *The Awkward State of Utah,* Chapters 10 and 11. See also Jorge Iber, *Hispanics in the Mormon Zion: 1912–1999* (College Station: Texas A&M University Press, 2000), 40–41.
74. Peterson and Cannon argue that in 1920, there were approximately 20,400 Roman Catholics, 13,800 Protestants, and 6,000 other religious people in Utah. There were also 80,000 unchurched Utahns. See Peterson and Cannon, *The Awkward State of Utah,* 250–1. The *Salt Lake Telegram* published a survey of religion taken in 1939. See "Religion Plays Constant Part in State History," *Salt Lake Telegram,* July 8, 1942, 20. In the article, it reported denominational affiliations lower than the estimates given by Peterson and Cannon. For example, Peterson and Cannon estimate that in 1920, there were 20,400 Catholics, 3,550 Presbyterians, 3,220 Methodists, and 2,295 Congregationalists and Episcopalians apiece. The 1939 survey reported there were 14,000 Catholics, 2,500 Presbyterians, 2,500 Methodists, 1,600 Congregationalists, and 3,500 Episcopalians. It may be the case that many non-Mormons left Utah during the 1920s and 1930s. This is hard to determine on denominational statistics alone. Compare also the religious statistics compiled in the table "Membership of Religious Denominations in Utah—1870–1975," in Richard D. Poll, general ed., *Utah's History* (Logan: Utah State University Press, 1989), 692–93.
75. L. Vere Elliott, Deceased Ministers File, Flower Pentecostal Heritage Center (Springfield, MO); L. Vere Elliott, "Salt Lake City, Utah," *The Pentecostal Evangel,* October 23, 1926, 13. For the Full Gospel Mission, see "Sunday Services in Salt Lake Churches," *Salt Lake Telegram,* September 15, 1928, 3. Pastor Constantine Nicholas and the Full Gospel Mission are discussed in Chapter 2.
76. "Sunday Services in Salt Lake Churches," *Salt Lake Telegram,* September 14, 1929, 3; Paul Kienel, Deceased Ministers File, Flower Pentecostal Heritage Center (Springfield, MO).
77. For Benjamin H. Caudle, see the Constitution and By-Laws of the General Council of the Assemblies of God, September 1933, Flower Pentecostal Heritage Center (Springfield, MO), 122, and also Benjamin H. Caudle, Deceased Ministers File, Flower Pentecostal Heritage Center (Springfield, MO). Caudle would return briefly to pastor in Provo, Utah in 1953. For Gilbert T. Thompson, see the Official List of Ministers and Missionaries of the General Council of the Assemblies of God, January 1937, Flower Pentecostal Heritage Center (Springfield, MO), 59, and also Gilbert T. Thompson, Deceased Ministers File, Flower Pentecostal Heritage

Center (Springfield, MO). For Joe Clapper, see "Assembly of God (Pentecostal)," *San Juan Record*, July 14, 1938, 20; "Cedar Point," *San Juan Record*, July 28, 1938, 8; and "Ucolo," *San Juan Record*, May 4, 1939, 8.

78. See the Constitution and By-Laws of the General Council of the Assemblies of God reports from the late 1920s and early 1930s, Flower Pentecostal Heritage Center (Springfield, MO).
79. For a more complete analysis of this subject, see Chapters 6 and 7.
80. Patricia Limerick made the language of conquest famous as it relates to the history of the American West in her seminal work *The Legacy of Conquest: The Unbroken Past of the American West* (New York: W. W. Norton & Company, 1987). Religious actors also participated in this conquest to some extent, albeit perhaps in a less successful way at times. Many Pentecostals entered Utah hoping to conquer the Mormon kingdom, only to reveal a cycle of failure in Limerick's analytical principle of conquest.
81. Ronald G. Watt, *History of Carbon County* (Salt Lake City: Utah State Historical Society, 1997), 107–33.
82. Robert Smith, interview conducted by the author, October 2013. The reference is to Acts 16:9. Paul received a request to help the Christians in Macedonia. Immediately they accepted the request. Robert Smith expressed feeling called in a similar way.
83. The details concerning Robert Smith and the Valley Assembly of God come from interviews conducted by the author with Robert Smith, Phil Smith, and Alex Lucero, October 2013.
84. Peterson and Cannon, *The Awkward State of Utah*, 355. For additional analysis on the incorporation of Utah into the United States through federal spending and wartime economy, see all of Chapter 13, 316–50.
85. "Pastors Note More Interest In Religions," *Ogden Standard-Examiner*, February 7, 1943, 44.
86. "Reports from the Reapers," *The Pentecostal Evangel*, November 9, 1940, 12. See also "Assembly of God," *Salt Lake Tribune*, May 19, 1940, 13, and "Assembly of God," *Ogden Standard-Examiner*, September 14, 1940, 3.
87. "Assembly of God," *Salt Lake Tribune*, August 18, 1940, 11.
88. "Reports from the Reapers," *The Pentecostal Evangel*, November 9, 1940, 13.
89. For more detail on Ogden's nineteenth and early twentieth century religious diversity, see Richard C. Roberts and Richard W. Sadler, *A History of Weber County*, Utah Centennial County History Series (Salt Lake City: Utah State Historical Society, 1997), 157–64.
90. See "Assemblies of God Church", *Ogden Standard-Examiner*, August 19, 1933, 3; "Assemblies of God Revival," *Ogden Standard-Examiner*, September 9, 1933, 3; "Assemblies of God Revival," *Ogden Standard-Examiner*, September 16, 1933, 3; "Assemblies of God Church," *Ogden Standard-Examiner*, October 7, 1933, 3; and Benjamin H Caudle, Deceased Ministers File, Flower Pentecostal Heritage Center (Springfield, MO).
91. Ogden Application for Affiliation with the General Council of the Assemblies of God, Rocky Mountain District offices of the Assemblies of God, Colorado Springs, CO.

92. Salt Lake City Application for Affiliation with the General Council of the Assemblies of God, Rocky Mountain District offices of the Assemblies of God, Colorado Springs, CO; "Concise history of First Assembly Salt Lake," Rocky Mountain District offices of the Assemblies of God, Colorado Springs, CO; and also "Assembly of God," *Salt Lake Tribune*, May 19, 1940, 13, and "Assembly of God," *Salt Lake Tribune*, November 9, 1941, 35.
93. "Assembly of God," *Salt Lake Tribune*, January 9, 1944, 22.
94. "Assembly of God," *Ogden Standard-Examiner*, March 3, 1944, 18, and "The Assembly of God Church," *Ogden Standard-Examiner*, March 24, 1945, 8.
95. "Assembly of God Church," *Ogden Standard-Examiner*, March 27, 1943, 3.
96. "Assembly of God Church," *Ogden Standard-Examiner*, October 9, 1943, 3.
97. Dwight C. Ritchie, "The Case Against Polygamy," published by Dwight C. Ritchie, Church History Library, The Church of Jesus Christ of Latter-day Saints, Salt Lake City, UT. An analysis of Dwight C. Ritchie's writings are included in Chapter 7.
98. Leona Bryant, "Salt Lake City, Utah," *Pentecostal Evangel*, November 11, 1944, 13.
99. Angela Tarango, *Choosing the Jesus Way: American Indian Pentecostals and the Fight for the Indigenous Principle* (Chapel Hill: University of North Carolina Press, 2014), 44.
100. History provided by Max Croasmun, the son of Addie B. and Grant Croasmun, interview conducted by the author, October 2013. Addie died in a car accident in 1968. See "Tucumcari Woman, Baby Die In Traffic Accident," *Clovis News Journal*, June 25, 1968, 12.
101. Howard Ray Antes, as cited by Bob McPherson, "Howard Antes and the Navajo Faith Mission: Evangelist of Southeastern Utah," *Blue Mountain Shadows: The Magazine of San Juan County History* 17 (Summer 1996): 15.
102. For additional information on Samuel Antes, see Bob McPherson, "Howard Antes and the Navajo Faith Mission: Evangelist of Southeastern Utah," *Blue Mountain Shadows: The Magazine of San Juan County History* 17 (Summer 1996): 14–24. For his evangelistic efforts in Utah, see "Indian Evangelist to Preach Sunday at Assembly of God," *Salt Lake Telegram*, May 27, 1950, 7.
103. "Church Readies 1st Camp Meet," *Salt Lake Telegram*, August 20, 1945, 10, and "Ministers of 4 States Attend Camp Meet," *Salt Lake Telegram*, August 22, 1945, 7.
104. J. E. Austell, "First Utah State Camp Meeting," *Pentecostal Evangel*, October 6, 1945, 14. It is likely the sixth congregation not listed was the Spanish congregation in the Dragerton/Price area. A history of the Spanish AG congregations is provided in Chapter 3.
105. J. E. Austell, "First Utah State Camp Meeting," *Pentecostal Evangel*, October 6, 1945, 14.
106. Oliver McMahan, "Spiritual Direction in the Pentecostal/Charismatic Tradition," in Gary W. Moon and David G. Benner, eds., *Spiritual Direction and the Care of Souls: A Guide to Christian Approaches and Practices* (Downers Grove, IL: InterVarsity Press, 2004), 152–53.
107. Daniel E. Albrecht and Evan B. Howard, "Pentecostal Spirituality," in Cecil M. Robeck Jr. and Amos Yong, eds., *The Cambridge Companion to Pentecostalism* (New York: Cambridge University Press, 2014), 239.
108. "Assembly of God Sets State Camp Meeting," *Salt Lake Telegram*, July 5, 1946, 19; "Assembly of God Sets State-Wide Sessions in Provo," *Daily Herald*, June 3, 1948, 3; "Camp Sunday," *Salt Lake Telegram*, June 11, 1949, 7; "Camp Meeting Slated by

S. L. Church," *Salt Lake Telegram*, July 1, 1950, 7; "Camp Meeting Sets Final Talks Sunday," *Salt Lake Telegram*, July 15, 1950, 7; "Utah Assembly Sets Annual Camp Meeting," *Salt Lake Telegram*, June 30, 1951, 5; and "Camp Meeting Draws 300 to Sessions," *Salt Lake Telegram*, July 14, 1951, 5.

109. Guy M. Heath, "Salt Lake City, Utah," *Pentecostal Evangel*, March 16, 1946, 14.
110. Guy M. Heath, "Tent Meetings Continued for Five Weeks in Salt Lake City," *Pentecostal Evangel*, October 19, 1952, 16.
111. For examples of early fellowship meetings, see *Ogden Standard*, November 14, 1942, 3; "Church to be Host to State Fellowship Meet," *American Fork Citizen*, November 22, 1946, 1; "Local Church Holds Fellowship Rally," *American Fork Citizen*, March 19, 1948, 4; "Church Shares Three-Day Meet Series," *Salt Lake Telegram*, September 2, 1950, 7; "Church Services", *Pleasant Grove Review*, April 16, 1954, 4; "Assembly of God Church to Host SLC 'Teen Choir,'" *Vernal Express*, June 4, 1970, 14; and "Assemblies of God Plan Bountiful Fellowship Rally," *Davis County Clipper*, November 19, 1971, 25.
112. "This Week's Cover," *Pentecostal Evangel*, May 30, 1954, 10.
113. "This Week's Cover," 10.
114. The politics of planting churches in Utah will be covered in depth in Chapter 6.
115. Doris Karren Burton, *The History of Uintah County* (Salt Lake City: Utah County Commission, 1996), 243.
116. For further information, visit http://lcaeagle.org/welcome/.
117. See Myke Crowder, "History of First Assembly of God Layton, Utah," (M. Div., Southwestern Assemblies of God College, 1988).
118. For additional information, see http://vernalchristianchurch.com/connect/christian-seminary/.
119. For an overview of the Episcopalian schools in Utah, see Paul La Mar Martin, "A Historical Study of the Religious Education Program of the Episcopal Church in Utah," (master's thesis, Brigham Young University, 1967). Westminster College, originally founded by the Presbyterian Church, is one of the few schools from the late nineteenth century still in operation today.
120. Information taken from the "Refugees in Utah" fact sheet, April 2017, produced by the Kem C. Gardner Policy Institute, University of Utah. Available at http://gardner.utah.edu/wp-content/uploads/Refugee-Fact-Sheet-Final.pdf, accessed January 14, 2018.
121. For current information, visit http://www.saltlakechristiancenter.org/international-churches/.
122. A discussion about Latino and African American Pentecostal communities is available in Chapters 3 and 4.
123. "Religious Landscape Study," Pew Research Center, Washington, DC (2014), http://www.pewforum.org/religious-landscape-study/state/utah/, accessed December 21, 2017.
124. Elizabeth Drescher, *Choosing Our Religion: The Spiritual Lives of America's Nones* (New York: Oxford University Press, 2016), 9.
125. Under the category "Who Are You Trying to Reach?" available at https://www.k2thechurch.com/check-us-out/, accessed October 19, 2018.
126. Available at https://alpinechurch.org/, accessed October 19, 2018.

127. While the Genesis Project is not an affiliated Assemblies of God church, its campus in Provo retains some affiliation with the Assemblies of God.
128. Greg Johnson's organization focuses on Evangelicals and Latter-day Saints in dialogue. Within the purview of Evangelicalism, many Pentecostals have also participated in these events, sometimes even holding the events at their churches.
129. For additional information about Standing Together, visit http://standingtogether.org/. Politics and interfaith dialogue will be discussed in greater detail in Chapters 6 and 7.
130. Notes from the author, Alan J. Clark, who attended the installation of Dan Gilboy, January 14, 2018, Canyon Road Assembly of God, 1390 Canyon Road, Ogden UT 84404-6021.
131. "Religious Landscape Study," Pew Research Center, Washington, DC (2014), http://www.pewforum.org/religious-landscape-study/state/utah/, accessed December 21, 2017.

CHAPTER 2: UNDERNEATH THE RADAR

1. "Former Ogden Rescue Mission Leader Dies," *Ogden Standard-Examiner,* February 8, 1974, 22.
2. "Youth Evangelist," *Ogden Standard-Examiner,* September 25, 1949, 7, and "Full Gospel Assembly," *Ogden Standard-Examiner,* October 16, 1949, 4. Forrest Stinson would later appear in the Assemblies of God directory of licensed ministers in the early 1960s. See "Ministers Directory General Council," 1961, Flower Pentecostal heritage Center (Springfield, MO). He held credentials with the International Church of the Foursquare Gospel, however, near the end of his life. See Reverend Forrest Stinson Assembly of God Church Guest," *Vernal Express,* June 14, 1973, 12.
3. *Ogden Standard-Examiner,* February 12, 1953, 13, and "Pentecostal Church of God," *Ogden Standard-Examiner,* May 9, 1953, 3.
4. "Moments with the Master," *Ogden Standard-Examiner,* March 29, 1958, 3.
5. "Gospel Rites to Feature Bible Charts," *Ogden Standard-Examiner,* April 8, 1961, 3.
6. "Observance Points Up Rescue Mission Work," *Ogden Standard-Examiner,* October 2, 1972, 17. The article points out the relationship between the Ogden Rescue Mission and the International Union of Gospel Missions.
7. "Ogden Rescue Mission Will Host Open House For Public on Sunday," *Ogden Standard-Examiner,* November 4, 1967, 10.
8. "Rescue Mission Aims To Aid Area Families," *Ogden Standard-Examiner,* August 14, 1969, 14.
9. ". . . Mercy Mission Aids," *Hill Top Times,* September 5, 1969, 30, and "Air Force Association Starts '70 Version of 'Project Navajo,'" *Ogden Standard-Examiner,* November 16, 1970, 17.
10. "Thanksgiving Dinner," *Ogden Standard-Examiner,* November 22, 1969, 10.
11. "Rescue Mission Leader Ends 7 Years of Duties," *Ogden Standard-Examiner,* December 15, 1973, 3.
12. "Winning Souls Main Goal of Local Mission," *Ogden Standard-Examiner,* January 22, 1972, 8.

13. "Assembly of God Gets New Pastor, Rev. David Stinson," *Vernal Express*, December 25, 1969, 11.
14. "Local Woman To Translate Bible Works," *Ogden Standard-Examiner*, June 17, 1972, 10.
15. Grant Wacker, *Heaven Below: Early Pentecostals and American Culture* (Cambridge, MA: Harvard University Press, 2001), 10.
16. Gastón Espinosa, *William J. Seymour and the Origins of Global Pentecostalism: A Biography and Documentary History* (Durham, NC: Duke University Press, 2014), 31.
17. The church is known as the Church of God, Cleveland, because of the many different churches with a similar name. The most complete history is Charles W. Conn, *Like A Mighty Army: A History of the Church of God, 1886–1996* (Cleveland, TN: Pathway Press, 1996). See also Mickey Crews, *The Church of God: A Social History* (Knoxville: University of Tennessee Press, 1990), and Wade H. Phillips, *Quest to Restore God's House—A Theological History of the Church of God Volume 1* (Cleveland, TN: CPT Press, 2015).
18. For a conversation about their early engagement with Latter-day Saints, see Chapter 7, which discusses interfaith relations between Pentecostals and Latter-day Saints in Utah.
19. "Every Foot of Ground Must be Covered by Our Workers," *The Church of God Evangel*, March 19, 1921, 1.
20. "Every Foot of Ground Must be Covered by Our Workers," *The Church of God Evangel*, March 19, 1921, 1.
21. A. J. Tomlinson, editorial, *Church of God Evangel*, June 4, 1921, 2.
22. Tracking historical congregations with the name "Church of God" can be troublesome due to the various organizations that have used the name over the years. It is important to distinguish the *Church of God*, located in Cleveland, Tennessee. There was a Church of God congregation established in Salt Lake City in 1925 by R. E. Schmidt and Otto Doebert. Located at 803 West 100 South, this congregation remained for several decades. According to the survey done by the Works Progress Administration, however, this church was affiliated with the Church of God located in Anderson, Indiana. They are a Holiness church. See "Inventory of the Church Archives of Utah: Volume 3 Smaller Denominations," Salt Lake City: Utah Historical Records Survey, 1940–1941, 7. Utah State History Research Center, PAM1489.
23. Loretta Boyd and Grace Hall, "Great Victory In Summit Point, Utah," *Church of God Evangel*, December 7, 1929, 1.
24. Grace Hall, "Pray For The Gospel Light To Shine In Utah," *Church of God Evangel*, February 21, 1931, 2.
25. Jess W. Kinsey, "Future Prospects Looking Good For Church In Utah," *Church of God Evangel*, February 7, 1931, 3.
26. S. W. Latimer, "Notices & Specials," *Church of God Evangel*, February 21, 1931, 1. Simmons would be followed by J. H. Ingram (1933), John E. Douglas (1934–1937), S. J. Wood (1938–1939), H. E. Ramsey (1940–1942), D. A. Biggs (1943–1944), R. C. Muncy (1945–1947), and W. J. Cohen (1948–1951). List courtesy of the Dixon Pentecostal Research Center, Cleveland, TN.

27. *Minutes of the Twenty-Fifth Annual Assembly*, Church of God (Cleveland, TN: Church of God Publishing House, 1930), 32. Located at the Dixon Pentecostal Research Center, Cleveland, TN.
28. E. L. Moore, "Notices & Specials," *Church of God Evangel*, July 4, 1931, 2.
29. Elizabeth Summers, cited in Harold George and Fay Lunceford Muhlestein, *Monticello Journal: A History of Monticello until 1937* (Monticello, UT: Harold George and Fay Lunceford Muhlestein, 1988), 197.
30. E. L. Simmons, "Church Growing In Utah," *Church of God Evangel*, January 23, 1932, 3.
31. "Church of God Adds Several Members," *San Juan Record*, May 26, 1938, 16.
32. Frank Silvey, "Written for the Historical Survey of San Juan County, Utah, Frank Silvey, July 6, 1936, Monticello, Utah," Salt Lake City, Utah State History Research Center, MSSB57, Box 188, folder 4.
33. For more about the Gallegos family and the Assemblies of God in Monticello, see Chapter 3.
34. Grace Hall, Loretta Boyd, Ethel Perry, and Elizabeth Prickett probably made up what Frank Silvey referred to as the "Big Four" who led the Church of God in San Juan County. Frank Silvey, "Written for the Historical Survey of San Juan County, Utah, Frank Silvey, July 6, 1936, Monticello, Utah."
35. There are many brief articles and mentions of the comings and goings, revivals, and services made mention throughout the 1930s in the *San Juan Record*. They are often quite short, but it is a very helpful source of information on early Church of God activities.
36. S. J. Wood, "Church of God to Hold Revival Services," *San Juan Record*, May 19, 1938, 16, and "Local News," *San Juan Record*, May 26, 1938, 16.
37. "Church of God Adds Several Members," *San Juan Record*, May 26, 1938, 16.
38. "Local News," *San Juan Record*, July 14, 1938, 20.
39. "Bible Contest to Be Held," *San Juan Record*, December 7, 1939, 8, and "Local News," *San Juan Record*, January 4, 1940, 16.
40. Mary V. Brumley, "Northdale," *San Juan Record*, December 12, 1940, 8.
41. J. H. Walker, "Notes From My Letters . . . ," *Church of God Evangel*, June 20, 1942, 9. See also Grace Hall, "Summit Point," *San Juan Record*, May 21, 1942, 5.
42. H. E. Ramsey, "Greetings from Utah," *Church of God Evangel*, July 4, 1942, 16.
43. Ethel M. Perry, "Eyes Set in Death—Instantly Healed," *Church of God Evangel*, June 30, 1945, 13.
44. John C. Jernigan, "The General Overseer Speaks," *Church of God Evangel*, October 7, 1944, 3.
45. H. L. Chesser, "Assistant General Overseer's Convention Work," *Church of God Evangel*, August 28, 1948, 4.
46. James B. Allen and Jesse Bushman make note of a few congregations in James B. Allen, *Still the Right Place: Utah's Second Half-Century of Statehood, 1945–1995* (Provo, UT: Charles Redd Center for Western Studies and the Utah State Historical Society, 2016), 584–85. The data comes from various church directories of the 1980s and 1990s.
47. This inference comes from interviews and conversations with long time members of Pentecostal churches around Utah. Many individuals attended Pentecostal

congregations of various denominations because they were limited in options where they lived.

48. Current congregations available at https://churchofgod.org/church-locator/.
49. "'Four-Square' Temple Ready," *Salt Lake Telegram*, January 8, 1923, 3. There is one possible reference to an earlier ICFG church in Utah. A church directory from 1938 suggests there was a "Four Square" church at 554 South State Street in Salt Lake City. The pastor is listed as unknown. I have not been able to uncover any additional information about this church or mission. It may very well be the first attempt at planting an ICFG church in the state, but there are no details beyond a date and an address. See *Directory of Churches and Religious Organizations in Utah (Not Including the Church of Jesus Christ of Latter-day Saints)*, (Ogden, UT: Historical Records Survey of the Works Progress Administration, 1938), 12.
50. Matthew Avery Sutton, *Aimee Semple McPherson and the Resurrection of Christian America* (Cambridge, MA: Harvard University Press, 2007), 49.
51. For Sutton's complete argument concerning McPherson's influence on American Pentecostalism and Evangelicalism, see Sutton, *Aimee Semple McPherson and the Resurrection of Christian America*, 277–80.
52. Peter J. Scarlet, "Fraternal Organization Is Host for New Church in Granger," *Salt Lake Tribune*, April 24, 1976, 13.
53. James B. Allen, *Still the Right Place: Utah's Second Half-Century of Statehood, 1945–1995*, 584.
54. Membership statistics are available at https://www.foursquare.org/about/stats, accessed May 8, 2018.
55. Information collected through Pete Akins, personal interview, July 23, 2013.
56. Quote taken from the mission statement on their website, http://www.ccfutah.org/home/who/about/, accessed on May 8, 2018. Additional information about the North Park Foursquare Church and the Crossroads Christian Fellowship are based on visits to the churches and conversations with the pastors, April 2018.
57. The data and analysis in this paragraph come from personal conversations with pastors and congregation members, and visits to church services.
58. Larry Martin, *We've Come This Far By Faith: Readings on the Early Leaders of the Pentecostal Church of God* (Pensacola, FL: Christian Life Books, 2009), 14–15.
59. National statistics taken from "Transformation Proposal 2015," *Pentecostal Messenger*, Spring 2015, 24, available at http://docs.wixstatic.com/ugd/18e4e6_8e0317bcacd94d64b061c1beae251ecc.pdf, accessed June 19, 2018. Utah statistics are estimated through interviews with pastors and church visits.
60. "Field Representatives," *Pentecostal Herald*, March 1917, 2.
61. For more on Robert H. Lowe, see Chapter 1. It is not entirely certain that Robert Lowe is the same individual listed in the *Pentecostal Herald*, but the Pentecostal community in Salt Lake during this period is quite small, and it is very likely that they are the same individual.
62. Larry Martin, *We've Come This Far By Faith*, 24.
63. "Pentecostal Church of God," *Salt Lake Telegram*, January 3, 1920, 5.
64. "Series for Pastors," *Salt Lake Tribune*, March 3, 1951, 31. See also "Churches Ready Services To Usher In New Year," *Salt Lake Telegram*, December 30, 1950, 12. Another Pentecostal church, called the Full Gospel Assembly, previously met at 517 South 200 East

in Salt Lake City. They are discussed below. It is likely that the Pentecostal Church of God rented or purchased the building from the Full Gospel Assembly.

65. "Revival Meets to End," *Salt Lake Tribune*, October 20, 1949, 28.
66. For a later reference to this church, see *Polk's Salt Lake City Directory* (Salt Lake City: R. L. Polk & Co., 1953), 196. Identifying denominational ties to specific churches can be complicated at times. The Pentecostal Church of God was occasionally advertised as the "Church of God (Pentecostal)." In other cases, the Church of God referred to the Pentecostal denomination based out of Cleveland, discussed earlier in this chapter. At other times, the Church of God referred to non-Pentecostal churches, such as the Church of God based in Anderson, Indiana. As early as 1925, Pastor Otto Doebert organized a Church of God located at 803 West 100 South, Salt Lake City. This congregation persisted through the 1940s, and then ads with the same address began appearing for the "Church of God, Pentecostal," pastored by Charles F. Keener. See *Salt Lake Tribune*, December 7, 1947, 26. With little more than newspapers and WPA records, it is complicated to differentiate between advertisements for the various churches that use "Church of God" in their title. For additional information on Doebert's denomination, see "Inventory of the Church Archives of Utah: Smaller Denominations," Volume 3, Utah Historical Records Survey, prepared by the Utah Historical Records Survey Division of Professional and Service Projects, Works Progress Administration, Ogden, Utah, February 1941, available at the Utah State Historic Research Center (Salt Lake City), PAM 1489.
67. "Listen To The Gospel Hour," *Helper Journal*, March 28, 1946, 5. J. R. Green, pastor for the Church of God in Christ in Helper, and Lee Francis, pastor for the Assemblies of God in Price, also participated in "The Gospel Hour" radio program.
68. The congregation still functions as of 2018. It is the only remaining Pentecostal church in East Carbon, Utah. The city was renamed East Carbon after a series of mergers between the cities of Dragerton, Columbia, and Sunnyside. Michael Cowan pastors the Calvary Faith Pentecostal Church of God at the present.
69. "Revival Service," *Ogden Standard-Examiner*, March 20, 1951, 11.
70. "Death Takes Pentecostal Pastor, 61," *Ogden Standard-Examiner*, November 29, 1970, 24.
71. For Leo Waggoner's church, see "Full Gospel Tabernacle, Pentecostal Church of God," *Ogden Standard-Examiner*, September 4, 1954, 3. For the Sunset Church, see "Pentecostal Church of God," *Ogden Standard-Examiner*, May 21, 1955, 3. For the Pentecostal Church of God in Salt Lake, see *Polk's Salt Lake City Directory* (Salt Lake City: R. L. Polk & Co., 1955), 834.
72. "Spanish Pentecostal Church of God," *Ogden Standard-Examiner*, April 9, 1955, 2; and "Revival Center Opened on 25th," *Ogden Standard-Examiner*, July 14, 1956, 1.
73. "Continue Rally," *Salt Lake Tribune*, May 11, 1963, 14, and "Pentecostal Church of God," *Salt Lake Tribune*, February 15, 1975, 5.
74. Information provided through interviews with Harley Boyles, January, 2018, and Ed Jones, April, 2018, interview notes in my possession.
75. David A. Reed, *"In Jesus' Name": The History and Beliefs of Oneness Pentecostals* (Dorset, UK: Deo Publishing, 2008), 165. Oneness theology is similar to the Modalism or Sabellianism that existed in early Christianity and Eastern Christianity respectively.

76. For more on these theological developments and the history of Oneness Pentecostalism, see David A. Reed, *"In Jesus' Name": The History and Beliefs of Oneness Pentecostals* (Dorset, UK: Deo Publishing, 2008), Chapters 4 and 6. See also Donald W. Dayton, *Theological Roots of Pentecostalism* (Grand Rapids, MI: Baker Academic, 1987), 18–21.
77. For more on the history of G. T. Haywood, see Talmadge L. French, *Early Interracial Oneness Pentecostalism: G. T. Haywood and the Pentecostal Assemblies of the World* (Eugene, OR: Pickwick Publications, 2014).
78. David A. Reed, *"In Jesus' Name": The History and Beliefs of Oneness Pentecostals* (Dorset, UK: Deo Publishing, 2008), 207–21. There are no PAW churches in Utah at present.
79. Ivan Johnson, interview, July 26, 2013, interview notes in my possession. Pastor Johnson could not recall Pastor Covey's first name. Another UPC church existed in the mid-1950s in Ogden on Lake Street. It was pastored by the Reverend J. Paul Thomas. I have not, however, been able to find many details about the church. It operated during the late 1950s and early 1960s, according to Bishop Tommy Vigil of the Apostolic Assembly. Tommy Vigil, interview, December 21, 2018, interview notes in my possession.
80. Information provided through interviews with John Russell, July 17, 2013, Ivan Johnson, July 26, 2013, and William Fitzgerel, July 25, 2013, interview notes in my possession.
81. See ads for the congregation in the "Church News," *Times Independent*, during the late 1960s.
82. Information provided through interviews with Ivan Johnson, July 26, 2013, and Erik Johnson, July 31, 2013, interview notes in my possession.
83. "'Ripe Harvest' In Utah," *Outreach* IV (1969): 6, available at the Center for the Study of Oneness Pentecostalism, Urshan College (Florissant, MO). *Outreach* is the magazine for the UPCI Home Missions.
84. J. T. Pugh, "New Church is opened in Salt Lake City, Utah," *Outreach* VIII, no. 8 (November 1973): 3, available at the Center for the Study of Oneness Pentecostalism, Urshan College (Florissant, MO).
85. The Landmark Apostolic Church in West Valley, presently pastored by Daniel Gill, is likely the oldest continuously operating UPC church in Utah.
86. Information provided through interviews with Eugene Guerrero, July 29, 2018, and Ronald Rice, March 8, 2017, interview notes in my possession. Eugene Guerrero currently pastors the New Life Center in West Valley, Utah, and Ronald Rice currently pastors the Pentecostals of Salt Lake in Salt Lake City, Utah.
87. Helen Papanikolas wrote many books and articles on the topic. One of her best-known collections is *The Peoples of Utah*, edited by Helen Papanikolas (Salt Lake City: Utah State Historical Society, 1981). For additional information on the Hellenic community in Salt Lake, see Constantine J. Skedros, *100 Years of Faith and Fervor: A History of the Greek Orthodox Church Community of Greater Salt Lake City, Utah 1905–2005* (Salt Lake City, UT: Greek Orthodox Church of Greater Salt Lake, 2005).
88. "Open Meeting Approved," *Salt Lake Tribune*, April 26, 1946, 8, and "Greek Minister, 62, Succumbs," *Salt Lake Telegram*, July 9, 1947, 15. Unfortunately very

little other information survives concerning the origins of the congregation and its founding minister.

89. There are a handful of advertisements in the *Salt Lake Telegram* from the 1920s for a church called the Full Gospel Assembly. Pastor Constantine A. Nicholas is attached to a few of these, as well as a Pastor named W. McGhehey. They are probably separate churches. McGhehey's ads appear briefly in 1926, while articles about Nicholas's church would continue until his death. Leah Larratt McDermott is also recognized as a long-time member and assistant pastor for the Full Gospel Assembly in her obituary, "Leah Larratt McDermott," *Salt Lake Tribune*, June 6, 1939, 5.
90. "Full Gospel Assembly," *Salt Lake Tribune*, November 26, 1966, 19, and "Full Gospel Church Emphasizes Spirit," *Salt Lake Tribune*, July 13, 1968, 10.
91. Information available in records of the "National Register of Historic Places Registration Form" for the building at 1840 East 800 South, Salt Lake City, Utah. Documentation is available at npgallery.nps.gov. Search for "Adventist" historic sites in the state of Utah, accessed July 16, 2018. The historical summary for the structure at 1840 South 800 East appears to have some errors in it concerning the time period that the building is owned by the Full Gospel Assembly. It is noted in this source, however, that the Full Gospel Assembly sold the building in 1993 and moved to a location in West Valley after the sale.
92. The information is a little conflicting concerning its original affiliation. In "Inventory of the Church Archives of Utah: Volume 3 Smaller Denominations," (Salt Lake City: Utah Historical Records Survey, 1940–1941), 53, Utah State History Research Center, PAM1489. This source states that the Full Gospel Assembly is affiliated with the Pentecostal Assemblies of the World. However, in the original interview form filled out by the WPA for this publication, the affiliation listed is the Hellenic Protogonos Apostolic Ecclesia. See the WPA Form 20HR completed for the Full Gospel Assembly, Works Progress Administration collection, Mss B 57, Box 192 Folder 8, Utah State History Research Center, Salt Lake City, UT. There is no explanation for the discrepancy from the original form to the printed collection. It may be that when Constantine A. Nicholas immigrated to the United States, he received his ministerial license from the Pentecostal Assemblies of the World. Yet given the ethnic makeup of the congregation, the theological differences between the Pentecostal Assemblies of the World and the Assemblies of God, and the content of the original form, it makes much more sense for the congregation to be associated with the Hellenic Protogonos Apostolic Ecclesia.
93. "Religious Rites to Dedicate New Year," *Salt Lake Telegram*, December 29, 1951, 6. The Full Gospel Assembly met with six Assemblies of God congregations, as well as the Spanish-speaking Assembly of God church of Salt Lake City, to celebrate New Year's Eve.
94. Darrin Rodgers, "Speaking in Tongues: The Proliferation of Assemblies of God Language Branches Among Immigrants in the 1940s and 1950s," as part of the Flower Pentecostal Heritage Center blog, November 11, 2014, available at https://ifphc.wordpress.com/2014/11/11/speaking-in-tongues-the-proliferation-of-assemblies-of-god-language-branches-among-immigrants-in-the-1940s-and-1950s/, accessed July 17, 2018.
95. "Full Gospel Church Emphasizes Spirit," *Salt Lake Tribune*, July 13, 1968, 10.

96. It is not entirely clear when the congregation ceased holding Sunday meetings. It would have been the longest continuously operating Pentecostal congregation if it were still organized, because the Assembly of God congregation organized in 1916 temporarily shuttered at times during the 1920s and 1930s. The author is not familiar with the exact reasons for the closure of the Full Gospel Assembly, nor where its final meetinghouse was located.
97. Teri Orr, "Strike a Vein: Unseen Forces at Work," *Park Record,* October 22, 1992, 14.
98. "Pentecostal Preacher Busy Following God's Message to 'Go Seek Souls,'" *Deseret News,* July 2, 1988. See also "Death: Dr. Rosemary 'Redmon' Cosby," *Deseret News,* January 9, 1997, available at deseretnews.com, accessed July 24, 2018.
99. "Death: Dr. Rosemary 'Redmon' Cosby." For more information on the Faith Temple Pentecostal church, see http://tletsinger2.wixsite.com/website.
100. Information concerning the First Apostolic Church and the Gospel Tabernacle come from interviews. Interview with William Fitzgerel, July 25, 2013. Interview with Erik Johnson, July 31, 2013.
101. Margaret M. Poloma and John C. Green, *The Assemblies of God: Godly Love and the Revitalization of American Pentecostalism* (New York: New York University Press, 2010), 204–5.
102. For more specific data on religious populations in Utah, see the Introduction and Chapter 1. The statistics here are estimated from various sources including Richard D. Poll, general ed., *Utah's History* (Logan: Utah State University, 1989), 692–3; Nils Bloch-Hoell, *The Pentecostal Movement: Its Origin, Development, and Distinctive Character* (New York: Humanities Press, 1964), 57; and the "Religious Landscape Study," Pew Research Center, Washington, DC (2014), http://www.pewforum.org/religious-landscape-study/state/utah/, accessed on December 21, 2017. While the growth among Utah Pentecostals identified here is marginal, almost all other churches in the state of Utah have experienced decline in membership, making sustained growth more significant overall.

CHAPTER 3: STRUGGLING ON THE FRINGES

1. Guy M. Heath, "Salt Lake City, Utah," *Pentecostal Evangel,* January 21, 1950, 14.
2. Néstor Bazán, "Dragerton, Utah," *La Luz Apostólica,* August 1949, 11. For this and all following Spanish quotations, I have translated the text into English. In the footnotes, I will provide the Spanish text, as well as the citation. "El culto por la noche fué un culto Pentecostal. Había más de 300 almas en esta occasion, de tal manera cayó el poder de Dios que nuestro hermano Joaquin no pudo predicar."
3. See Chapter 4 for more information on African American Pentecostalism in Utah.
4. According to Robert P. Jones and Daniel Cox, *America's Changing Religious Identity,* Public Religion Research Institute, released on September 6, 2017, available at https://www.prri.org/research/american-religious-landscape-christian-religiously-unaffiliated/. For a more nuanced study of the data, see Robert P. Jones, *The End of White Christian America* (New York: Simon & Schuster, 2016).
5. Néstor Bazán, "Dragerton, Utah," *La Luz Apostólica,* August 1949, 11. "Thus far Jehovah has helped us."

6. For the ancestral history, see Armando Solórzano, *We Remember, We Celebrate, We Believe: Recuerdo, Celebración, y Esperanza: Latinos in Utah* (Salt Lake City: University of Utah Press, 2014).
7. Paul Morgan and Vincent Mayer, "The Spanish-Speaking Population of Utah: From 1900 to 1935," in *Working Papers Toward a History of the Spanish-Speaking Peoples of Utah*, ed. Vincent Mayer (Salt Lake City, UT: American West Center, Mexican American Documentation Project, University of Utah, 1973), 17–32. See also Jorge Iber, *Hispanics in the Mormon Zion, 1912–1999* (College Station: Texas A&M University Press, 2000), 7.
8. Pamela S. Perlich, "Utah Minorities: The Story Told by 150 Years of Census Data," published by the Bureau of Economic and Business Research, David S. Eccles School of Business, University of Utah, October 2002, available at http://gardner.utah.edu/bebr/Documents/studies/Utah_Minorities.pdf, accessed February 1, 2018; Armando Solórzano, "The Making of Latino Families in Utah," in *Beehive History* 25 (1999): 18–21; and Lee Davidson, "Census: Utah's Latino population grows to more than 400,000," *Salt Lake Tribune*, June 23, 2016, available at http://archive.sltrib.com/article.php?id=4035282&itype=CMSID, accessed February 1, 2018. See also Emily Harris, "First Insights—2020 Census Race and Hispanic or Latino Origin in Utah," published by the Kem C. Gardner Policy Institute, David Eccles School of Business, University of Utah, August 2021, available at https://gardner.utah.edu/wp-content/uploads/C2020-RceEth-FS-Aug2021.pdf?x71849, accessed March 2, 2022.
9. Gastón Espinosa, *Latino Pentecostals in America: Faith and Politics in Action* (Cambridge, MA: Harvard University Press, 2014), 51–53.
10. Espinosa, *Latino Pentecostals in America*, 83–108. Chapter 3 tells the story of the integration of these congregations into the structure of the Assemblies of God. Chapter 4 includes the origins of Latino AG congregations around the southwest, with the exception of Utah.
11. See Mrs. H. E. Blake, "Narcizo Gallegos Called by Reaper," *San Juan Record*, November 23, 1944, 1; and William H. González and Genaro M. Padilla, "Monticello, the Hispanic Cultural Gateway to Utah," in John S. McCormick and John R. Sillito, eds., *A World We Thought We Knew: Readings in Utah History* (Salt Lake City: University of Utah Press, 1995): 228. Several of the Gallegos children did not live to adulthood.
12. José Facundo Marez, "Testifica un Veterano," *La Luz Apostólica*, December 1966, 7.
13. A. T. Salazar, "Historia," *La Luz Apostólica*, June 1969, 11. "Los actos de adoración eran acompañados por el poder de Dios y pronto hubo resultados. La hermana Romana Gallegos y sus hijos, y abrieron sus puertas para que otros también en Monticello aceptasen a Cristo y Su grande salvación."
14. For some brief, additional information on religion in Monticello, see Robert S. McPherson, *A History of San Juan County: In the Palm of Time* (Salt Lake City: Utah State Historical Society, 1995), 300–305.
15. "Local News," *San Juan Record*, October 12, 1939, 13; "News Items," *San Juan Record*, December 3, 1942, 8; and "News Items," *San Juan Record*, July 29, 1943, 8.
16. "Local Happenings," *San Juan Record*, January 31, 1935, 5.
17. "Local News," *San Juan Record*, June 2, 1938, 16.

18. "Assembly of God," *San Juan Record*, July 14, 1938, 20.
19. Simón R. Franco, "Embajadores de Cristo," *La Luz Apostólica*, April 1937, 7.
20. "Local Happenings," *San Juan Record*, August 20, 1936, 5. The Hall and Perry families held meetings under the name of the Church of God in the home of the Enriquez family. This may have been the family of Vidal Enriquez, who would shortly become a pastor for the Assemblies of God.
21. "'Assembly of God' Holds Revival Meets," *San Juan Record*, June 2, 1938, 13.
22. Jorge Iber, *Hispanics in the Mormon Zion*, 40–41. See also Charles L. Peterson and Brian Q. Cannon, *The Awkward State of Utah: Coming of Age in the Nation 1896–1945* (Salt Lake City: University of Utah Press, 2015), Chapter 11.
23. Daniel Ramírez, *Migrating Faith: Pentecostalism in the United States and Mexico in the Twentieth Century* (Chapel Hill: University of North Carolina Press, 2015), 86.
24. For examples, see "3 Aliens on Way To Be Deported," *Salt Lake Telegram*, January 27, 1932, 16; "Man Will Face Fifth Deportation Action," *Salt Lake Telegram*, September 26, 1933, 12; "Aliens on Way Home After Terms in Cells," *Salt Lake Telegram*, March 15, 1935, 16; and "Returned Deportee Arrested in Ogden," *Salt Lake Telegram*, January 6, 1937, 10.
25. A. T. Salazar, "Historia," *La Luz Apostólica*, July 1969, 7. "En la iglesia de Monticello, Utah, ese mismo año, Bonifacio Hernández sequia al frente como pastor de la nueva grey [sic] y un joven con el nombre de Vidal Enriquez hacía su consagración para ir a esos lugares." Vidal's name is often misspelled in English periodicals. It comes up as Bidol or Bidal fairly often.
26. Vidal Enriquez, Deceased Ministers File, Flower Pentecostal Heritage Center (Springfield, MO); and also *La Luz Apostólica*, September 1940, 16.
27. According to Mike Archuleta, phone interview completed by the author, June 2015.
28. *Salt Lake Tribune*, May 19, 1940, 13. James Summerton and E. F. Chopper arrived in Salt Lake in 1940 with plans to restart a congregation. See Chapter 1 for more details.
29. Vidal Enriquez, "Salt Lake City, Utah," *La Luz Apostólica*, February 1942, 7. "Un verdadero triunfo para la obra."
30. Vidal Enriquez, "Salt Lake City, Utah," *La Luz Apostólica*, May 1942, 13. "Tenemos dos años de estar aquí trabajando en esta ciudad. El primer año no vimos ningunos resultados alentadores."
31. Jorge Iber, *Hispanics in the Mormon Zion*, 15, 17. Iber uses the term *Hispanic*, whereas I have chosen to use the term *Latino*. I understand them interchangeably in the sense used here.
32. Jorge Iber, *Hispanics in the Mormon Zion*, 134.
33. Joseph Elmer Allen, "A Sociological Study of Mexican Assimilation in Salt Lake City," (master's thesis, University of Utah, 1947), 48.
34. Gastón Espinosa, *Latino Pentecostals in America*, 147–51.
35. Allen, "A Sociological Study of Mexican Assimilation in Salt Lake City," 69.
36. For additional information on Mexican Latter-day Saint history, see Jason H. Dormady and Jared M. Tamez, eds., *Just South of Zion: The Mormons in Mexico and Its Borderlands* (Albuquerque: University of New Mexico Press, 2015), and Elisa Eastwood Pulido, *The Spiritual Evolution of Margarito Bautista* (New York: Oxford University Press, 2020).

37. Vidal Enriquez, "Salt Lake City, Utah," *La Luz Apostólica,* May 1942, 13.
38. José Marez, "Conferencia del Oeste de Colorado," *La Luz Apostólica,* March 1943, 8.
39. Demetrio Bazán, "Concilio de Distrito," *La Luz Apostólica,* January 1946, 7. "La obra en la capital mormona promote mucho."
40. Eugenio Girón, "Dragerton, Utah," *La Luz Apostólica,* July 1945, 8.
41. Fidel Martínez, "Una Gloriosa Junta de Confraternidad," *La Luz Apostólica,* February 1947, 11. "Desde luego la atmósfera fué liviana y gloriosa en medio de la congregación, y hubo preciosas y singulares manifestaciones del poder del Epíritu Santo entre nosotros. Mientras estuvimos bajo las olas de bendiciones de lo alto unos lloraban, otros bailaban en el Espíritu, otros oraban y aún otros gritaban del gozo celestial que embargaba sus corazones."
42. Néstor Bazán, Deceased Ministers File, Flower Pentecostal Heritage Center (Springfield, MO); and Néstor Bazán, "Nota Necrológica," *La Luz Apostólica,* November 1948, 6. Demetrio Bazán, Néstor's father, was the superintendent of the AG Latin District from 1939 to 1958. Bazán was the first Latino to hold the position.
43. Ronald G. Watt, *A History of Carbon County,* Utah Centennial County History Series (Salt Lake City: Utah State Historical Society, 1997), 122–24.
44. Néstor Bazán, "Dragerton, Utah," *La Luz Apostólica,* April 1949, 7.
45. Alberto Medina, "Price, Utah," *La Luz Apostólica,* May 1950, 10. "No había ni obra ni iglesia aqui." And "y cada domingo nuestro número pasa de cien . . . 104, 108, y hasta 120, en asistencia."
46. *Ogden Standard-Examiner,* March 27, 1943, 3.
47. Interview with Inez Perea, Becky Cazares, and Virginia Vigil, conducted by the author, July 2015.
48. Of the pastors and long-time Pentecostal Utah residents, almost all agreed that very rarely did the English and Spanish congregations interact. They most often asserted the language barrier as a probable cause for the dissociation.
49. While it is true that the English-speaking AG congregations also sacrificed their time and finances, they received support from AG headquarters that the Spanish congregations did not.
50. "In the name of Christ Jesus." In reference to the belief in the Oneness of Jesus Christ, observed by the Apostolic Assembly of the Faith in Christ Jesus.
51. Originating first in Spanish, the denomination is now recognized as the Asamblea Apostólica de la Fe en Cristo Jesús in Spanish, and as the Apostolic Assembly of the Faith in Christ Jesus in English.
52. Ismael Martín Del Campo, ed., *The First Sixty Years of the Apostolic Assembly: 1906–1966* (Rancho Cucamonga, CA: Apostolic Assembly of the Faith in Christ Jesus, 2014), 22.
53. For additional information, see *The First Sixty Years of the Apostolic Assembly: 1906–1966,* and Daniel Ramírez, *Migrating Faith: Pentecostalism in the United States and Mexico in the Twentieth Century* (Chapel Hill: University of North Carolina Press, 2015), 33–81.
54. Information provided through an interview with Tommy Vigil, December 21, 2018, interview notes in my possession.

55. Jamie Buckingham, "The Return of the Heresy Hunters," *Charisma and Christian Life*, January 1988, 82. In the article, Buckingham discusses how the fundamentalist Christian magazine *Moody Monthly* included the United Pentecostal Church on the list of suspect religious organizations, alongside Latter-day Saints and Jehovah's Witnesses.
56. Elena Martinez, as cited by Allen, ""A Sociological Study of Mexican Assimilation in Salt Lake City," 109.
57. Jorge Iber, *Hispanics in the Mormon Zion, 1912–1999* (College Station: Texas A&M University Press, 2000), 86.
58. For additional information, see Armando Solórzano, *We Remember, We Celebrate, We Believe: Latinos in Utah* (Salt Lake City: University of Utah Press, 2014), 145–51; and Jorge Iber, *Hispanics in the Mormon Zion, 1912–1999* (College Station: Texas A&M University Press, 2000), 85–114.
59. David Velasquez. Information provided through an interview with David Velasquez, March 22, 2019, interview notes in my possession.
60. David's daughter Jaci Velasquez would become nationally recognized for her singing and acting. For more information, see www.jacivelasquez.com.
61. David Velasquez, interview, March 22, 2019.
62. Information provided through an interview with Tommy Vigil, December 21, 2018, interview notes in my possession.
63. Pastor Cazares mentioned that the Church of Jesus Christ of Latter-day Saints also offered a small amount of monetary assistance for the construction of their new building. Roy Cazares, interview with the author, May 2018.
64. For demographic data, see Armando Solórzano, *We Remember, We Celebrate, We Believe: Latinos in Utah* (Salt Lake City: University of Utah Press, 2014), 207–9. The information concerning the history of the Spanish Assemblies of God and returning to Spanish worship services comes from Roy Cazares in an interview with the author, May 2018.
65. The Pentecostal Church of God and the Church of God Cleveland have also offered services in Spanish or maintained Latino congregations at different times. As of 2020, the Church of God had eight Spanish congregations. More research needs to be done to follow the rapid growth more closely among Latino Pentecostals in Utah.
66. Roy Cazares, interview with the author, May 2018.

CHAPTER 4: "TAKING US HIGHER"

1. Henry McAllister, "Soldier's Story," originally published in *The Whole Truth*, November 1985, reprinted in "Obsequies of Superintendent Emeritus David F. Griffin," 1989, on the occasion of David F. Griffin's funeral.
2. Recollection of the event provided by the Reverend France A. Davis, pastor emeritus of the Calvary Baptist Church, Salt Lake City, Utah, interview conducted by the author, February 22, 2020.
3. Ronald G. Coleman, "Blacks in Utah History: An Unknown Legacy," in *The Peoples of Utah*, ed. Helen Z. Papanikolas (Salt Lake City: Utah State Historical Society,

1976), 117. Coleman notes that the 1850 Territorial census probably came up short on the total number of slaves in Utah, but it is difficult to be certain.

4. The data for population come from census data collected in various publications. See Pamela S. Perlich, "Utah Minorities: The Story Told by 150 Years of Census Data," 10–11. October 2002, Bureau of Economic and Business Research, David S. Eccles School of Business, University of Utah; and "Race and Ethnicity in Utah: 2016," fact sheet produced by the Kem C. Gardner Policy Institute, University of Utah, July 2017, available at http://gardner.utah.edu/wp-content/uploads/RaceandEthnicity_FactSheet20170825.pdf. See also US Census Bureau quick facts for the state of Utah, available at https://www.census.gov/quickfacts/fact/table/UT/RHI225216#viewtop. For nineteenth century African American history in Utah, see Coleman, "Blacks in Utah," 115–40. For more recent studies of African American Latter-day Saints, see W. Paul Reeve, *Religion of a Different Color: Race and the Mormon Struggle for Whiteness* (New York: Oxford University Press, 2015); and Russell W. Stevenson, *For the Cause of Righteousness: A Global History of Blacks and Mormonism, 1830–2013* (Draper, UT: Greg Kofford Books, 2014).
5. "1990 Census Brief: Minorities of Utah," prepared by Demographic and Economic Analysis, Office of Planning and Budget, Salt Lake City, April 1991.
6. Utah State Profile, created by the US Census Bureau, available at https://www.census.gov/library/stories/state-by-state/utah-population-change-between-census-decade.html, accessed August 31, 2021. See also Emily Harris, "First Insights—2020 Census Race and Hispanic or Latino Origin in Utah," published by the Kem C. Gardner Policy Institute, David Eccles School of Business, University of Utah, August 2021, available at https://gardner.utah.edu/wp-content/uploads/C2020-RceEth-FS-Aug2021.pdf?x71849, accessed March 2, 2022.
7. France A. Davis, "Utah in the '40s: An African American Perspective," *Beehive History* 25 (1999): 26.
8. Anna Belle Weakley, "Interviews with African Americans in Utah, AnnaBelle Mattson, Part 1," J. Willard Marriott Digital Library, University of Utah, available at https://collections.lib.utah.edu/details?id=893667&q=AnnaBelle+Mattson, accessed August 29, 2021.
9. Eric Stene, "The African-American Community of Ogden, Utah: 1910–1950" (master's thesis, Utah State University, 1994), 58.
10. James B. Allen, *Still the Right Place: Utah's Second Half-Century of Statehood, 1945–1995* (Provo, UT: Charles Redd Center for Western Studies at Brigham Young University and Utah State Historical Society, 2016), 425, 461.
11. Stene, "African-American Community of Ogden, Utah," 58–59.
12. "African Americans Built Churches in Utah," *The History Blazer* (July 1996), available at https://issuu.com/utah10/docs/historyblazers_1996_7_july, accessed May 5, 2021.
13. France Davis, *Light in the Midst of Zion* (Salt Lake City, UT: University Publishing, LLC, 1997), 13–15.
14. For a history of the Baptist in Utah, see Davis, "Utah in the '40s: An African American Perspective," 25. For Seventh Day Adventists history, see Maxine Goins, "History of the Central SDA Church," available at https://slccentral.adventistfaith.org/central-history, accessed May 5, 2021.

15. There are many histories of Pentecostalism available. For a focused history of the Azusa Street Revival and William J. Seymour, see Cecil M. Robeck Jr., *Azusa Street Mission and Revival: The Birth of the Global Pentecostal Movement* (Nashville, TN: Thomas Nelson, Inc., 2006), and Gastón Espinosa, *William J. Seymour and the Origins of Global Pentecostalism: A Biography and Documentary History* (Durham, NC: Duke University Press, 2014).
16. Bishop Ithiel C. Clemmons, *Bishop C. H. Mason and the Roots of the Church of God in Christ,* Centennial Edition (Bakersfield, CA: Pneuma Life Publishing, 1996), 26.
17. Clemmons, *Bishop C. H. Mason,* 61–71.
18. For Church of God in Christ membership statistics, see "Church of God in Christ (COGIC)," Center for Religion and Civic Culture, University of Southern California, available at https://crcc.usc.edu/report/national-association-of-real-estate-brokers-nareb-religious-literacy-primer-2019/church-of-god-in-christ-cogic/, accessed May 6, 2021. See also https://www.cogic.org/about-company/.
19. The Assemblies of God has more members globally, but it has only approximately three million members in the United States. For additional details on Assemblies of God statistics, see https://ag.org/about/statistics, accessed May 6, 2021.
20. The African American population in Utah is very small. Although members of the various African American churches hold differing views on religious practice and Christian theology, they celebrate special events together. Historically, Pentecostal churches did not receive support from other Protestant or Evangelical churches. Even though COGIC members did not initially worship with Black members of other denominations, this disposition changed over the years. Especially in remote areas like Utah with small African American populations, COGIC churches learned to adapt and participate in more interfaith social activities.
21. These estimates are for 2021 and come from Pastor Henry McAllister. For context and comparison, a *Salt Lake Tribune* article estimated membership of the Trinity AME Church to be approximately sixty members in 2018. See Peggy Fletcher Stack, "Utah Pastor at Historic Black Church Retires after a Grueling but Gratifying Tenure," *Salt Lake Tribune,* August 25, 2018. France Davis estimates that as of March 2020, there were approximately 2,300 weekly attendees among the eight predominantly African American Baptist congregations in Utah. Estimates provided via personal communication with authors, May 4, 2021.
22. "Obsequies of Superintendent Emeritus David F. Griffin," 1989, on the occasion of David F. Griffin's funeral.
23. Clemmons, *Bishop C. H. Mason,* 99.
24. From "Mother Alberta Harris Jennings Trail Blazer," local history from the history collection of the Utah Church of God in Christ.
25. Alberta Harris would marry Elder Jack R. Jennings in October 1942. See "Statistics," *Salt Lake Telegram,* October 14, 1942, 21. The article includes an announcement for the wedding of Jack Roy Jennings and Alberta Harris.
26. Within the Utah COGIC community, Mother Harris's encounter with the Salt Lake City Council is an oft-recited anecdote. We have not yet found historical evidence beyond these cultural memories to elaborate on these encounters, but believe that due to the nature of her outdoor ministry at public parks, it is probable that she had meetings with the city council to authorize her services.

Other examples of this type of encounter occurred in Ogden and elsewhere in the state.

27. Biographical details from "Mother Alberta Harris Jennings Trail Blazer," local history from the history collection of the Utah Church of God in Christ.
28. In the Church of God in Christ today, women are not called as elders or pastors. They do, however, have the ability to share spiritual messages with the congregations in which they reside.
29. Anthea D. Butler, *Women in the Church of God in Christ: Making a Sanctified World* (Chapel Hill: University of North Carolina Press, 2007), 59.
30. Clemmons, *Bishop C. H. Mason*, 100.
31. Butler, *Women in the Church of God in Christ*, 3.
32. Biographical details from "Mother Alberta Harris Jennings Trail Blazer."
33. Very little is currently known about Elder Caldwell. He is included in the "History of Mount Zion Church of God in Christ," written by Henry McAllister, and a few newspaper articles mention him in the early 1940s. He seems to have assisted in the early stages of the church and then moved on to another location outside Utah.
34. From "Jurisdictional Prelate Bishop Isaac Finley," local history from the history collection of the Utah Church of God in Christ.
35. "Meeting Called to Protest Lynching," *Salt Lake Telegram*, July 4, 1925, 3. See also Dean L. May, *Utah: A People's History* (Salt Lake City: University of Utah Press, 1987), 144–45. There is not a great deal of data available on lynchings that occurred in the state of Utah, but it appears to have been quite rare. Larry Gerlach provided some context from his research in 1981: "A study of early Utah executions–legal as well as illegal–reveals that at least twelve lynchings have taken place in the state. Except for the lynching of Robert Marshall in Price on June 18, 1925, mob justice in Utah was confined to the territorial period." See Larry R. Gerlach, "Ogden's 'Horrible Tragedy': The Lynching of George Segal," *Utah Historical Quarterly* 49 (Spring 1981): 159.
36. Larry R. Gerlach, "The Klan in Salt Lake City," in *The Invisible Empire in the West: Toward a New Historical Appraisal of the Ku Klux Klan of the 1920s*, edited by Shawn Lay (Urbana: University of Illinois Press, 1992), 146.
37. Doris Fry, "Interviews with African Americans in Utah, Doris Fry Interview," Ms0453, Interviews with Blacks in Utah, 1982–1988, J. Willard Marriott Library, University of Utah, Salt Lake City.
38. Danny Burnett, "Interviews with African Americans in Utah, Danny Burnett Interview," Ms0453, Interviews with Blacks in Utah, 1982–1988, J. Willard Marriott Library, University of Utah, Salt Lake City. Burnett spoke of priesthood limitations elsewhere in his interview as a point of concern with the Salt Lake area.
39. Howard Browne, "Interviews with African Americans in Utah, Howard Browne Interview 2," Ms0453, Interviews with Blacks in Utah, 1982–1988, J. Willard Marriott Library, University of Utah, Salt Lake City, Utah. Howard Browne lived in the mining area of Helper and Price, Utah. The visit to southern Utah was for recreation.
40. Fry, "Interviews with African Americans in Utah, Doris Fry Interview."
41. James Gillespie, quoted by Eric Stene, "The African-American Community of Ogden, Utah: 1910–1950," (master's thesis, Utah State University, 1994), 52.

42. Thomas G. Alexander, *Utah, the Right Place: The Official Centennial History* (Salt Lake City, UT: Gibbs Smith Publisher in association with the Utah State Historical Society, 1995), 388–89.
43. Charles Nabors would become the first African American faculty member at the University of Utah. He also volunteered with the Salt Lake chapter of the NAACP during the 1960s.
44. Joan Nabors, "Interviews with African Americans in Utah, Joan Nabors Interview," Ms0453, Interviews with Blacks in Utah, 1982–1988, J. Willard Marriott Library, University of Utah, Salt Lake City, Utah.
45. This meeting is recorded in "Mother Alberta Harris Jennings Trail Blazer," local history from the history collection of the Utah Church of God in Christ. We have not been able to corroborate the reminiscence with records from the Church History Library of the Church of Jesus Christ of Latter-day Saints. There may be additional information on this meeting, but records and meeting minutes for the activities of the Quorum of the Twelve are restricted to most researchers.
46. See "Permit Granted," *Salt Lake Tribune*, March 25, 1943, 10, and "Assembly of God," *Salt Lake Tribune*, August 18, 1940, 11. The tent meetings continued on and off for several months. See "S. L. Church Sets Nightly Revival Meetings," *Salt Lake Telegram*, April 29, 1943, 12.
47. "Board Approves Tent Tabernacle," *Ogden Standard-Examiner*, April 7, 1943, 18; "Church of God in Christ," *Ogden Standard-Examiner*, August 7, 1943, 3.
48. "28th & Wall Avenue/Emmanuel Church of God in Christ History," local history from the history collection of the Utah Church of God in Christ.
49. "Griffin Temple/Memorial History," from the history collection of the Utah Church of God in Christ.
50. Over the years, the congregation had quite a few assistant pastors, including Elders Sylvester V. Miller, Hasie Owens, Lafayette Mosely, Johnathan St. Thomas, James Shaw, and Bishop Richard Paige.
51. Elder R. E. Hurrington served as pastor of Mount Zion from 1953 to 1983. He was followed by Elder James Shaw and Elder Ronald Norman.
52. A few other congregations existed at one time or another before dissolving. Bishop Melvin Givens led the Deliverance Temple Church of God in Christ in Salt Lake City in the 1970s. The Fresh Start COGIC existed under Apostle Dennis Newsome and the New Life COGIC was pastored by Elder H. J. Lilly. Elder Clifton Melvin oversaw the Victory COGIC, Robert Harris pastored the St. Paul COGIC, and Mother Leona Thomas led the Shiloh COGIC. At the time of this publication, four congregations hold weekly services in Utah: Griffin Memorial COGIC under Bishop Bobby Allen, Emmanuel COGIC under Elder John Miller, Journey of New Beginnings COGIC under Elder Henry McAllister, and Holiness Tabernacle COGIC under Elder George Green. From the history collection of the Utah Church of God in Christ.
53. Biographical information on Latter-day Saint African Americans living in Utah in the late nineteenth and early twentieth centuries has recently been made available online through the University of Utah. The database, called "Century of Black Mormons," is available at https://exhibits.lib.utah.edu/s/century-of-black-mormons/page/welcome. The database includes biographical profiles

of Latter-day Saints, as well as individuals who at one time associated with the Church of Jesus Christ of Latter-day Saints but later left it. It is a very helpful collection for understanding the life of African Americans in Utah.

54. Various strikes occurred in the early twentieth century, but one of the largest strikes in Carbon County occurred in 1922–1923. Quite a few outsiders including African Americans moved in as strike breakers during these years. See Ronald G. Watt, *A History of Carbon County*, Utah Centennial County History Series (Salt Lake City: Utah State Historical Society, 1997), 171–73. See also Howard Browne, "Interviews with African Americans in Utah, Howard Browne Interview," Ms0453, Interviews with Blacks in Utah, 1982–1988, J. Willard Marriott Library, University of Utah, Salt Lake City.
55. "Listen To the Gospel Hour," *Helper Journal*, March 28, 1946, 5. Although it is not clear exactly when Green began his ministry in Helper, he is listed as a participating pastor in this 1946 ad for the Gospel Hour radio broadcast.
56. "Church of God and Christ Services," *Helper Journal*, January 16, 1947, 5. The name of the church was misprinted as the "Church of God and Christ" in the earliest announcements.
57. "Religious Group Slates Chair Rally in Helper," *Helper Journal*, October 2, 1947, 8. St. Anthony's Catholic Church burned down in a fire in 1936. Green received permission to use its foundation in the construction of his church. See "Community Church of God in Christ, Building New Church," *Helper Journal*, July 17, 1947, 3.
58. "Community Church Here Plans Barbecue Aug. 26," *Helper Journal*, August 18, 1949, 8.
59. "New Schedule Listed For Colored Church; LDS Head Sends Check," *Helper Journal*, May 6, 1948, 4. There is very little further information available on the Church of God in Christ in Helper, Utah. Advertisements for the church continued in the newspaper through 1951. There is no information concerning J. R. Green or his church within the Utah Church of God in Christ history. Likely Green operated independently from the other churches in the state.
60. Browne, "Interviews with African Americans in Utah, Howard Browne Interview 2."
61. Browne, "Interviews with African Americans in Utah, Howard Browne Interview 2." Browne recalled a conversation turned argument with an Italian miner who unintentionally targeted Browne with racist language. Although not out of spite, the example once again highlighted the subtle kind of racism rampant in Utah during much of the twentieth century.
62. Bishop Bobby Allen, opening statement in the pamphlet for the "Utah Jurisdiction Church of God in Christ Holy Convocation," 2013. The year 2013 celebrated seventy-five years of history for the Church of God in Christ in the state of Utah.
63. For additional details, see Robert R. Owens, *Never Forget! The Dark Years of COGIC History* (Fairfax, VA: Xulon Press, 2002), 32–33.
64. As noted, Lincoln Avenue changed its name from Lincoln Avenue to Finley Temple. Eventually it would become the Journey of New Beginnings Church of God in Christ. Other pastors of this congregation include Elder R. E. Hurrington (1983–1992), Elder Leon Lewis (1992–1993), Bishop William Whitehead (1993–1994), Bishop Bobby Allen (1994–1996), and Elder Henry McAllister (1996–present).

65. The major exception to this is the social activism of Elder Robert L. Harris, which was mentioned in the beginning of this section.
66. "Utah Jurisdiction Church of God in Christ Holy convocation: Celebrating 75 Years," from the history collection of the Utah Church of God in Christ.
67. Recollections from Tommy Vigil, interview conducted by the author, December 21, 2018.
68. Reverend France A. Davis, interview conducted by the author, February 22, 2020.
69. Bishop Bobby Allen, interview conducted by the author, September 30, 2020.
70. "History of Deliverance Temple Church of God in Christ," from the history collection of the Utah Church of God in Christ.
71. "Y Groups To Join Singer," *Daily Herald*, March 1, 1970, 20.
72. "Mormon Teens Raise $33,000 to Aid Salt Lake Negro Church," *Daily Herald*, June 11, 1970, 13.
73. "Mormon Teens Raise $33,000 to Aid Salt Lake Negro Church."
74. Stevenson, *For the Cause of Righteousness*, 157.
75. Stevenson, *For the Cause of Righteousness*, 156.
76. "Mormon Teens Raise $33,000 to Aid Salt Lake Negro Church," *Daily Herald*, June 11, 1970, 13.
77. Henry McAllister, interview conducted by the authors on March 8, 2017.
78. Robert L. Harris, quoted by David Briscoe, "Capitol Officials Take Minister's Lying Down Protest Lying Down," *Ogden Standard-Examiner*, June 6, 1973, 19.
79. The Church of God in Christ Congregational broke away from the main body of the Church of God in Christ after the death of Bishop Charles H. Mason due to various concerns over the leadership structure of the church. Although Robert Harris ministered within the Church of God in Christ Congregational, he also participated in the events and services held by the Utah Church of God in Christ. For more about the schism, see Owens, *Never Forget!*
80. Robert L. Harris, quoted by Amy Donaldson, "Grocer, Reverend Enjoys Feeding Hungry," *Deseret News*, February 3, 1994.
81. The Church of God in Christ Congregational formed in 1932 when it separated from the Church of God in Christ. Its first bishop was Bishop J. Bowe. Some additional information on the Church of God in Christ Congregational is available from Sherry Sherrod DuPree, *African-American Holiness Pentecostal Movement: An Annotated Bibliography* (New York: Garland Publishing, Inc., 1996), 142.
82. Biographical data on Robert L. Harris comes from "Pastor to Tell History of 19 Peace Marches Without Violence," *Ogden Standard-Examiner*, November 21, 1968, 4; Cliff Thompson, "'No Protests Planned,' Reverend Harris Says," *Ogden Standard-Examiner*, January 5, 1977, 24; and Donaldson, "Grocer, Reverend Enjoys Feeding Hungry."
83. "Preacher Lodges Protest," *Daily Herald*, January 15, 1975, 23.
84. "Protest is Costly For Pastor," *Daily Herald*, January 30, 1974, 9; David Briscoe, "Capitol Officials Take Minister's Lying Down Protest Lying Down," *Ogden Standard-Examiner*, June 6, 1973, 19; and "Church Prepares for Third Peace March," *Ogden Standard-Examiner*, August 31, 1967, 2
85. "Pastor Asks Election to City Council," *Ogden Standard-Examiner*, August 12, 1971, 7.
86. Thompson, "'No Protests Planned,' Reverend Harris Says," 24.

87. Thompson, "'No Protests Planned,' Reverend Harris Says," 24.
88. James B. Allen, *Still the Right Place*, 423.
89. Joan Nabors, "Interviews with African Americans in Utah, Joan Nabors Interview," Ms0453, Interviews with Blacks in Utah, 1982–1988, J. Willard Marriott Library, University of Utah, Salt Lake City.
90. Henry McAllister, interview conducted by the author on March 8, 2017.
91. Terry Williams, "Interviews with African Americans in Utah, Terry Williams Interview," Ms0453, Interviews with Blacks in Utah, 1982–1988, J. Willard Marriott Library, University of Utah, Salt Lake City.
92. Information received from La'Mae Ervin and Henry McAllister, November 2020, notes in the authors' possession; and "Rev. Robert Lee Harris" obituary, *Ogden Standard-Examiner*, February 27, 2005, 7B.
93. Recollections from Bishop Bobby Allen, interview conducted by the authors, September 30, 2020. Bishop Isaac Finley served as Jurisdictional Bishop from 1942 to 1970. Bishop Allen will soon be the longest serving Jurisdictional Bishop in Utah's history.
94. Recollections from Bishop Bobby Allen, interview conducted by the authors, September 30, 2020.
95. Bishop Bobby Allen, opening statement in the pamphlet for the "Utah Jurisdiction Church of God in Christ Holy Convocation," 2013.
96. Although not all members of the congregations of the Church of God in Christ are African Americans, most are. The denomination holds an important place in African American religious history in the United States.

CHAPTER 5: "LABORERS ARE NEEDED IN THESE WESTERN STATES"

1. Carrie A. Moore, "Evangelist to speak at Tabernacle," *Deseret News*, September 11, 2004, available at https://www.deseretnews.com/article/595090586/Evangelist-to-speak-at-Tabernacle.html, accessed August 14, 2018.
2. Edith L. Blumhofer, "Selected Letters of Mae Eleanore Frey," *Pneuma* 17, no. 1 (Spring 1995): 67.
3. Mae Eleanor Frey, "Preaching to the Mormons," *Pentecostal Evangel*, October 9, 1926, 9. The article does not give Miss Harrington's first name, nor does it give the name of the bishop who invited them to speak at the Tabernacle.
4. Mae Eleanor Frey, "Preaching to the Mormons," *Pentecostal Evangel*, October 9, 1926, 9.
5. Joel 2:28 has played a role in the theological development of women's place in institutional structures throughout the Pentecostal movement. The verse states, "And it shall come to pass afterward, that I will pour out my spirit upon all flesh; and your sons and your daughters shall prophesy."
6. Joy E. A. Qualls, *God Forgive Us for Being Women: Rhetoric, Theology, and the Pentecostal Tradition* (Eugene, OR: Pickwick Publications, 2018), 15.
7. 1914 General Council Minutes, as cited by Qualls, *God Forgive Us for Being Women*, 16.
8. "Minutes of the General Council of the Assemblies of God in the United States of America, Canada, and Foreign Lands," April 1914, 12, available at ifphc.org.

9. August Feick, "The Etter Meeting at Salt Lake City," *The Weekly Evangel*, November 4, 1916, 15.
10. "Loretta Boyd and Grace Hall, "Great Victory In Summit Point, Utah," *Church of God Evangel*, December 7, 1929, 1.
11. Bob Aguilar, interview, February 2017, interview notes in my possession. See also A. T. Salazar, "Historia," *La Luz Apostólica*, June 1969, 11.
12. "Obituaries: Alberta H. Jennings," *Ogden Standard-Examiner*, February 21, 1970, 11.
13. See *Daily Herald*, May 7, 1942, 3; "Lilly May Strayer," *Davis County Clipper*, February 23, 1991, 14; and Max Croasmun, interview, October 2013, interview notes in my possession.
14. "Pentecostal Preacher Busy Following God's Message to 'Go Seek Souls,'" *Deseret News*, July 2, 1988.
15. Estrelda Alexander, "Introduction," in *Philip's Daughters: Women in Pentecostal-Charismatic Leadership*, eds. Estrelda Alexander and Amos Yong (Eugene, OR: Pickwick Publications, 2009), 7.
16. Barbara Brown Zikmund, Adair T. Lummis, and Patricia M. Y. Chang, "Women, Men and Styles of Clergy Leadership," *Christian Century* 115, no. 14 (May 6, 1998), available at http://hirr.hartsem.edu/research/quick_question3.html, accessed December 7, 2018. See also Qualls, *God Forgive Us for Being Women*, 143. She found in the Assemblies of God that "in 1936, one female was ordained a minister for every four males. By 1986, the number was one female for every eight of her male counterparts."
17. Pentecostal Assemblies of Canada Fellowship Statistics, available at https://www.paoc.org/docs/default-source/fellowship-services-documents/fellowship-stats.pdf?sfvrsn=284ae76a_2, accessed December 7, 2018.
18. See Dean R. Hoge and Jacqueline E. Wenger, *Pastors in Transition: Why Clergy Leave Local Church Ministry* (Grand Rapids, Michigan: William B. Eerdmans Publishing Co., 2005) 173–85; and Qualls, *God Forgive Us for Being Women*, 135–45. Qualls summarized the arguments of various scholars including Margaret Poloma, Edith Blumhofer, and Barfoot and Sheppard as she concluded that "women's participation in church ministry at nearly every level saw rapid decline in the 1960s."
19. Charles H. Barfoot and Gerald T. Sheppard, "Prophetic vs. Priestly Religion: The Changing Role of Women Clergy in Classical Pentecostal Churches, *Review of Religious Research* 22, no. 1 (September 1980): 4.
20. For a few examples, see Gastón Espinsoa, "'Third Class Soldiers': A History of Hispanic Pentecostal Clergywomen in the Assemblies of God," in *Philip's Daughters: Women in Pentecostal-Charismatic Leadership*, Estrelda Alexander and Amos Yong, eds. (Eugene, OR: Pickwick Publications, 2009): 97–98; and Qualls, *God Forgive Us for Being Women*, 30–32.
21. Qualls, *God Forgive Us for Being Women*, 31.
22. Qualls, *God Forgive Us for Being Women*, 120.
23. Alexander, "Introduction," 7.
24. Kathleen Sprows Cummings, *New Women of the Old Faith: Gender and American Catholicism in the Progressive Era* (Chapel Hill: University of North Carolina Press, 2009), 4.
25. Barbara Burrows, daughter of Lilly May Strayer, interview, February 8, 2017, interview notes in my possession.

26. Lilly May Strayer, testimony written in her personal Bible, from the collection of Barbara Burrows.
27. Lilly May Strayer, testimony written in her personal Bible, from the collection of Barbara Burrows.
28. "Hunting Funeral Held Friday In American Fork," *Vernal Express*, August 24, 1950, 8.
29. Qualls, *God Forgive Us for Being Women*, 16.
30. Barbara Burrows, interview, February 8, 2017, interview notes in my possession.
31. Lilly Strayer, letter to Russel G. Fulford, June 25, 1953, Layton, Utah, from the collection of Barbara Burrows.
32. Lilly May Strayer, "Application for District Credentials of the Rocky Mountain District Council of the Assemblies of God," 1952, from the collection of Barbara Burrows.
33. Strayer, Letter to Russel G. Fulford.
34. Strayer, Letter to Russel G. Fulford.
35. Strayer, Letter to Russel G. Fulford.
36. Qualls, *God Forgive Us for Being Women*, 202.
37. David G. Roebuck, "Limiting Liberty: The Church of God and Women Ministers, 1986–1996," (PhD diss., Vanderbilt University, 1997), 146–65.
38. Myke Crowder, "History of First Assembly of God Layton, Utah," Divinity degree, Southwestern Assemblies of God College, 1988, 3.
39. "Assembly of God Church Pushes Building Program to Completion," *American Fork Citizen*, December 25, 1958, 6.
40. For examples, see "Ruben Dean, Native of A. F. Dies in Lehi," *American Fork Citizen*, November 7, 1957, 9; and "Greetings: 'No Room,'" *American Fork Citizen*, December 25, 1958, 2.
41. For examples of each, see *Daily Herald*, May 7, 1942, 3; "Sunday Services," *Sunday Herald*, August 30, 1942, 3; and "Sunday Services," *Sunday Herald*, September 12, 1943, 6. Only in the later ads would she take the title of pastor.
42. H. E. Ramsey, "Greetings from Utah," *The Church of God Evangel*, July 4, 1942, 16.
43. Lilly May Strayer, "Highest Authority," *Salt Lake Tribune*, August 8, 1957, 18.
44. Lilly May Strayer, "Misusing the Bible," *Salt Lake Tribune*, April 25, 1958, 7.
45. See Lilly May Strayer, "Wants Freedom of Choice," *Salt Lake Tribune*, February 2, 1967, 9; and Lilly May Strayer, "According to Word," *Ogden Standard-Examiner*, November 14, 1977, 4.
46. Barfoot and Sheppard, "Prophetic vs. Priestly Religion," 2–17.
47. Qualls, *God Forgive Us for Being Women*, 134–35. Qualls analyzes the gendered language of various advertisements and articles published by the *Pentecostal Evangel*.
48. David T. Holden, Letter to Lilly Strayer, April 6, 1976, from the collection of Barbara Burrows. This complex situation is, of course, not entirely the result of gender dynamics. However, it did present her leaders with an opportunity to carefully remove her from her position despite her long years of service. Additional details received through an interview with Barbara Burrows, February 8, 2017, interview notes in my possession.
49. See the Minutes and Revised Constitution and Bylaws of the General Council of the Assemblies of God, Thirty-Sixth General Council, August 14–19, 1975, 103–5, available at the Flower Pentecostal Heritage Center.

50. Strayer, Letter to Russel G. Fulford.
51. Joy Langford, "Feminism and Leadership in the Pentecostal Movement," *Feminist Theology* 26, no. 1 (September 2017): 73.
52. Langford, "Feminism and Leadership in the Pentecostal Movement," 75.
53. Alexander, "Introduction," 7.
54. For a more detailed discussion on the tension between a spiritual call and denominational authority, see Qualls, *God Forgive Us for Being Women*, 182–84.
55. For examples, see "Recreation Program Gets Off With A Bang," *Davis County Clipper*, June 20, 1969, 22; "For Nutrition," *Davis County Clipper*, February 13, 1976, 30; "Zucchini Pickles," *Davis County Clipper*, October 1, 1980, 26; and "Volunteers Honored," *Davis County Clipper*, December 15, 1987, 12.
56. "Lilly May Strayer," *Davis County Clipper*, February 23, 1991, 14.
57. Of the approximately twenty-five pastors I have interviewed who work or worked in the state of Utah, I have not interviewed any women who are currently pastors. There may be a few pastoring in smaller or independent congregations. If so, that would make sense according to the historical role women have played in planting congregations in the state. But to my knowledge, there are very few female pastors at present.
58. Biographical sketch of Mother Janie B. Thomas, from the history collection of the Utah Church of God in Christ.
59. Data for the Assemblies of God comes from "Rocky Mountain Ministry Network 100th Celebration History," 2017. Produced by the Rocky Mountain Ministry Network, Colorado Springs, CO.
60. See https://ordainwomen.org/mission/, accessed September 27, 2018.
61. Sprows Cummings, *New Women of the Old Faith*, 193.
62. Strayer, Letter to Russel G. Fulford.

CHAPTER 6: GROWING PAINS

1. I address the theological and evangelistic relationship between Pentecostals and Latter-day Saints at length in Chapter 7.
2. It is probable that Pentecostals might have acted in the same way to Latter-day Saints, but because of the sheer size of the Latter-day Saint community in Utah compared to the Pentecostal community, rarely if ever did Pentecostals find themselves in a position to meet the needs of the Latter-day Saint community financially or socially.
3. A significant amount of the information provided in this chapter comes from interviews with and local histories of Pentecostals in Utah. Because of the anecdotal nature of the information, inferences must be made about the experience of the Pentecostal community over the twentieth century in relation to other religious groups and institutions. There are very few published records relating local prejudice and discrimination. As such, this chapter might best be understood as a reflection of the personal experiences and memories of the Utah Pentecostal community. Where possible, I have supported the content of interviews and local histories with newspaper accounts and other publications.

4. Grant Wacker, "Travail of a Broken Family: Radical Evangelical Responses to the Emergence of Pentecostalism in America, 1906–1916," in *Pentecostal Currents in American Protestantism*, Edith L. Blumhofer, Russell P. Spittler, and Grant A. Wacker, eds. (Urbana: University of Illinois Press, 1999), 23.
5. Wacker, "Travail of a Broken Family," 29.
6. The term *radical evangelical* is borrowed from Grant Wacker to describe those evangelical movements that sat on the edges of the evangelical churches in the early 1900s. Holiness churches pursued a greater spiritual experience than that which they found in the established denominations, often using revivalist practices to encourage a "holier" Christian experience. Fundamentalists believed it important to support a small set of doctrines as fundamental to and unchangeable within Christianity. Most early Pentecostals defected from these groups to join the new movement. See Grant Wacker, "Travail of a Broken Family," 23–49.
7. Wacker, "Travail of a Broken Family," 40.
8. Grant Wacker, *Heaven Below: Early Pentecostals and American Culture* (Cambridge, MA: Harvard University Press, 2001), 201.
9. Wacker, *Heaven Below*, 197–216.
10. Charles Randall Paul, "Converting the Saints: An Investigation of Religious Conflict Using a Study of Protestant Missionary Methods in an Early 20th Century Engagement with Mormonism," (PhD diss., University of Chicago, 2000), 703. Paul's dissertation is now also available in a revised form, as Charles Randall Paul, *Converting the Saints: A Study of Religious Rivalry in America* (Draper, UT: Greg Kofford Books, 2018).
11. Paul, "Converting the Saints," 710–804. Paul offers an excellent analysis of the efforts of Nutting, Paden, and Spalding, which is long overdue.
12. Paul, "Converting the Saints," 712.
13. Paul, "Converting the Saints," 742. The Articles of Organization for the Comity Council are reproduced on page 809.
14. James B. Allen, "Religion in Twentieth-century Utah," in *Utah's History*, Richard D. Poll, general ed. (Provo, UT: Brigham Young University Press, 1978), 611.
15. Second principle from "Utah Home Missions Council Articles of Organization," reprinted in Paul, "Converting the Saints," 809.
16. "Utah Home Missions Council Articles of Organization," reprinted in Charles Randall Paul, "Converting the Saints," 809.
17. Paul, "Converting the Saints," 735–60.
18. Max Croasmun, interview, October 2013, interview notes in the author's possession.
19. Vinson Synan, *The Holiness-Pentecostal Tradition: Charismatic Movements in the Twentieth Century* (Grand Rapids, MI: William B. Eerdman's Publishing Company, 1997), 146.
20. Gastón Espinosa, *Latino Pentecostals in America: Faith and Politics in Action* (Cambridge, MA: Harvard University Press, 2014), 147–51.
21. Daniel Ramírez, *Migrating Faith: Pentecostalism in the United States and Mexico in the Twentieth Century* (Chapel Hill: University of North Carolina Press, 2015), 92.
22. Timothy H. Wadkins, *The Rise of Pentecostalism in Modern El Salvador: From the Blood of the Martyrs to the Baptism of the Spirit* (Waco, TX: Baylor University Press, 2017), 75–76, 85–86.

23. Nephi Jensen, in *Ninetieth Annual Conference Report of the Church of Jesus Christ of Latter-day Saints* (Salt Lake City: *Deseret News,* April 1920), 82.
24. R. Laurence Moore, *Religious Outsiders and the Making of Americans* (New York: Oxford University Press, 1986), 208.
25. Wacker, *Heaven Below: Early Pentecostals and American Culture,* 196.
26. Most Latter-day Saint communal living projects ended during the nineteenth century, with the exception of some unauthorized Utah communities. Nevertheless, the culture of church community continued through the Progressive Era. Only in the 1920s did church leaders begin encouraging church members to stop gathering to the state of Utah. See Orson F. Whitney, "Stay Where You Are!", *Millennial Star* 83, no. 37 (September 15, 1921): 584–86.
27. "This Week's Cover," *Pentecostal Evangel,* May 30, 1954, 10.
28. "This Week's Cover," 10.
29. Willard Coleman, interview, September 21, 2018, interview notes in the author's possession.
30. Alex Lucero, interview, July 31, 2013.
31. Max Croasmun, interview, October 2013, interview notes in the author's possession.
32. Sandy Markham, interview, August 1, 2013, interview notes in the author's possession.
33. Willard Coleman, interview, September 21, 2018, interview notes in the author's possession.
34. Barbara Burrows, interview, October 2013, interview notes in the author's possession.
35. "This Week's Cover," 10.
36. William Fitzgerel, interview, July 25, 2013, interview notes in the author's possession.
37. Willard Coleman, interview, September 21, 2018, interview notes in the author's possession.
38. Most individuals interviewed preferred not to share the names of individuals or groups that harassed them, but many did acknowledge difficulties with the Latter-day Saint community. In none of the interviews did Pentecostals identify non-Latter-day Saints as the culprits of discrimination or harassment. It is assumed, based on the interviews and the representative population, that a majority of the incidents identified in this chapter probably included either a member of the Church of Jesus Christ of Latter-day Saints or individuals culturally associated with the same. But as in most studies of this kind, it is difficult to know for certain.
39. Sandy Markham, interview, August 1, 2013, interview notes in the author's possession.
40. Max Croasmun, interview, October 2013, interview notes in the author's possession.
41. Willard Coleman, interview, September 21, 2018, interview notes in the author's possession.
42. "28th & Wall Avenue/Emmanuel Church of God in Christ History," local history from the history collection of the Utah Church of God in Christ.
43. Max Croasmun, interview, October 2013, interview notes in the author's possession.
44. Sandy Markham, interview, August 1, 2013, interview notes in the author's possession.

45. Alex Lucero, interview, July 31, 2013, interview notes in the author's possession.
46. *Garfield County News,* May 3, 1979, 13.
47. Willard Coleman, interview, September 21, 2018, interview notes in my possession.
48. "Building Sale Stirs Controversy," *Garfield County News,* May 17, 1979, 1.
49. "Garfield Area Events Included Progress During the Year 1979," *Garfield County News,* January 3, 1980, 1.
50. "Church Efforts Fail to Find Land for Disputed Building," *Garfield County News,* May 31, 1979, 1.
51. "Information concerning Paul Harvey's visit to Brigham Young University," L. Tom Perry Special Collections, Harold B. Lee Library, Brigham Young University, MSS SC 2941, Provo, Utah.
52. "Paul Harvey News Broadcast," December 8, 1967, L. Tom Perry Special Collections, Harold B. Lee Library, Brigham Young University, MSS SC 2941, Provo, Utah.
53. Mike Huckabee, author of the foreword to Paul J. Batura, *Good Day! The Paul Harvey Story* (Washington, DC: Regnery Publishing, Inc., 2009), ix. Paul Harvey's biographer wrote that "Harvey was not overly concerned about the doctrinal differences within particular Christian denominations." He and his wife attended various different churches over the years and shared a close, personal friendship with Billy and Ruth Graham. In this sense, he might be understood as a nondenominational evangelical. See Paul J. Batura, *Good Day! The Paul Harvey Story* (Washington, DC: Regnery Publishing, Inc., 2009), 182.
54. Batura, *Good Day! The Paul Harvey,* 185. Throughout the early 1970s, the *Daily Herald* printed Harvey's column every Friday. Like newspapers across the country, the *Daily Herald*'s Latter-day Saint readers.
55. "Paul Harvey, Noted Commentator, to Speak at Fund-Raising Event for Provo Church," *Daily Herald,* March 12, 1972, 6; and "Paul Harvey Special," *Daily Herald,* March 15, 1972, 7.
56. Raymond Ansel, interview conducted by the author, September 2017. With only $20 in the bank, Pastor Ansel wrote a check to Paul Harvey for $5,000. He did not know how he would come up with the money for the check to clear. Through what Pastor Ansel understood to be a miracle, within twenty-four hours a couple from Denver, Colorado, called him offering to pay the cost of Harvey's visit to Utah. Despite the fundraiser being a failure, the Rock Canyon Assembly of God managed to complete their building on 3410 Canyon Road in 1974. For additional history, see Charles Hidenshield, "Rock Canyon Assembly of God," in *Protestant and Catholic Churches of Provo: A Study of the Non-LDS Christian Congregations,* by David M. Walden (Provo, UT: Center for Family and Community History at Brigham Young University, 1986), 140–49.
57. "Y Groups to Join Singer," *Daily Herald,* March 1, 1970, 20.
58. "Mormon Teens Raise $33,000 to Aid Salt Lake Negro Church," *Daily Herald,* June 11, 1970, 13. For more on this event, see Chapter 4 of this dissertation.
59. "Mormon Teens Raise $33,000 to Aid Salt Lake Negro Church," 13; and "Negro Faith, LDS End Fund Campaign," *Ogden Standard-Examiner,* June 11, 1970, 10.
60. "Mormon Teens Raise $33,000 to Aid Salt Lake Negro Church," 13.
61. Raymond Ansel, interview conducted by the author, September 2017.

62. J. Reuben Clark Jr., "All Roads Lead to Rome," *The Improvement Era* 63, no. 6 (June 1960): 399.
63. "Elder LeGrand Richards," *One Hundred Thirtieth Annual Conference Report of the Church of Jesus Christ of Latter-day Saints* (Salt Lake City: *Deseret News,* April 1960), 104. LeGrand Richards explained, "By appointment from the First Presidency and at their request, I was privileged to meet with a group of ministers here in Salt Lake City who were holding a convention. They gave me two hours and a half to explain Mormonism to them." The denominational background of the convention is not entirely clear, but they appear at least to be Christian.
64. J. Reuben Clark Jr., "All Roads Lead to Rome," *The Improvement Era* 63, no. 6, (June 1960): 398–99. Neil J. Young also cites this speech and discusses the effects of this kind of rhetoric on Latter-day Saint ecumenical practice in Neil J. Young, *We Gather Together: The Religious Right and the Problem of Interfaith Politics* (New York: Oxford University Press, 2016), 34.
65. Interview with Raymond Ansel, September 2017, interview notes in the author's possession.
66. Most Pentecostals in Utah that I interviewed stated they usually agreed with their Latter-day Saint neighbors when it came to national politics. Robert Smith, a long-time pastor in Utah, also worked with W. Cleon Skousen speaking for the National Center for Constitutional Studies (NCCS). Interview with Robert Smith, October 2013, interview notes in the author's possession.
67. Interview with Raymond Ansel, September 2017, interview notes in the author's possession.
68. Gustav Niebuhr, "Mormons Intensify Missionary Effort in Utah," *New York Times,* March 29, 2001, available at https://www.nytimes.com/2001/03/29/us/mormons-intensify-missionary-effort-in-utah.html, accessed December 14, 2018. Niebuhr notes that the Church of Jesus Christ of Latter-day Saints began assigning proselytizing missionaries to Utah in 1975. Temple Square in Salt Lake City had missionaries earlier, but they did not proselytize in the rest of the state.
69. Interview with Judy Williams, October 2017, interview notes in the author's possession.
70. Kristine Hoyt, "Catholic Utahns Share Experiences Living Within LDS Community," *Daily Universe,* May 12, 2017, available at https://universe.byu.edu/2017/05/12/final-story-catholic-utahns-share-their-experiences-while-living-among-lds-people/, accessed December 18, 2018.
71. Dean Merrill, "A Peacemaker in Provo: How One Pentecostal Pastor Taught His Congregation to Love Mormons," *Christianity Today,* February 7, 2000, available at https://www.christianitytoday.com/ct/2000/february7/7.66.html, accessed April 16, 2017. Dean Jackson served as an Assemblies of God pastor in Provo, Utah, during the 1990s.

CHAPTER 7: MEET THE MORMONS

1. Roberto Gonzalez, "Assembly of God CEO addresses BYU students," *Daily Universe,* September 17 2013; and "Rev. Campbell Addresses BYU Religion Class," *The American Fork Citizen,* March 17, 1949, 5.

2. Robert Wuthnow, *The Restructuring of American Religion: Society and Faith Since World War II* (Princeton, NJ: Princeton University Press, 1988).
3. Neil J. Young, *We Gather Together: The Religious Right and the Problem of Interfaith Politics* (New York: Oxford University Press, 2016), 3–4.
4. Much of Neil J. Young's analysis focuses on the evangelical movement centered around Billy Graham and the publication *Christianity Today*. He is right to include Pentecostals as evangelicals, but he rarely discusses Pentecostal views or behaviors separately from his arguments about the more generalized population of evangelicals.
5. "The Growth of Mormonism," *The Bridegroom's Messenger*, November 15, 1912, 4; and George O. Wood as cited by Roberto Gonzalez, "Assembly of God CEO Addresses BYU Students," *Daily Universe*, September 17, 2013, available at http://universe.byu.edu/2013/09/17/assembly-of-god-ceo-addresses-byu-students/.
6. "The Love of the Truth and What it Will Save Us From," *The Bridegroom's Messenger*, February 1, 1914, 1.
7. "Doctrine and Covenants, 1835," *The Joseph Smith Papers*, 73, available at http://www.josephsmithpapers.org/paper-summary/doctrine-and-covenants-1835/81?highlight=%22train%20of%20attendants%22, accessed August 3, 2018.
8. A distinction is sometimes used within the differing branches of Mormonism. The Church of Jesus Christ of Latter-day Saints sometimes uses the term *Latter-day Saint* to refer to its membership. Other churches, such as the Community of Christ (formerly the Reorganized Church of Jesus Christ of Latter Day Saints) sometimes use the term *Latter Day Saint* to refer to its membership. Note the absence of a hyphen in the latter term.
9. John Powell, "The Church Rejected—When?", *Improvement Era* 7, no. 11 (September 1904): 821.
10. "In an Unknown Tongue," *Deseret News*, April 13, 1908, 8.
11. "Pentecostal Jumpers Here," *Ogden Standard*, June 14, 1905, 7.
12. There are various articles in Utah papers about Alexander Dowie and his religious movement. For examples, see "Dowie Is Coming," *Deseret Evening News*, September 9, 1903, 4; "Drummers from Zion City," *Ogden Daily Standard*, April 21, 1904, 8; "Dowie Drives Away Mormon Missionaries," *Salt Lake Tribune*, January 10, 1905, 2; and "Dowie Wanted Plural Wives," *Salt Lake Herald Republican*, April 3, 1906, 1. There is also an analysis of John Alexander Dowie's relationship to the Church of Jesus Christ of Latter-day Saints. See D. William Faupel, "What Has Pentecostalism to Do with Mormonism?: The Case of John Alexander Dowie," in *New Perspectives in Mormon Studies*, Quincy D. Newell and Eric F. Mason, eds. (Norman: University of Oklahoma Press, 2013), 85–100.
13. "Elder Andrew Jenson," *Seventy-sixth Semi-annual Conference Report of the Church of Jesus Christ of Latter-day Saints* (Salt Lake City, UT: *Deseret News*, October 1905), 66.
14. "Elder John W. Taylor," *Seventy-fourth Semi-annual Conference Report of the Church of Jesus Christ of Latter-day Saints* (Salt Lake City, UT: *Deseret News*, October 1903), 41.
15. There are various commentaries on charismatic expression within the Church of Jesus Christ of Latter-day Saints. Two recent examples are Mark L. Staker, *Hearken, O Ye People: The Historical Setting of Joseph Smith's Ohio Revelations* (Draper,

UT: Greg Kofford Books, Inc., 2009), and Terryl Givens, *Feeding the Flock: The Foundations of Mormon Thought: Church and Praxis* (New York: Oxford University Press, 2017). For analyses on the decline of charismatic expression within the church, see Thomas G. Alexander, *Mormonism in Transition: A History of the Latter-day Saints, 1890–1930* (3rd ed.), (Draper, UT: Greg Kofford Books, Inc., 2012); John G. Turner, *Brigham Young: Pioneer Prophet* (Cambridge, MA: Belknap Press, 2012); and Jonathan A. Stapley, *The Power of Godliness: Mormon Liturgy and Cosmology* (New York: Oxford University Press, 2018).

16. This fourfold understanding of Pentecostalism is best explored and explained by Donald W. Dayton, *Theological Roots of Pentecostalism* (Grand Rapids, MI: Baker Academic, 1987). The spiritual gifts manifest themselves prominently in the notions of Christ as Baptizer in the Holy Spirit (a reference to speaking in tongues and other spiritual manifestations which occur to the believer) and Christ as Healer (a reference to Christ's ability to cleanse an individual bodily of disease and spiritually of sin). A fivefold understanding also includes Christ as sanctifier.
17. Dayton, *Theological Roots of Pentecostalism*, 22.
18. Gilbert E. Farr, as cited in "Claim Strange Gift," *American Fork Citizen*, March 16, 1907, 4.
19. "Missionaries to Jerusalem," *Apostolic Faith*, September, 1906, 4.
20. "Missionaries Claim 'Gift of Tongues,'" *Salt Lake Tribune*, July 19, 1907, 3; and "'Apostolic Light' Mission," *Deseret News*, July 19, 1907, 10.
21. Thomas W. Simpson recently argued about the importance of these Latter-day Saints who received their education at secular universities in the early twentieth century. While Claude T. Barnes is not specifically highlighted in Simpson's work, his writings are definitely representative of the new generation of Latter-day Saints who would contend with Pentecostal theology in their adult years. For more on the importance of secular education among early twentieth century Latter-day Saints, see Thomas W. Simpson, *American Universities and the Birth of Modern Mormonism, 1867–1940* (Chapel Hill: University of North Carolina Press, 2016).
22. Claude T. Barnes, "The Unconscious Illapse," *Improvement Era* 10, no. 10 (August 1907): 783.
23. Barnes, "The Unconscious Illapse," 784.
24. Barnes, "The Unconscious Illapse," 789.
25. Barnes, "The Unconscious Illapse," 789.
26. "Spiritual Signs," *Liahona The Elders' Journal* 5, no. 17 (October 1907): 465.
27. "Spiritual Signs," *Liahona The Elders' Journal*, 466. The editorials do not list authors, but they may be written by B. F. Cummings, editor of the *Liahona* at this time, or perhaps by Samuel O. Bennion, the mission president and manager of the *Liahona*.
28. "The Marvelous," *Liahona The Elders' Journal* 5, no. 30 (January 1908): 806.
29. "The Marvelous," *Liahona*, 807.
30. "Speaking in Tongues," *Liahona The Elders' Journal* 5, no. 36 (February 1908): 954–9. Matthew Davies identifies the Pentecostal missionaries mentioned in this article, in his research. See Matthew Davies, "The Tongues of the Saints: The Azusa Street Revival and the Changing Definition of Tongues," in *Joseph F. Smith: Reflections on the Man and His Times*, ed. by Craig K. Manscill, Brian D.

Reeves, Guy L. Dorius, and J. B. Haws, (Provo, UT: Religious Studies Center and Deseret Book, 2013), 470–83. For additional analysis, see also Alan J. Clark, "'We Believe in the Gift of Tongues': The 1906 Pentecostal Revolution and Its Effects on the LDS Use of the Gift of Tongues in the Twentieth Century," *Mormon Historical Studies* 14, no. 1 (Spring 2013): 67–80.

31. "Speaking in Tongues," *Liahona*, 958.
32. "Spirits," *Liahona The Elders' Journal* 6, no. 48 (May 1909): 1149–52; and "Spirits," *Liahona The Elders' Journal* 6, no. 49 (May 1909): 1175–78. While there is no specific mention of the Pentecostal movement with the reprinted article, the timing of its reprinting, as well as the articles being printed around the same time, suggests that they are responding to the growing Pentecostal movement in the United States.
33. "The Gift of Tongues," *Goodwins Weekly*, February 8, 1908, 2.
34. Very few works examine the decline of charismatic expression among Latter-day Saints. There is much yet to be explored on this subject. As mentioned in footnote 16 of this chapter, Thomas G. Alexander's *Mormonism in Transition* is the most complete examination of doctrinal transitions among Latter-day Saints in the early twentieth century. He argues, "By the early 1920s the general authorities were actively discouraging such Pentecostal experience within the church." Alexander provides only about ten pages of analysis concerning the lived religion and spiritual practices of church members during this period. Although it leaves much to be desired, it does suggest that fewer Latter-day Saints continued publicly participating in charismatic worship. See Thomas G. Alexander, *Mormonism in Transition*, 288–98.
35. "The Love of the Truth and What it Will Save Us From," *The Bridegroom's Messenger*, February 1, 1914, 1.
36. "Questions Concerning Tongues," *The Bridegroom's Messenger*, May 15, 1908, 2.
37. "Questions Concerning Tongues," *The Bridegroom's Messenger*, 2.
38. E. N. Bell, "What Is Mormonism?," *Pentecostal Evangel*, March 6, 1920, 5.
39. E. N. Bell, "Questions and Answers," *The Pentecostal Evangel*, January 22, 1921, 10.
40. G. F. Taylor, "Mormons," *The Pentecostal Holiness Advocate* 2, no. 6 (June 6, 1918): 4; and Andrew L. Fraser, "Marriage and Divorce," *The Latter Rain Evangel*, October 1915, 8. My appreciation to John Christopher Thomas for pointing out these references. A discussion about Pentecostal perception of the Church of Jesus Christ of Latter-day Saints can be found in John Christopher Thomas, *A Pentecostal Reads the Book of Mormon: A Literary and Theological Introduction* (Cleveland, TN: CPT Press, 2016), 359–68.
41. Bell, "What Is Mormonism?,"5.
42. "The Growth of Mormonism," *The Bridegroom's Messenger*, November 15, 1912, 4; and Bell, "What Is Mormonism?," 5.
43. "Mormonism! A Survey of Its Blasphemous Pretentions and Evil Practices," *The Latter Rain Evangel*, February 1920, 20.
44. Several silent films, beginning with *A Victim of the Mormons*, promoted anti-Mormon concerns about polygamy throughout the early twentieth century. *Trapped by the Mormons*, released in 1922, continued the stereotype of Latter-day Saint missionaries in pursuit of polygamist wives more than a decade after the

Reed Smoot hearings gave a sort of finality to the continuing practice of polygamy within the Church of Jesus Christ of Latter-day Saints.

45. "Are Home Missions Needed?", *The Latter Rain Evangel*, September 1925, 12.
46. "Mormonism Today," *The Bridegroom's Messenger*, March 1, 1911, 2.
47. J. Spencer Fluhman, *"A Peculiar People": Anti-Mormonism and the Making of Religion in Nineteenth-Century America* (Chapel Hill: University of North Carolina Press, 2012), 146.
48. "The Love of the Truth and What it Will Save Us From," *The Bridegroom's Messenger*, February 1, 1914, 1.
49. Jamie Buckingham, "The Return of the Heresy Hunters," *Charisma and Christian Life*, January 1988, 82. In the article, Buckingham discusses how the fundamentalist Christian magazine *Moody Monthly* included the United Pentecostal Church on the list of "Pseudo-Christian churches," alongside Latter-day Saints and Jehovah's Witnesses.
50. A. A. Boddy, "Christian Science," *Confidence* 4, no. 7 (July 1911), 165.
51. "God's Word versus Man's Word," *The Latter Rain Evangel*, December 1912, 14.
52. "False Doctrine," *The Bridegroom's Messenger*, April 15, 1911, 1.
53. See Spencer Fluhman's discussion on the reevaluation of Mormonism in the late 1800s in J. Spencer Fluhman, *A Peculiar People*, 127–47.
54. Robert Mapes Anderson, *Vision of the Disinherited* (New York: Oxford University Press, 1979), 141.
55. A spokesperson for the Southern Baptist church described their concern over Pentecostalism in the following language: "Most of the folks who belong to this cult have been turned out of the churches. Not all, but most all. Those who have gone from our churches to walk this road of heresy have been worthless to the church when they belonged." As cited by Robert Mapes Anderson, *Vision of the Disinherited*, 141. It is likely they felt the same way about Latter-day Saints. With polygamy properly regulated, many people felt they no longer threatened the moral fabric of society.
56. The name of a missionary tract published by the Church of Jesus Christ of Latter-day Saints in 1922. L. Tom Perry Special Collections, Harold B. Lee Library, Brigham Young University, Provo, UT.
57. "Elder Nephi Jensen," *Ninetieth Annual Conference Report of the Church of Jesus Christ of Latter-day Saints* (Salt Lake City, UT: *Deseret News*, April 1920), 82.
58. For examples of early congregations in Utah, see Chapters 1–4.
59. "The Missions: Eastern States," *Liahona The Elders' Journal* 10, no. 36 (February 1913): 571.
60. "News from the Missions: Eastern States Mission," Helga Pederson, *Liahona The Elders' Journal* 13, no. 13 (September 1915): 202.
61. "The Missions: Eastern States," *Liahona The Elders' Journal* 10, no. 36 (February 1913): 571.
62. "News from the Missions," *Liahona The Elders Journal* 24, no. 14 (December 28, 1926): 328.
63. "News from the Missions: Eastern States," Helga Pederson, *Liahona The Elders' Journal* 13, no. 49 (May 1916): 783.

64. "News from the Missions: Western States Mission," Zelma Shaw stenographer, *Liahona The Elders' Journal* 16, no. 11 (September 1918): 1005.
65. Frank I. Kooyman, "Tract On!", in *Tracts and Tracting* (Liverpool, England: Church of Jesus Christ of Latter-day Saints European Mission Office, 1932), 20–21. L. Tom Perry Special Collections, Harold B. Lee Library, Brigham Young University, Provo, UT.
66. Many of these tracts are available in the archives of the L. Tom Perry Special Collections of the Harold B. Lee library at Brigham Young University. Others of these tracts are discussed in Jay E. Jensen, "Proselyting Techniques of Mormon Missionaries," (master's thesis, Brigham Young University, 1974).
67. In many interviews with Pentecostal pastors in Utah, they recalled how Latter-day Saints desiring to be called Christians felt like a relatively new and recent trend. Previously, they preferred to be called Mormons. This came up especially with older pastors that had resided in Utah since the mid-nineteenth century.
68. Dwight C. Ritchie, "The Case Against Polygamy," (Salt Lake City, UT: Published by Dwight C. Ritchie), 3, Church History Library, The Church of Jesus Christ of Latter-day Saints, Salt Lake City, UT.
69. Dwight C. Ritchie, Deceased Ministers File, Flower Pentecostal Heritage Center (Springfield, MO).
70. Dwight C. Ritchie, "Signs!," in a collection titled "Poems by Dwight C. Ritchie," December 1963, no page, Flower Pentecostal Heritage Center (Springfield, MO).
71. For more on William Paden, see Chapter 6. See also Charles Randall Paul, "Converting the Saints: An Investigation of Religious Conflict Using a Study of Protestant Missionary Methods in an Early 20th Century Engagement with Mormonism," (PhD diss., University of Chicago, 2000), 762–64. Paul argued that Paden believed "the Mormons were only playing possum until they grew large enough to have things their own way again." Other ministers in Utah, aware of continued polygamy in the state, held similar beliefs.
72. For additional details, see Jerold A. Hilton, "Polygamy in Utah and Surrounding Area Since the Manifesto," (master's thesis, Brigham Young University, 1965), 79–83. See also Martha Sonntag Bradley, *Kidnapped From That Land: The Government Raids on the Short Creek Polygamists* (Salt Lake City: University of Utah Press, 1993), 74–76. William Chatwin persuaded Dorothy Wyler, deemed mentally disabled, to leave her family and become one of his plural wives.
73. Dwight C. Ritchie, "An Exposure of False Teachers," (Salt Lake City, UT: Published by Dwight C. Ritchie, 1944), Church History Library, Church of Jesus Christ of Latter-day Saints, Salt Lake City, UT.
74. There is a collection of Dwight C. Ritchie's tracts in the Church History Library in Salt Lake City, Utah.
75. Dwight C. Ritchie, "Polygamy Disproved," (Salt Lake City, UT: Published by Dwight C. Ritchie, 1944), Church History Library, Church of Jesus Christ of Latter-day Saints.
76. Dwight C. Ritchie, "Revival of Polygamy Presents a Challenge to the Mormon Church," (Salt Lake City, UT: Published by Dwight C. Ritchie, 1944), Church History Library, Church of Jesus Christ of Latter-day Saints, Salt Lake City, UT.

77. Ritchie comments on the letters he wrote and the responses he received in his tracts from the period. While there are no other extant sources concerning the letters, the tracts appear to present a fairly reliable timeline of events from which to reconstruct his interactions with church and city leaders.
78. Ritchie, "An Exposure of False Teachers."
79. Ritchie, "An Exposure of False Teachers."
80. Dwight C. Ritchie, "Mormonism Disproved," (Salt Lake City, UT: Published by Dwight C. Ritchie, Salt Lake City, 1944), Church History Library, Church of Jesus Christ of Latter-day Saints, Salt Lake City, UT. For the content of the addresses, see Dwight C. Ritchie, "Friendly Open Letters to a Latter-day Saint," (Salt Lake City, UT: Published by Dwight C. Ritchie, Salt Lake City, 1944), Church History Library, Church of Jesus Christ of Latter-day Saints, Salt Lake City, UT.
81. There are examples of these bulletins in the archives of the Flower Pentecostal Heritage Center (Springfield, MO), including a collection of his poems cited earlier in this chapter.
82. Ritchie, "Friendly Open Letters to a Latter-day Saint."
83. Ritchie, "Friendly Open Letters to a Latter-day Saint."
84. Dwight C. Ritchie, "The Mind of Joseph Smith: A Study of the Words of the Founder of Mormonism Revealing 24 Symptoms of Mental Derangement," (Montana: Published by Dwight C. Ritchie, 1954), Church History Library, Church of Jesus Christ of Latter-day Saints, Salt Lake City, UT.
85. Dwight C. Ritchie, "The 'Book of Mormon' Hoax: An Exposure of One of the World's Wickedest Religious Frauds" (Montana: Published by Dwight C. Ritchie, 1956), Church History Library, Church of Jesus Christ of Latter-day Saints, Salt Lake City, UT.
86. Dwight C. Ritchie, letter from Hamilton, Montana, to J. Reuben Clark Jr., Salt Lake City, Utah, April 5, 1956, Church History Library, Church of Jesus Christ of Latter-day Saints, Salt Lake City, UT.
87. Dwight C. Ritchie, "Friendly Open Letters to a Latter-day Saint," Letter No. 4, (Salt Lake City, UT: Published by Dwight C. Ritchie, 1944), Church History Library, Church of Jesus Christ of Latter-day Saints, Salt Lake City, UT.
88. This phrase served as the slogan for the 1973 General Conference of the United Pentecostal Church, held at the Salt Palace in Salt Lake City, Utah.
89. "Religious Rites to Dedicate New Year," *Salt Lake Telegram*, December 29, 1951, 6. Even though the Spanish Assembly of God was part of the same denomination as the predominantly English speaking and white congregations, they seldom came together for fellowship meetings.
90. "Series for Pastors," *Salt Lake Tribune*, March 3, 1951, 31.
91. "Easter Sunrise Services Scheduled," *Hill Top Times*, April 5, 1957, 13. For commentary on the effect of the military chaplaincy on American religious trends, see Ronit Y. Stahl, *Enlisting Faith: How the Military Chaplaincy Shaped Religion and State in Modern America* (Cambridge, MA: Harvard University Press, 2017).
92. See *Pentecostal Evangel*, January 29, 1956, 29. *Who Are the False Prophets?* by Oswald J. Smith and *Mormonism Under the Searchlight* by William E. Biederwolf. These books were sold through the Gospel Publishing House of the Assemblies of God. Many books of this genre existed among Pentecostals.

93. Neil J. Young, *We Gather Together,* 34. The McKay era refers to the years 1951–1970, when David O. McKay presided as president of the Church of Jesus Christ of Latter-day Saints.
94. Neil J. Young, *We Gather Together,* 35.
95. "The Melchizedek Priesthood Now in Action," *Salt Lake Tribune,* January 19, 1974, 6. The reference to "Melchizedek priesthood" played suggestively with the Latter-day Saint doctrine of priesthood origins and restrictions.
96. R. G. Fulford, "Home Missions in Rocky Mountain District," *Pentecostal Evangel,* June 30, 1957, 20.
97. "Announcements," *Pentecostal Evangel,* February 23, 1964, 25.
98. "Youth Lends a Big Hand," *Pentecostal Evangel,* April 12, 1964, 20.
99. "Youth Lends a Big Hand," 20.
100. D. V. Hurst, "The Big 'Hi'—Operation Utah," *Pentecostal Evangel,* November 8, 1964, 10.
101. Hurst, "The Big 'Hi'," 11.
102. "The Utah Story," *Pentecostal Evangel,* February 13, 1972, 12.
103. Details of these missionary efforts are found in interviews with Robert Smith and Phil and Angie Smith, notes in the author's possession.
104. "'Herods' Fail, Evangelist Says," *Deseret News,* October 20, 1973, 4A.
105. "Pentecostal Crusade," *Outreach* VIII, no. 8 (November 1973), 1.
106. "Pentecostal Crusade," 4.
107. "Pentecostal Church Lists Growth," *Salt Lake Tribune,* January 19, 1974, 6.
108. Jessica Ravitz, "Moved by the Spirit: Fast-Growing Pentecostal Church Takes Root in 'The Last Frontier'", *Salt Lake Tribune,* May 6, 2006, available at archive.sltrib.com, accessed January 13, 2018.
109. A full discussion of the subject is in Chapter 5. Willard Coleman experienced significant pushback from the Tropic community as he worked to establish a physical location for the church in the community. See Anne Roberts, "Injustice Done," *Garfield County News,* May 24, 1979, 1.
110. Dean Jackson, as cited by Dean Merrill, "A Peacemaker in Provo: How One Pentecostal Pastor Taught His Congregation to Love Mormons," available at https://www.christianitytoday.com/ct/2000/february7/7.66.html, accessed April 16, 2017.
111. Roberto Gonzalez, "Assembly of God CEO Addresses BYU students," *Daily Universe,* September 17 2013.
112. "Narcizo Gallegos Called by Reaper," *San Juan Record,* November 23, 1944, 1.
113. "300 Attend First Vernal All-Faith Thanksgiving Service by Kiwanis," *Vernal Express,* December 2, 1954, 8.
114. Bob Mims, "'Master Mender,' Musical Passion Play, Marks 35th Year in Utah." *Salt Lake Tribune,* April 5, 2017, available at http://archive.sltrib.com/article.php?id=5138078&itype=CMSID, accessed May 14, 2018. Additional introductory information on the Master Mender production can be found at http://www.saltlakechristiancenter.org/ministries/mastermender/.
115. Jackson, as cited by Merrill, "A Peacemaker in Provo."
116. Jackson, as cited by Merrill, "A Peacemaker in Provo."
117. Jackson, as cited by Merrill, "A Peacemaker in Provo."
118. Stephen Robinson, as cited by Merrill, "A Peacemaker in Provo."

119. Jackson, as cited by Merrill, "A Peacemaker in Provo."
120. Laura Hancock, "Reel Place of Worship," *Deseret News*, November 6, 2007, available at https://www.deseretnews.com/article/705384091/Reel-place-of-worship.html, accessed July 9, 2018.
121. Gregory Johnson, from an interview conducted by the author, June 2017. A similar sentiment is shared by many pastors I have interviewed in the state.
122. Ray Smith, from an interview by the author, October 2013.
123. Alex Lucero, from an interview by the author, February 2017.
124. Chapter 5 discusses Pentecostal influence on local politics in more depth.
125. Roy Cazares, from an interview by the author, May 2018.
126. Greg Johnson, from an interview by the author, June 2017.
127. Greg Johnson, from an interview by the author, June 2017.
128. Carrie A. Moore, "Evangelical Preaches at Salt Lake Tabernacle," *Deseret News*, November 15, 2004, available at https://www.deseretnews.com/article/595105580/Evangelical-preaches-at-Salt-Lake-Tabernacle.html, accessed August 14, 2018. See also Carrie A. Moore, "Evangelist to speak at Tabernacle," *Deseret News*, September 11, 2004, available at https://www.deseretnews.com/article/595090586/Evangelist-to-speak-at-Tabernacle.html, accessed August 14, 2018. In the article Greg Johnson believed that the last non-Mormon to speak in the Tabernacle may have been Dwight L. Moody in 1871. Yet there are other examples. Pentecostal evangelist Mae Eleanor Frey described her experience preaching in the tabernacle in 1926. See Mae Eleanor Frey, "Preaching to the Mormons," *Pentecostal Evangel*, October 9, 1926, 9.
129. Richard Mouw, as cited by Carrie A. Moore, "Evangelical Preaches at Salt Lake Tabernacle."
130. Ronald V. Huggins, as cited by Carrie A. Moore, "Speaker's Apology to LDS Stirs Up Fuss," *Deseret News*, January 15, 2005, available at https://www.deseretnews.com/article/600104625/Speakers-apology-to-LDS-stirs-up-fuss.html, accessed August 14, 2018.
131. Michelle A. Vu, "Evangelicals, Mormons Search for Common Ground in Utah," *The Christian Post*, March 10, 2011, available at https://www.christianpost.com/news/evangelicals-mormon-search-for-common-ground-in-utah-49351/, accessed August 15, 2018.
132. C. H. Fisher, "George Wood Explains His Involvement with the LDS," September 26, 2013, available at http://www.truthkeepers.com/?p=228, accessed April 23, 2017.
133. Fisher, "George Wood Explains His Involvement with the LDS."
134. Robert D. Putnam and David E. Campbell, *American Grace: How Religion Divides and Unites Us* (New York: Simon and Schuster, 2010), 550; and Laurie Goodstein, "Mormons' Ad Campaign May Play Out on the '12 Campaign Trail," *New York Times*, November 17, 2011, available at https://www.nytimes.com/2011/11/18/us/mormon-ad-campaign-seeks-to-improve-perceptions.html, accessed August 20, 2018.
135. See Quentin L. Cook, "LDS Women are Incredible!," footnote 2. Available at https://www.lds.org/languages/eng/content/general-conference/2011/04/lds-women-are-incredible.

136. Putnam and Campbell, *American Grace*, 547.
137. George O. Wood, "Response to the 2016 Election," November 9, 2016, available at https://news.ag.org/en/News/Response-to-the-2016-Election, accessed December 29, 2018.
138. Fisher, "George Wood Explains his Involvement with the LDS."
139. Neil J. Young, *We Gather Together: The Religious Right and the Problem of Interfaith Politics* (New York: Oxford University Press, 2016), 297.
140. In many of the interviews with pastors and individuals in Utah, Pentecostals often made a point of noting how they do not and will not agree with Latter-day Saints on points of doctrine, even if they find value in the recent forms of engagement between the two religious communities.

EPILOGUE

1. Robert Orsi, *Between Heaven and Earth: The Religious Worlds People Make and the Scholars Who Study Them* (Princeton, NJ: Princeton University Press, 2005), 161.
2. Orsi, *Between Heaven and Earth*, 192.
3. Orsi, *Between Heaven and Earth*, 166.
4. Orsi, *Between Heaven and Earth*, 167.

BIBLIOGRAPHY

INTERVIEWS

The following includes interviews I collected from individuals within the Utah Pentecostal community. There are also a few interviews listed in this section concerning the experience of African Americans in Utah from the Special Collections Department of the J. Willard Marriott Library, University of Utah.

Aguilar, Bob. Interview by Alan J. Clark. February 13, 2017.
Akins, Pete. Interview by Alan J. Clark. July 23, 2013.
Allen, Bobby. Interview by Alan J. Clark. September 30, 2020.
Ansel, Raymond. Interview by Alan J. Clark. September 20, 2017.
Archuleta, Mike. Interview by Alan J. Clark. June 7, 2015.
Ayers, Jim. Interview by Alan J. Clark. July 26, 2013.
Boyles, Harley. Interview by Alan J. Clark. January 17, 2018.
Browne, Howard. "Interviews with African Americans in Utah, Howard Browne Interview 2." Ms0453, Interviews with Blacks in Utah, 1982–1988. J. Willard Marriott Library. University of Utah (Salt Lake City).
Burnett, Danny. "Interviews with African Americans in Utah, Danny Burnett Interview," Ms0453, Interviews with Blacks in Utah, 1982–1988. J. Willard Marriott Library. University of Utah (Salt Lake City).
Burrows, Leon, and Barbara Burrows. Interview by Alan J. Clark. October 25, 2013.
Burrows, Leon, and Barbara Burrows. Interview by Alan J. Clark. June 6, 2015.
Burrows, Leon, and Barbara Burrows. Interview by Alan J. Clark. February 8, 2017.
Cairoli, Dario. Interview by Alan J. Clark. June 9, 2015.
Cazares, Becky. Interview by Alan J. Clark. July 23, 2015.
Cazares, Roy. Interview by Alan J. Clark. May 2, 2018.
Christensen, Pat. Interview by Alan J. Clark. January 17, 2018.
Clark, Andrew. Interview by Alan J. Clark. March 8, 2017.
Coleman, Willard. Interview by Alan J. Clark. September 21 and 24, 2018.
Croasmun, Max. Interview by Alan J. Clark. October 25, 2013.
Fitzgerel, William. Interview by Alan J. Clark. July 25, 2013.
Fry, Doris. "Interviews with African Americans in Utah, Doris Fry Interview." Ms0453, Interviews with Blacks in Utah, 1982–1988. J. Willard Marriott Library. University of Utah (Salt Lake City).
Guerrero, Eugene. Interview by Alan J. Clark. July 29, 2018.
Iwaarden, Jerry van. Interview by Alan J. Clark. July 23, 2013.
Johns, Terry. Interview by Alan J. Clark. April 18, 2019.

Johnson, Erik. Interview by Alan J. Clark. July 31, 2013.
Johnson, Gregory. Interview by Alan J. Clark. June 27, 2017.
Johnson, Ivan. Interview by Alan J. Clark. July 26, 2013.
Jones, Ed. Interview by Alan J. Clark. April 2018.
Lautenschlager, Jerry. Interview by Alan J. Clark. July 31, 2013.
Lopez, Fred. Interview by Alan J. Clark. June 17, 2018.
Lucero, Alex. Interview by Alan J. Clark. July 31, 2013.
Lucero, Alex. Interview by Alan J. Clark. October 25, 2013.
Lucero, Alex. Interview by Alan J. Clark. February 22, 2017.
Markham, Sandy. Interview by Alan J. Clark. August 1, 2013.
McCallister, Henry. Interview by Alan J. Clark. March 8, 2017.
McIntosh, Ray, and Loretta McIntosh. Interview by Alan J. Clark. January 24, 2018.
Nabors, Joan. "Interviews with African Americans in Utah, Joan Nabors Interview." Ms0453, Interviews with Blacks in Utah, 1982–1988. J. Willard Marriott Library. University of Utah (Salt Lake City).
Nicholson, David. Interview by Alan J. Clark. July 16, 2013.
Perea, Inez. Interview by Alan J. Clark. July 23, 2015.
Rice, Ronald. Interview by Alan J. Clark. March 8, 2017.
Russell, John. Interview by Alan J. Clark. July 17, 2013.
Smith, Fred. Interview by Alan J. Clark. March 11, 2018.
Smith, Phil, and Angie Smith. Interview by Alan J. Clark. October 24, 2013.
Smith, Ray. Interview by Alan J. Clark. October 26, 2013.
Smith, Ray. Interview by Alan J. Clark. February 22, 2017.
Smith, Robert. Interview by Alan J. Clark. October 26, 2013.
Smith, Robert. Interview by Alan J. Clark. February 11, 2017.
Sparger, James. Interview by Alan J. Clark. March 11, 2017.
Velasquez, David. Interview by Alan J. Clark. March 22, 2019.
Vigil, Tommy. Interview by Alan J. Clark. December 21, 2018.
Vigil, Virginia. Interview by Alan J. Clark. July 23, 2015.
Williams, Judy. Interview by Alan J. Clark. October 26, 2017.
Williams, Terry. "Interviews with African Americans in Utah, Terry Williams Interview." Ms0453, Interviews with Blacks in Utah, 1982–1988. J. Willard Marriott Library. University of Utah (Salt Lake City).

NEWSPAPER ARTICLES

Unraveling the story of Pentecostalism in Utah required using hundreds of newspaper articles. References throughout the book come from newspapers across the state of Utah at various times during the twentieth and twenty-first centuries. I have chosen not to list every newspaper article here. However, I am indebted to the work of the Utah Digital Newspapers Archive at the J. Willard Marriott Library, University of Utah. Although many articles came from the archives of local newspapers around the state, the vast majority of the articles are publicly available and searchable through the ongoing efforts of the archive. The religion columns and advertisements for churches were also used from various Utah newspapers throughout the twentieth century to locate and identify church communities over the decades.

PENTECOSTAL PUBLICATIONS AND ARCHIVAL RECORDS

The sources in this section are unique sources on Pentecostal history in Utah, written by Pentecostals about their work. Academic sources concerning Pentecostalism will be found among the general list of publications.

"Announcements." *Pentecostal Evangel.* February 23, 1964.

"Are Home Missions Needed?" *The Latter Rain Evangel.* September 1925.

Austell, J. E. "First Utah State Camp Meeting." *Pentecostal Evangel.* October 6, 1945.

Bazán, Demetrio. "Concilio de Distrito." *La Luz Apostólica.* January 1946.

Bazán, Néstor. Deceased Ministers File. Flower Pentecostal Heritage Center (Springfield, MO).

Bazán, Néstor. "Dragerton, Utah." *La Luz Apostólica.* April 1949.

Bazán, Néstor. "Dragerton, Utah." *La Luz Apostólica.* August 1949.

Bazán, Néstor. "Nota Necrológica." *La Luz Apostólica.* November 1948.

Bell, E. N. "Questions and Answers." *The Pentecostal Evangel.* January 22, 1921.

Bell, E. N. "What Is Mormonism?" *Pentecostal Evangel.* March 6, 1920.

Boddy, A. A. "Christian Science." *Confidence* 4, no. 7 (July 1911): 165.

Boyd, Loretta, and Grace Hall. "Great Victory in Summit Point, Utah." *Church of God Evangel.* December 7, 1929.

Boyles, William H. Correspondence to J. W. Welch. August 9, 1923. Flower Pentecostal Heritage Center (Springfield, MO).

Bryant, Leona. "Salt Lake City, Utah." *Pentecostal Evangel.* November 11, 1944.

Caudle, Benjamin H. Deceased Ministers File. Flower Pentecostal Heritage Center (Springfield, MO).

Chesser, H. L. "Assistant General Overseer's Convention Work." *Church of God Evangel.* August 28, 1948.

Combined Minutes of the General Council of the Assemblies of God in the United States of America, Canada, and Foreign Lands 1914–1917. Flower Pentecostal Heritage Center (Springfield, MO).

"Concise History of First Assembly Salt Lake." Rocky Mountain District Offices of the Assemblies of God (Colorado Springs, CO).

Constitution and Bylaws of the General Council of the Assemblies of God. September 1933. Flower Pentecostal Heritage Center (Springfield, MO).

Eiting, Fred. "The Largest Untouched Field in the United States." *Weekly Evangel.* December 9, 1916.

Elliott, L. Vere. Deceased Ministers File. Flower Pentecostal Heritage Center (Springfield, MO).

Elliott, L. Vere. "Salt Lake City, Utah." *The Pentecostal Evangel.* October 23, 1926.

Enriquez, Vidal. Deceased Ministers File. Flower Pentecostal Heritage Center (Springfield, MO).

Enriquez, Vidal. "Salt Lake City, Utah." *La Luz Apostólica.* February 1942.

Enriquez, Vidal. "Salt Lake City, Utah." *La Luz Apostólica.* May 1942.

"Every Foot of Ground Must Be Covered by Our Workers." *The Church of God Evangel.* March 19, 1921.

"False Doctrine." *The Bridegroom's Messenger.* April 15, 1911.

Feick, August. "The Etter Meeting at Salt Lake City." *The Weekly Evangel.* November 4, 1916.
"Field Representatives." *Pentecostal Herald.* March 1917.
Franco, Simón R. "Embajadores de Cristo." *La Luz Apostólica.* April 1937.
Fraser, Andrew L. "Marriage and Divorce." *The Latter Rain Evangel.* October 1915.
Frey, Mae Eleanor. "Preaching to the Mormons." *Pentecostal Evangel.* October 9, 1926.
Fulford, R. G. "Home Missions in Rocky Mountain District." *Pentecostal Evangel,* June 30, 1957, 20–21.
Girón, Eugenio. "Dragerton, Utah." *La Luz Apostólica.* July 1945.
"God's Word Versus Man's Word." *The Latter Rain Evangel.* December 1912.
Griffin, Thomas. "Salt Lake City, Utah." *The Weekly Evangel.* May 5, 1917.
Griffin, Thomas. "A Word of Cheer from Salt Lake City, Utah." *The Weekly Evangel.* May 19, 1917.
Hall, Grace. "Pray for the Gospel Light to Shine in Utah." *Church of God Evangel.* February 21, 1931.
Heath, Guy M. "Salt Lake City, Utah." *Pentecostal Evangel.* March 16, 1946.
Heath, Guy M. "Salt Lake City, Utah." *Pentecostal Evangel.* January 21, 1950.
Heath, Guy M. "Tent Meetings Continued for Five Weeks in Salt Lake City." *Pentecostal Evangel.* October 19, 1952.
History Collection of the Utah Church of God in Christ. Ogden, UT.
Holden, David T. Letter to Lilly Strayer. April 6, 1976. From the collection of Barbara Burrows.
Hurst, D. V. "The Big 'Hi'—Operation Utah." *Pentecostal Evangel.* November 8, 1964.
Jernigan, John C. "The General Overseer Speaks." *Church of God Evangel.* October 7, 1944.
Kienel, Paul. Deceased Ministers File. Flower Pentecostal Heritage Center (Springfield, MO).
Kinsey, Jess W. "Future Prospects Looking Good For Church in Utah." *Church of God Evangel.* February 7, 1931.
Latimer, S. W. "Notices & Specials." *Church of God Evangel.* February 21, 1931.
Linden, Gordon, Isaac Linden, and Martin Linden. Correspondence to N. R. Nichols. September 20, 1923. Flower Pentecostal Heritage Center (Springfield, MO).
Lowe, Robert H. "Woodworth-Etter Meeting at Salt Lake City, Utah." *The Weekly Evangel.* September 16, 1916.
Lowe, Robert H. "Fellowship in Christ." *The Weekly Evangel.* April 21, 1917.
Lowe, Robert H. Correspondence to J. W. Welch. August 21, 1923. Flower Pentecostal Heritage Center (Springfield, MO).
Marez, José Facundo. "Conferencia del Oeste de Colorado." *La Luz Apostólica.* March 1943.
Marez, José Facundo. "Testifica un Veterano," *La Luz Apostólica,* December 1966.
Martínez, Fidel. "Una Gloriosa Junta de Confraternidad." *La Luz Apostólica.* February 1947.
McCabe, P. D. "Reports from the Field." *Pentecostal Evangel.* December 27, 1919.
Medina, Alberto. "Price, Utah." *La Luz Apostólica.* May 1950.
Merrill, Dean. "A Peacemaker in Provo: How One Pentecostal Pastor Taught his Congregation to Love Mormons." *Christianity Today.* February 7, 2000. Available at https://www.christianitytoday.com/ct/2000/february7/7.66.html. Accessed April 16, 2017.
Ministers Directory General Council, 1914–1917. Flower Pentecostal Heritage Center (Springfield, MO).
Minutes of the General Council of the Assemblies of God in the United States of America, Canada, and Foreign Lands. April 1914. Flower Pentecostal Heritage Center (Springfield, MO).

Minutes of the General Council of the Assemblies of God. October 1916. Flower Pentecostal Heritage Center (Springfield, MO).

Minutes of the Twenty-fifth Annual Assembly. Cleveland, TN: Church of God Publishing House, 1930. Dixon Pentecostal Research Center (Cleveland, TN).

"Missionaries to Jerusalem." *Apostolic Faith*. September 1906.

Moore, E. L. "Notices & Specials." *Church of God Evangel*. July 4, 1931.

"Mormonism! A Survey of Its Blasphemous Pretentions and Evil Practices." *The Latter Rain Evangel*. February 1920.

"Mormonism Today." *The Bridegroom's Messenger*. March 1, 1911.

Official List of Ministers and Missionaries of the General Council of the Assemblies of God. January 1937. Flower Pentecostal Heritage Center (Springfield, MO).

Ogden Application for Affiliation with the General Council of the Assemblies of God. Rocky Mountain District offices of the Assemblies of God (Colorado Springs, CO).

"Pentecostal Crusade." *Outreach* VIII, no. 8 (November 1973): 1, 4.

Perry, Ethel M. "Eyes Set in Death—Instantly Healed." *Church of God Evangel*. June 30, 1945.

Pugh, J. T. "New Church Is Opened in Salt Lake City, Utah." *Outreach* VIII, no. 8, November 1973. Center for the Study of Oneness Pentecostalism, Urshan College (Florissant, MO).

"Questions Concerning Tongues." *The Bridegroom's Messenger*. May 15, 1908.

Ramsey, H. E. "Greetings from Utah." *Church of God Evangel*. July 4, 1942.

"Reports from the Reapers." *The Pentecostal Evangel*. November 9, 1940.

"Requests for Prayer." *The Weekly Evangel*. May 20, 1916.

"'Ripe Harvest' In Utah." *Outreach* IV, (1969). Center for the Study of Oneness Pentecostalism, Urshan College (Florissant, MO).

Ritchie, Dwight C. "An Exposure of False Teachers." Salt Lake City, UT: Published by Dwight C. Ritchie, 1944. Church History Library, The Church of Jesus Christ of Latter-day Saints (Salt Lake City).

Ritchie, Dwight C. Deceased Ministers File. Flower Pentecostal Heritage Center (Springfield, MO).

Ritchie, Dwight C. "Friendly Open Letters to a Latter-day Saint." Salt Lake City, UT: Published by Dwight C. Ritchie, 1944. Church History Library, The Church of Jesus Christ of Latter-day Saints (Salt Lake City).

Ritchie, Dwight C. Letter to J. Reuben Clark Jr. April 5, 1956. Church History Library, The Church of Jesus Christ of Latter-day Saints (Salt Lake City).

Ritchie, Dwight C. "Mormonism Disproved." Salt Lake City, UT: Published by Dwight C. Ritchie, 1944. Church History Library, The Church of Jesus Christ of Latter-day Saints (Salt Lake City).

Ritchie, Dwight C. "Poems by Dwight C. Ritchie." December 1963. Flower Pentecostal Heritage Center (Springfield, MO).

Ritchie, Dwight C. "Polygamy Disproved." Salt Lake City, UT: Published by Dwight C. Ritchie, 1944. Church History Library, The Church of Jesus Christ of Latter-day Saints (Salt Lake City).

Ritchie, Dwight C. "Revival of Polygamy Presents a Challenge to the Mormon Church." Salt Lake City, UT: Published by Dwight C. Ritchie, 1944. Church History Library, The Church of Jesus Christ of Latter-day Saints (Salt Lake City).

Ritchie, Dwight C. "The 'Book of Mormon' Hoax: An Exposure of One of the World's Wickedest Religious Frauds." Montana: Published by Dwight C. Ritchie, 1956. Church History Library, The Church of Jesus Christ of Latter-day Saints (Salt Lake City).

Ritchie, Dwight C. "The Case Against Polygamy." Salt Lake City, UT: Published by Dwight C. Ritchie, 1944. Church History Library, The Church of Jesus Christ of Latter-day Saints (Salt Lake City).

Ritchie, Dwight C. "The Mind of Joseph Smith: A Study of the Words of the Founder of Mormonism Revealing 24 Symptoms of Mental Derangement." Montana: Published by Dwight C. Ritchie, 1954. Church History Library, The Church of Jesus Christ of Latter-day Saints (Salt Lake City).

Salazar, A. T. "Historia." *La Luz Apostólica*. June 1969.

Salt Lake City Application for Affiliation with the General Council of the Assemblies of God. Rocky Mountain District Offices of the Assemblies of God (Colorado Springs, CO).

"Salt Lake City." *The Christian Evangel*. October 24, 1914.

Silvey, Frank. "Written for the Historical Survey of San Juan County, Utah, Frank Silvey, July 6, 1936, Monticello, Utah." MSSB57, Box 188, folder 4. Utah State History Research Center (Salt Lake City).

Simmons, E. L. "Church Growing in Utah." *Church of God Evangel*. January 23, 1932.

Steinkamp, Eric. "History of the Rocky Mountain District of the Assemblies of God." Flower Pentecostal Heritage Center (Springfield, MO).

Strayer, Lilly May. "Application for District Credentials of the Rocky Mountain District Council of the Assemblies of God." 1952. From the collection of Barbara Burrows.

Strayer, Lilly May. Letter to Russel G. Fulford. June 25, 1953. Layton, Utah. From the collection of Barbara Burrows.

Strayer, Lilly May. Testimony written in her personal Bible. In the possession of Barbara Burrows.

Taylor, G. F. "Mormons." *The Pentecostal Holiness Advocate* 2, no. 6 (June 6, 1918): 4.

"The End of the Sidney, Iowa Meeting." *The Weekly Evangel*. October 28, 1916.

"The Growth of Mormonism." *The Bridegroom's Messenger*. November 15, 1912.

"The Love of the Truth and What It Will Save Us From." *The Bridegroom's Messenger*. February 1, 1914.

"This Week's Cover." *Pentecostal Evangel*. May 30, 1954.

Thompson, Gilbert T. Deceased Ministers File. Flower Pentecostal Heritage Center (Springfield, MO).

Tomlinson, A. J. "Editorial." *Church of God Evangel*. June 4, 1921.

"The Utah Story." *Pentecostal Evangel*. February 13, 1972.

Wagner, G. W. "Reports from the Field." *Pentecostal Evangel*. June 21, 1924.

Walker, J. H. "Notes From My Letters. . . ." *Church of God Evangel*. June 20, 1942.

Wells, J. D. "Young Man, Go West!" *Pentecostal Evangel*. April 28, 1923.

Wood, George O. "Response to the 2016 Election." November 9, 2016. Available at https://news.ag.org/en/News/Response-to-the-2016-Election. Accessed December 29, 2018.

"Youth Lends a Big Hand." *Pentecostal Evangel*. April 12, 1964.

BOOKS, ARTICLES, DISSERTATIONS

Alder, Douglas D., and Karl F. Brooks. *A History of Washington County: From Isolation to Destination*. Utah Centennial County History Series (2nd ed.). Salt Lake City: Utah State Historical Society and Zion Natural History Association, 2007.

Alexander, Estrelda, and Amos Yong, eds. *Philip's Daughters: Women in Pentecostal-Charismatic Leadership*. Eugene, OR: Pickwick Publications, 2009.

Alexander, Thomas G. *Mormonism in Transition: A History of the Latter-day Saints, 1890–1930* (3rd ed.). Draper, UT: Greg Kofford Books, Inc., 2012.

Alexander, Thomas G., and James B. Allen. *Mormons and Gentiles: A History of Salt Lake City.* Boulder, CO: Pruett Publishing Co., 1984.

Alexander, Thomas G., and James B. Allen. *Utah, the Right Place: The Official Centennial History*. Salt Lake City, UT: Gibbs Smith Publisher in association with the Utah State Historical Society, 1995.

Allen, James B. *Still the Right Place: Utah's Second Half-Century of Statehood, 1945–1995*. Salt Lake City, UT: Charles Redd Center for Western Studies and the Utah State Historical Society, 2017.

Allen, Joseph Elmer. "A Sociological Study of Mexican Assimilation in Salt Lake City." Master's thesis, University of Utah, 1947.

"America's Changing Religious Landscape." Pew Research Center, Washington, DC (May 12, 2015).

Anderson, Allen. *An Introduction to Pentecostalism: Global Charismatic Christianity* (2nd ed.). New York: Cambridge University Press, 2014.

Anderson, Robert Mapes. *Vision of the Disinherited: The Making of American Pentecostalism.* Peabody, MA: Hendrickson Publishers, 1992.

Antrei, Albert C. T., and Allen D. Roberts. *A History of Sanpete County*. Utah Centennial County History Series. Salt Lake City: Utah State Historical Society, 1999.

Ballestero, Carl Joseph. *How High My Mountain*. Bloomington, CA: Carl Joseph Ballestero, 1991.

Barfoot, Charles H., and Gerald T. Sheppard. "Prophetic vs. Priestly Religion: The Changing Role of Women Clergy in Classical Pentecostal Churches." *Review of Religious Research* 22, no. 1 (September 1980): 2–17.

Barnes, Claude T. "The Unconscious Illapse." *Improvement Era* 10, no. 10 (August 1907): 783–89.

Barton, John D. *A History of Duchesne County*. Utah Centennial County History Series. Salt Lake City: Utah State Historical Society, 1998.

Batura, Paul J. *Good Day! The Paul Harvey Story*. Washington, DC: Regnery Publishing, Inc., 2009.

Bishop, M. Guy. *A History of Sevier County*. Utah Centennial County History Series. Salt Lake City: Utah State Historical Society, 1997.

Blanthorn, Ouida, ed. *A History of Tooele County*. Utah Centennial County History Series. Salt Lake City: Utah State Historical Society, 1998.

Bloch-Hoell, Nils. *The Pentecostal Movement: Its Origin, Development, and Distinctive Character*. New York: Humanities Press, 1964.

Blumhofer, Edith L., Russell P. Spittler, and Grant A. Wacker, eds. *Pentecostal Currents in American Protestantism*. Urbana: University of Illinois Press, 1999.

Blumhofer, Edith L. "Selected Letters of Mae Eleanore Frey." *Pneuma* 17, no. 1 (Spring 1995): 67.

Blumhofer, Edith L. *The Assemblies of God: A Chapter in the Story of American Pentecostalism* (two volumes). Springfield, MO: Gospel Publishing House, 1989.

Botham, Fay, and Sara M. Patterson, eds. *Race, Religion, Region: Landscapes of Encounter in the American West*. Tucson: University of Arizona Press, 2000.

Brackenridge, R. Douglas. "Hostile Mormons and Persecuted Presbyterians in Utah, 1870–1900: A Reappraisal." *Journal of Mormon History* 37, no. 3 (Summer 2011): 162–228.

Brackenridge, R. Douglas. "Presbyterians and Latter-day Saints in Utah: A Century of Conflict and Compromise, 1830–1930." *The Journal of Presbyterian History* 80, no. 4 (Winter 2002): 205–24.

Bradley, Martha Sonntag. *A History of Beaver County*. Utah Centennial County History Series. Salt Lake City: Utah State Historical Society, 1999.

Bradley, Martha Sonntag. *A History of Kane County*. Utah Centennial County History Series. Salt Lake City: Utah State Historical Society, 1999.

Bradley, Martha Sonntag. *Kidnapped From That Land: The Government Raids on the Short Creek Polygamists*. Salt Lake City: University of Utah Press, 1993.

Bringhurst, Newell G. *Saints, Slaves, and Blacks: The Changing Place of Black People Within Mormonism*. Westport, CT: Greenwood Press, 1981.

Brooks, Juanita. *The History of the Jews in Utah and Idaho*. Salt Lake City, UT: Western Epics, 1973.

Brown, Sara Black. "Krishna, Christians, and Colors: The Socially Binding Influence of Kirtan Singing at a Utah Hare Krishna Festival." *Ethnomusicology* 58, no. 3 (Fall 2014): 454–80.

Buckingham, Jamie. "The Return of the Heresy Hunters." *Charisma and Christian Life* (January 1988): 82.

Burton, Doris Karren. *A History of Uintah County: Scratching the Surface*. Utah Centennial County History Series. Salt Lake City: Utah State Historical Society, 1996.

Burton, Frederick G. *Presbyterians in Zion: History of the Presbyterian Church (USA) in Utah*. New York: Vantage Press, 2010.

Bushman, Jesse. "A Quantitative Analysis of the Non-LDS Experience in Utah." Master's thesis, Brigham Young University, 1995.

Butler, Anthea D. *Women in the Church of God in Christ: Making a Sanctified World*. Chapel Hill: University of North Carolina Press, 2007.

Campo, Ismael Martín Del, ed. *The First Sixty Years of the Apostolic Assembly: 1906–1966*. Rancho Cucamonga, CA: Apostolic Assembly of the Faith in Christ Jesus, 2014.

Clark, Alan J. "'We Believe in the Gift of Tongues': The 1906 Pentecostal Revolution and Its Effects on the LDS Use of the Gift of Tongues in the Twentieth Century." *Mormon Historical Studies* 14, no. 1 (Spring 2013): 67–80.

Clark Jr., J. Reuben. "All Roads Lead to Rome." *The Improvement Era* 63, no. 6 (June 1960): 398–99.

Coleman, Ronald G. "A History of Blacks in Utah, 1825–1910." PhD diss., University of Utah, 1980.

Conn, Charles W. *Like A Mighty Army: A History of the Church of God, 1886–1996*. Cleveland, TN: Pathway Press, 1996.

Cook, Quentin L. "LDS Women are Incredible!" Footnote 2. Available at https://www.lds.org/languages/eng/content/general-conference/2011/04/lds-women-are-incredible.

Cox, Harvey. *Fire from Heaven: The Rise of Pentecostal Spirituality and the Reshaping of Religion in the Twenty-First Century*. Cambridge, MA: Da Capo Press, 1995.

Cressler, Matthew J. *Authentically Black and Truly Catholic: The Rise of Black Catholicism in the Great Migration*. New York: New York University Press, 2017.

Crews, Mickey. *The Church of God: A Social History*. Knoxville: University of Tennessee Press, 1990.

Crowder, Myke. "History of First Assembly of God Layton, Utah." Master's thesis, Southwestern Assemblies of God College, 1988.

Cummings, Kathleen Sprows. *New Women of the Old Faith: Gender and American Catholicism in the Progressive Era*. Chapel Hill: University of North Carolina Press, 2009.

Darling, Dee Richard. "Cultures in Conflict: Congregationalism, Mormonism and Schooling in Utah, 1880–1893." PhD diss., University of Utah, 1991.

Davis, France. *Light in the Midst of Zion: A History of Black Baptists in Utah, 1892–1996*. Salt Lake City, UT: University Publishing, 1997.

Davis, France. "Utah in the '40s: An African American Perspective." *Beehive History* 25 (1999): 24–27.

Dayton, Donald W. *Theological Roots of Pentecostalism*. Grand Rapids, Michigan: Baker Academic, 1987.

Directory of Churches and Religious Organizations in Utah (Not Including the Church of Jesus Christ of Latter-day Saints). Historical Records Survey Division of Women's and Professional Projects Works Progress Administration. Ogden, UT: Historical Records Survey, 1938.

Ditmars, R. Maud. "A History of Baptist Missions in Utah, 1871–1931." Master's thesis, University of Colorado, 1931.

Donovan, Mary S. "Women Missionaries in Utah." *Anglican and Episcopal History* 66, no. 2 (June 1997): 154–74.

Dormady, Jason H., and Jared M. Tamez, eds. *Just South of Zion: The Mormons in Mexico and Its Borderlands*. Albuquerque: University of New Mexico Press, 2015.

Drescher, Elizabeth. *Choosing Our Religion: The Spiritual Lives of America's Nones*. New York: Oxford University Press, 2016.

DuPree, Sherry Sherrod. *African-American Holiness Pentecostal Movement: An Annotated Bibliography*. New York: Garland Publishing, Inc., 1996.

Dwyer, Robert J. *The Gentile Comes to Utah: A Study in Religious and Social Conflict, 1862–1890* (revised 2nd ed.). Salt Lake City, UT: Western Epics, 1971.

Embry, Jessie L. *A History of Wasatch County*. Utah Centennial County History Series. Salt Lake City: Utah State Historical Society, 1996.

Espinosa, Gastón. *Latino Pentecostals in America: Faith and Politics in Action*. Cambridge, MA: Harvard University Press, 2014.

Espinosa, Gastón. *William J. Seymour and the Origins of Global Pentecostalism: A Biography and Documentary History*. Durham, NC: Duke University Press, 2014.

Firmage, Richard A. *A History of Grand County*. Utah Centennial County History Series. Salt Lake City: Utah State Historical Society, 1996.

The First Century of the Methodist Church in Utah. Salt Lake City: Utah Methodism Centennial Committee, 1970.

Fisher, C. H. "George Wood Explains His Involvement with the LDS." September 26, 2013. Available at http://www.truthkeepers.com/?p=228. Accessed April 23, 2017.

Flake, Kathleen. *The Politics of American Religious Identity: The Seating of Senator Reed Smoot, Mormon Apostle*. Chapel Hill: University of North Carolina Press, 2004.

Fluhman, J. Spencer. *"A Peculiar People": Anti-Mormonism and the Making of Religion in Nineteenth-Century America*. Chapel Hill: University of North Carolina Press, 2012.

French, Talmadge L. *Early Interracial Oneness Pentecostalism: G. T. Haywood and the Pentecostal Assemblies of the World*. Eugene, OR: Pickwick Publications, 2014.

Friesen, Aaron T. *Norming the Abnormal: The Development and Function of the Doctrine of Initial Evidence in Classical Pentecostalism*. Eugene, OR: Pickwick Publications, 2013.

Geary, Edward A. *A History of Emery County*. Utah Centennial County History Series. Salt Lake City: Utah State Historical Society, 1996.

George, Harold, and Fay Lunceford Muhlestein. *Monticello Journal: A History of Monticello until 1937*. Monticello, UT: Published by Harold George and Fay Lunceford Muhlestein, 1988.

Givens, Terryl. *Feeding the Flock: The Foundations of Mormon Thought: Church and Praxis*. New York: Oxford University Press, 2017.

Guarneri, Carl, and David Alvarez Lanham, eds. *Religion and Society in the American West: Historical Essays*. Lanham, MD: University Press of America, 1987.

Hampshire, David, Martha Sonntag Bradley, and Allen Roberts. *A History of Summit County*. Utah Centennial County History Series. Salt Lake City: Utah State Historical Society, 1998.

Hilton, Jerold A. "Polygamy in Utah and Surrounding Area Since the Manifesto." Master of Arts, Brigham Young University, 1965.

Hine, Robert V., and John Mack Faragher. *The American West: A New Interpretive History*. New Haven, CT: Yale University Press, 2000.

Hobbs, Franklin, and Nicole Stoops. *Demographic Trends in the 20th Century: Census 2000 Special Reports*. Washington, DC: US Census Bureau, November 2002. Available at https://www.census.gov/prod/2002pubs/censr-4.pdf.

Hoge, Dean R., and Jacqueline E. Wenger. *Pastors in Transition: Why Clergy Leave Local Church Ministry*. Grand Rapids, MI: William B. Eerdmans Publishing Co., 2005.

Holzapfel, Richard Neitzel. *A History of Utah County*. Utah Centennial County History Series. Salt Lake City: Utah State Historical Society, 1999.

Huchel, Frederick M. *A History of Box Elder County*. Utah Centennial County History Series. Salt Lake City: Utah State Historical Society, 1999.

Hunke, Edmund W. *Southern Baptists in the Mountain West (1940–1989), A Fifty-Year History of Utah, Idaho, and Nevada Southern Baptists*. Franklin, TN: Providence House Publishers, 1998.

Hyde, Orson. "Discourse by President Orson Hyde." In *Journal of Discourses* 16, 230: 228–36. London: Latter-day Saints' Book Depot, 1874.

Iber, Jorge. *Hispanics in the Mormon Zion, 1912–1999*. College Station: Texas A&M University Press, 2000.

"Information Concerning Paul Harvey's Visit to Brigham Young University." L. Tom Perry Special Collections, Harold B. Lee Library, MSS SC 2941. Brigham Young University (Provo, UT).

"Inventory of the Church Archives of Utah: Smaller Denominations." Volume 3, Utah Historical Records Survey. Prepared by the Utah Historical Records Survey Division of Professional and Service Projects, Works Progress Administration. Ogden, Utah, February 1941. PAM1489. Utah State History Research Center (Salt Lake City).

Jensen, Jay E. "Proselyting Techniques of Mormon Missionaries." Master of Arts, Brigham Young University, 1974.

Jensen, Nephi. "Elder Nephi Jensen." In *Ninetieth Annual Conference Report of the Church of Jesus Christ of Latter-day Saints*. (Salt Lake City, UT: *Deseret News*, April 1920), 80–83.

Jenson, Andrew. "Elder Andrew Jenson." In *Seventy-sixth Semi-annual Conference Report of the Church of Jesus Christ of Latter-day Saints*. (Salt Lake City, UT: *Deseret News*, October 1905), 66–69.

Johnson, Michael W. *A History of Daggett County*. Utah Centennial County History Series. Salt Lake City: Utah State Historical Society, 1998.

Jones, Robert P. *The End of White Christian America*. New York: Simon & Schuster, 2016.

Jones, Robert P., and Daniel Cox *America's Changing Religious Identity*. Public Religion Research Institute, September 6, 2017. Available at https://www.prri.org/research/american-religious-landscape-christian-religiously-unaffiliated/.

Kerstetter, Todd M. *Inspiration and Innovation: Religion in the American West*. Malden, MA: John Wiley & Sons, Inc., 2015.

Kimball, Stanley B. "The Utah Gospel Mission, 1900–1950." *Utah Historical Quarterly* 44, no. 2 (Spring 1976): 149–55.

Langford, Joy. "Feminism and Leadership in the Pentecostal Movement." *Feminist Theology* 26, no. 1 (September 2017): 69–79.

Lay, Shawn, ed. *The Invisible Empire in the West: Toward a New Historical Appraisal of the Ku Klux Klan of the 1920s*. Urbana: University of Illinois Press, 1992.

Layton, Stanford J., ed. *Being Different: Stories of Utah's Minorities*. Salt Lake City, UT: Signature Books, 2001.

Leonard, Glen M. *A History of Davis County*. Utah Centennial County History Series. Salt Lake City: Utah State Historical Society, 1999.

Lewis, Robert E., Mark W. Fraser, and Peter J. Pecora. "Religiosity Among Indochinese Refugees in Utah." *Journal for the Scientific Study of Religion* 27, no. 2 (June 1988): 272–83.

Limerick, Patricia Nelson. *The Legacy of Conquest: The Unbroken Past of the American West*. New York: W. W. Norton & Company, 1987.

Lyford, C. P. *The Mormon Problem: An Appeal to the American People*. New York: Hunt & Eaton, 1886.

Lyman, Edward Leo, and Linda King Newell. *A History of Millard County*. Utah Centennial County History Series. Salt Lake City: Utah State Historical Society, 1999.

Lyon, T. Edgar. "Evangelical Protestant Missionary Activities in Mormon Dominated Areas, 1865–1900." PhD diss., University of Utah, 1962.

Maffly-Kipp, Laurie F. "Eastward Ho! American Religion from the Perspective of the Pacific Rim." In *Retelling U.S. Religious History*, edited by Thomas A. Tweed, 127–48. Berkeley: University of California Press, 1997.

Manscill, Craig K., Brian D. Reeves, Guy L. Dorius, and J. B. Haws, eds. *Joseph F. Smith: Reflections on the Man and His Times*. Provo, UT: Religious Studies Center and Deseret Book, 2013.

Martin, Larry. *We've Come This Far By Faith: Readings on the Early Leaders of the Pentecostal Church of God*. Pensacola, FL: Christian Life Books, 2009.

Martin, Paul La Mar. "A Historical Study of the Religious Education Program of the Episcopal Church in Utah." Master's thesis, Brigham Young University, 1967.

"The Marvelous." *Liahona The Elders' Journal* 5, no. 30 (January 1908): 806–8.

Mayer, Vincent, ed. *Working Papers Toward a History of the Spanish-Speaking Peoples of Utah*. Salt Lake City, UT: American West Center, Mexican American Documentation Project, University of Utah, 1973.

McCormick, John S., and John R. Sillito, eds. *A World We Thought We Knew: Readings in Utah History*. Salt Lake City: University of Utah Press, 1995.

McPherson, Robert S. *A History of San Juan County: In the Palm of Time*. Utah Centennial County History Series. Salt Lake City: Utah State Historical Society, 1995.

McPherson, Robert S. "Howard Antes and the Navajo Faith Mission: Evangelist of Southeastern Utah." *Blue Mountain Shadows: The Magazine of San Juan County History* 17 (Summer 1996): 14–24.

Merkel, Henry Martin. *History of Methodism in Utah*. Colorado Springs, CO: Dentan Printing Co., 1938.

Milner II, Clyde A., Carol A. O'Connor, and Martha A. Sandweiss, eds. *The Oxford History of the American West*. New York: Oxford University Press, 1994.

"The Missions: Eastern States." *Liahona The Elders' Journal* 10, no. 36 (February 1913): 571.

Mitchell, Martin. "Gentile Impressions of Salt Lake City, Utah, 1849–1870." *Geographical Review* 87, no. 3 (July 1997): 334–52.

Moon, Gary W., and David G. Benner, eds. *Spiritual Direction and the Care of Souls: A Guide to Christian Approaches and Practices*. Downers Grove, IL: InterVarsity Press, 2004.

Mooney, Bernice Maher. *Salt of the Earth: The History of the Catholic Church in Utah, 1776–2007* (3rd ed.). Salt Lake City: University of Utah Press, 2008.

Moore, R. Laurence. *Religious Outsiders and the Making of Americans*. New York: Oxford University Press, 1986.

Morrow, Carol Ann. "Catholics Among the Mormons." *St. Anthony Magazine Online* (October 1997). Available at www.americancatholic.org/messenger/oct1997/feature1.asp. Accessed June 26, 2012

Murphy, Miriam B. *A History of Wayne County*. Utah Centennial County History Series. Salt Lake City: Utah State Historical Society, 1999.

Newell, Linda King. *A History of Piute County*. Utah Centennial County History Series. Salt Lake City: Utah State Historical Society, 1999.

Newell, Linda King, and Vivian Linford Talbot. *A History of Garfield County*. Utah Centennial County History Series. Salt Lake City: Utah State Historical Society, 1998.

Newell, Quincy D., and Eric F. Mason, eds. *New Perspectives in Mormon Studies*. Norman: University of Oklahoma Press, 2013.

"News from the Missions." *Liahona The Elders Journal* 24, no. 14 (December 28, 1926): 328.

O'Dea, Thomas. *The Mormons*. Chicago: University of Chicago Press, 1957.

Orsi, Robert. *Between Heaven and Earth: The Religious Worlds People Make and the Scholars Who Study Them*. Princeton, NJ: Princeton University Press, 2005.

Owens, Dr. Robert R. *Never Forget! The Dark Years of COGIC History*. Fairfax, VA: Robert R. Owens and Xulon Press, 2002.

Papanikolas, Helen Z. *The Peoples of Utah*. Salt Lake City: Utah State Historical Society, 1976.

Parson, Robert E. *A History of Rich County*. Utah Centennial County History Series. Salt Lake City: Utah State Historical Society, 1996.

Pascoe, Peggy. *Relations of Rescue: The Search for Female Moral Authority in the American West, 1874–1939*. New York: Oxford University Press, 1990.

"Paul Harvey News Broadcast." December 8, 1967. MSS SC 2941. L. Tom Perry Special Collections, Harold B. Lee Library, Brigham Young University (Provo, UT).

Paul, Charles Randall. "Converting the Saints: An Investigation of Religious Conflict Using a Study of Protestant Missionary Methods in an Early 20th Century Engagement with Mormonism." PhD diss., University of Chicago, 2000.

Paul, Charles Randall. *Converting the Saints: A Study of Religious Rivalry in America*. Draper, UT: Greg Kofford Books, Inc., 2018.

Pederson, Helga. "News from the Missions: Eastern States Mission." *Liahona The Elders' Journal* 13, no. 13 (September 1915): 202.

Pederson, Helga. "News from the Missions: Eastern States." *Liahona The Elders' Journal* 13, no. 49 (May 1916): 783.

Perlich, Pamela S. "Utah Minorities: The Story Told by 150 Years of Census Data." Bureau of Economic and Business Research. David S. Eccles School of Business, University of Utah, October 2002. Available at http://gardner.utah.edu/bebr/Documents/studies/Utah_Minorities.pdf. Accessed February 1, 2018.

Peterson, Charles S., and Brian Q. Cannon. *The Awkward State of Utah: Coming of Age in the Nation 1896–1945*. Salt Lake City: University of Utah Press, 2015.

Peterson, F. Ross. *A History of Cache County*. Utah Centennial County History Series. Salt Lake City: Utah State Historical Society, 1997.

Phillips, Wade H. *Quest to Restore God's House—A Theological History of the Church of God* Vol. 1. Cleveland, TN: CPT Press, 2015.

Polk's Salt Lake Directory. Salt Lake City, UT: R. L. Polk & Co. of Utah, various years from the early to mid-twentieth century.

Poll, Richard D., Thomas G. Alexander, Eugene E. Campbell, and David E. Miller, eds. *Utah's History*. Provo, UT: Brigham Young University Press, 1978.

Poloma, Margaret M., and John C. Green. *The Assemblies of God: Godly Love and the Revitalization of American Pentecostalism*. New York: New York University Press, 2010.

Poloma, Margaret M., and Brian F. Pendleton. "Religious Experiences, Evangelism, and Institutional Growth Within the Assemblies of God." *Journal for the Scientific Study of Religion* 28, no. 4 (December 1989): 415–31.

Powell, John. "The Church Rejected—When?" *Improvement Era* 7, no. 11 (September 1904): 817–28.

Putnam, Robert D., and David E. Campbell. *American Grace: How Religion Divides and Unites Us*. New York: Simon and Schuster, 2010.

Qualls, Joy E. A. *God Forgive Us For Being Women: Rhetoric, Theology, and the Pentecostal Tradition*. Eugene, OR: Pickwick Publications, 2018.

Quinn, Frederick. *Building the "Goodly Fellowship of Faith": A History of the Episcopal Church in Utah, 1867–1996*. Logan: Utah State University Press, 2004.

Ramírez, Daniel. *Migrating Faith: Pentecostalism in the United States and Mexico in the Twentieth Century*. Chapel Hill: University of North Carolina Press, 2015.

Rathjen, Randall. "The Distribution of Major Non-Mormon Denominations in Utah." Master's thesis, University of Utah, 1966.

Reed, David A. *"In Jesus' Name": The History and Beliefs of Oneness Pentecostals*. Dorset, UK: Deo Publishing, 2008.

Reeve, W. Paul. *Religion of a Different Color: Race and the Mormon Struggle for Whiteness*. New York: Oxford University Press, 2015.

Reeve, W. Paul, and Jeffrey D. Nichols. "Klansmen at a Funeral and a Terrible Lynching." *History Blazer*, September 1995. Available at https://heritage.utah.gov/history/uhg-klansmen-funeral-terrible-lynching.

"Religious Landscape Study." Pew Research Center, Washington, DC (2014). Available at http://www.pewforum.org/religious-landscape-study/state/utah/. Accessed December 21, 2017.

Richards, LeGrand. "Elder LeGrand Richards." In *One Hundred Thirtieth Annual Conference Report of the Church of Jesus Christ of Latter-day Saints*. Salt Lake City, UT: *Deseret News* (April 1960): 103–5.

Riess, Jana Kathryn. "'Heathen in Our Fair Land': Presbyterian Women Missionaries in Utah, 1870–1890." *The Journal of Presbyterian History* 80, no. 4 (Winter 2002): 225–46.

Robeck, Cecil M. *The Azusa Street Mission and Revival: The Birth of the Global Pentecostal Movement.* Nashville, TN: Thomas Nelson, Inc., 2006.

Robeck, Cecil M., and Amos Yong, eds. *The Cambridge Companion to Pentecostalism.* New York: Cambridge University Press, 2014.

Roberts, Richard C., and Richard W. Sadler. *A History of Weber County.* Utah Centennial County History Series. Salt Lake City: Utah State Historical Society, 1997.

Rodgers, Darrin. "Speaking in Tongues: The Proliferation of Assemblies of God Language Branches Among Immigrants in the 1940s and 1950s." Flower Pentecostal Heritage Center blog. November 11, 2014. Available at https://ifphc.wordpress.com/2014/11/11/speaking-in-tongues-the-proliferation-of-assemblies-of-god-language-branches-among-immigrants-in-the-1940s-and-1950s/. Accessed July 17, 2018.

Roebuck, David G. "Limiting Liberty: The Church of God and Women Ministers, 1986–1996." PhD diss., Vanderbilt University, 1997.

Seegmiller, Janet Burton. *A History of Iron County: Community Above Self.* Utah Centennial County History Series. Salt Lake City: Utah State Historical Society, 1998.

Shaw, Zelma, stenographer. "News from the Missions: Western States Mission." *Liahona The Elders' Journal* 16, no. 11 (September 1918): 1005.

Shipps, Jan, and Mark Silk. *Religion and Public Life in the Mountain West: Sacred Landscapes in Transition.* Walnut Creek, CA: AltaMira Press, 2004.

Sillitoe, Linda. *A History of Salt Lake County.* Utah Centennial County History Series. Salt Lake City: Utah State Historical Society, 1996.

Simmonds, A. J. *The Gentile Comes to Cache Valley: A Study of the Logan Apostasies of 1874 and the Establishment of Non-Mormon Churches in Cache Valley, 1873–1913.* Logan: Utah State University Press, 1976.

Simpson, Thomas W. *American Universities and the Birth of Modern Mormonism, 1867–1940.* Chapel Hill: University of North Carolina Press, 2016.

Skedros, Constantine J. *100 Years of Faith and Fervor: A History of the Greek Orthodox Church Community of Greater Salt Lake City, Utah 1905–2005.* Salt Lake City, UT: Greek Orthodox Church of Greater Salt Lake, 2005.

Smith, Linda H. *A History of Morgan County.* Utah Centennial County History Series. Salt Lake City: Utah State Historical Society, 1999.

Solórzano, Armando. "The Making of Latino Families in Utah." *Beehive History* 25 (1999): 18–21.

Solórzano, Armando. *We Remember, We Celebrate, We Believe: Recuerdo, Celebración, y Esperanza: Latinos in Utah.* Salt Lake City: University of Utah Press, 2014.

"Speaking in Tongues." *Liahona The Elders' Journal* 5, no. 36 (February 1908): 954–59.

"Spirits." *Liahona The Elders' Journal* 6, no. 48 (May 1909): 1149–52.

"Spirits." *Liahona The Elders' Journal* 6, no. 49 (May 1909): 1175–78.

"Spiritual Signs." *Liahona The Elders' Journal* 5, no. 17 (October 1907): 465–67.

Stahl, Ronit Y. *Enlisting Faith: How the Military Chaplaincy Shaped Religion and State in Modern America.* Cambridge, MA: Harvard University Press, 2017.

Staker, Mark L. *Hearken, O Ye People: The Historical Setting of Joseph Smith's Ohio Revelations.* Draper, UT: Greg Kofford Books, Inc., 2009.

Stapley, Jonathan A. *The Power of Godliness: Mormon Liturgy and Cosmology.* New York: Oxford University Press, 2018.

Stene, Eric. "The African-American Community of Ogden, Utah: 1910–1950." Master's thesis, Utah State University, 1994.

Stevenson, Russell, W. *For the Cause of Righteousness: A Global History of Blacks and Mormonism, 1830–2013*. Draper, UT: Greg Kofford Books, 2014.

Stone, Eileen Hallet, ed. *A Homeland in the West: Utah Jews Remember*. Salt Lake City: University of Utah Press, 2001.

Sutton, Matthew Avery. *Aimee Semple McPherson and the Resurrection of Christian America*. Cambridge, MA: Harvard University Press, 2007.

Synan, Vinson. *The Holiness-Pentecostal Tradition: Charismatic Movements in the Twentieth Century*. Grand Rapids, MI: William B. Eerdman's Publishing Company, 1997.

Szasz, Ferenc M. *Religion in the Modern American West*. Tucson: University of Arizona Press, 2000.

Talmage, James E. "The Gifts of the Spirit Contrasted with the Spurious Manifestations of the Evil Power." *Liahona The Elders' Journal* 29, no. 5 (August 1931): 97–99.

Tarango, Angela. *Choosing the Jesus Way: American Indian Pentecostals and the Fight for the Indigenous Principle*. Chapel Hill: University of North Carolina Press, 2014.

Taylor, John W. "Elder John W. Taylor." In *Seventy-fourth Semi-annual Conference Report of the Church of Jesus Christ of Latter-day Saints*. Salt Lake City, UT: *Deseret News* (October 1903): 38–46.

Templin, J. Alton, Allen DuPont Breck, and Martin Rist, eds. *The Methodist, Evangelical, and United Brethren Churches in the Rockies, 1850–1976*. Rocky Mountain Conference of the United Methodist Church, 1977.

Thomas, John Christopher. *A Pentecostal Reads the Book of Mormon: A Literary and Theological Introduction*. Cleveland, TN: CPT Press, 2016.

Tracts and Tracting. Liverpool, UK: Church of Jesus Christ of Latter-day Saints European Mission Office, 1932. L. Tom Perry Special Collections, Harold B. Lee Library, Brigham Young University (Provo, UT).

"The Truth About the 'Mormons.'" L. Tom Perry Special Collections, Harold B. Lee Library, Brigham Young University (Provo, UT).

Turner, John G. *Brigham Young: Pioneer Prophet*. Cambridge, MA: Belknap Press of Harvard University Press, 2012.

Turner, Frederick Jackson. "The Significance of the Frontier in American History." Given at the American Historical Association in Chicago During the World Columbian Exposition, July 12, 1893.

Vu, Michelle A. "Evangelicals, Mormons Search for Common Ground in Utah." *The Christian Post*. March 10, 2011. Available at https://www.christianpost.com/news/evangelicals-mormon-search-for-common-ground-in-utah-49351/. Accessed August 15, 2018.

Wacker, Grant. *Heaven Below: Early Pentecostals and American Culture*. Cambridge, MA: Harvard University Press, 2001.

Wadkins, Timothy H. *The Rise of Pentecostalism in Modern El Salvador: From the Blood of the Martyrs to the Baptism of the Spirit*. Waco, TX: Baylor University Press, 2017.

Walden, David M. *Protestant and Catholic Churches of Provo: A Study of the Non-LDS Christian Congregations*. Provo, UT: Center for Family and Community History at Brigham Young University, 1986.

Watt, Ronald G. *A History of Carbon County*. Utah Centennial County History Series. Salt Lake City: Utah State Historical Society, 1997.

Weber, Francis J. "Catholicism Among the Mormons, 1875–79." *Utah Historical Quarterly* 44, no. 2 (Spring 1976): 141–48.

White, Richard. *It's Your Misfortune and None of My Own: A History of the American West*. Norman: University of Oklahoma Press, 1991.

Whitney, Orson F. "Stay Where You Are!", *Latter-day Saints' Millennial Star* 83 (September 15, 1921): 584–89.

Wilson, Pearl D. *A History of Juab County*. Utah Centennial County History Series. Salt Lake City: Utah State Historical Society, 1999.

Wuthnow, Robert. *The Restructuring of American Religion: Society and Faith Since World War II*. Princeton, NJ: Princeton University Press, 1988.

Yorgason, Ethan R. *Transformation of the Mormon Culture Region*. Urbana: University of Illinois Press, 2003.

Young, Neil J. *We Gather Together: The Religious Right and the Problem of Interfaith Politics*. New York: Oxford University Press, 2016.

Zikmund, Barbara Brown, Adair T. Lummis, and Patricia M. Y. Chang. "Women, Men and Styles of Clergy Leadership." *Christian Century* 115, no. 14 (May 6, 1998). Available at http://hirr.hartsem.edu/research/quick_question3.html.

INDEX

Entries printed in *italics* and preceded by a *P* (i.e. *P4*) refer to illustrations in the Photographic Gallery.

CPSIA information can be obtained
at www.ICGtesting.com
Printed in the USA
LVHW100111210123
737366LV00002B/3

9 781647 690939